# PRAISE FOR
# BRADLEY C. BIRKENFELD

"Bradley Birkenfeld—a name you will never forget."
—*New Haven Register*

"The most significant financial whistle-blower of all time."
—*CNBC*

"Simply put, Birkenfeld must be considered among the biggest whistle-blowers of all time."
—*Tax Notes*

"If a single person can be credited with drawing popular attention to the offshore world, it may be Bradley Birkenfeld."
—*Financial Times*

"In 2007, the veil of secrecy was shattered by a whistle-blower named Bradley Birkenfeld."
—*The Washington Post*

"UBS whistle-blower Bradley Birkenfeld deserves a statue on Wall Street, not a prison sentence."
—*New York Daily News*

"I will say that without Mr. Birkenfeld walking in the door of the Department of Justice in the summer of 2007, I doubt as of today this massive fraud scheme would have ever been discovered by the United States government."
—*Department of Justice Prosecutor*

"So does Mr. Birkenfeld deserve the award of $104 million . . . ? Every penny!"
—*Internal Revenue Service Agent*

WWW.LUCIFERSBANKER.COM

# LUCIFER'S
# BANKER

# LUCIFER'S BANKER

## THE UNTOLD STORY *of* HOW I DESTROYED SWISS BANK SECRECY

BRADLEY C. BIRKENFELD

GREENLEAF
BOOK GROUP PRESS

This is a work of nonfiction. While the stories in this book are true, some names and identifying details have been changed.

Published by Greenleaf Book Group Press
Austin, Texas
www.gbgpress.com

Distributed by Greenleaf Book Group

For ordering information or special discounts for bulk purchases, please contact Greenleaf Book Group at PO Box 91869, Austin, TX 78709, 512.891.6100.

Design and composition by Greenleaf Book Group and Sheila Parr
Cover design by Bradley C. Birkenfeld and Greenleaf Book Group

Cataloging-in-Publication data is available.

Print ISBN: 978-1-62634-371-9

eBook ISBN: 978-1-62634-372-6

Part of the Tree Neutral® program, which offsets the number of trees consumed in the production and printing of this book by taking proactive steps, such as planting trees in direct proportion to the number of trees used: www.treeneutral.com

TreeNeutral

Printed in the United States of America on acid-free paper

16 17 18 19 20 21    10 9 8 7 6 5 4 3 2 1

First Edition

*For my brother Doug, who has been with me from the first day I started on this roller-coaster ride. A loyal friend and brilliant lawyer, he witnessed the corruption, understood what was going on, and advised me along the way.*

*"An event has happened, upon which it is difficult to speak, and impossible to be silent."*

—EDMUND BURKE, IRISH PHILOSOPHER

**UBS** Wealth Management

**Bradley C. Birkenfeld**
Director, Key Clients

**UBS AG**
8, rue du Rhône
CH-1204 Geneva, Switzerland
Tel. +41-22-375 61 32
Fax +41-22-375 60 80
bradley.birkenfeld@ubs.com

www.ubs.com

# CONTENTS

# PROLOGUE

## FALL GUY

*"I fear that foreign bankers with their craftiness and tortuous tricks will entirely control the exuberant riches of America and use it to systematically corrupt civilization."*

—*OTTO VON BISMARCK,*
*GERMAN CHANCELLOR*

January 8, 2010
Minersville, Pennsylvania

ALL ROADS THAT LEAD to federal prisons are long.

There are no exits, no shortcuts to quicken the journey and dull the pain of anticipation. All such roads are built upon decisions, with hairpin turns and lost highways. That final leg might involve a quick mile's ride from a courthouse, or a six-hour trip aboard a fume-choked prison bus, but it's always the payoff of a life gone crazy, and it always ends the same way.

For me, the road to Schuylkill Federal Correctional Institution seemed fucking endless on that freezing Friday morning. It was only an hour's drive from my hotel in Scranton, Pennsylvania, to the prison in some backwater town, but it felt like a year. Inside the Lexus I could see my breath, and outside the snow fell in wind-whipped veils, making the blacktop slick and risky. I'd wanted to take the wheel myself, one last spin before they locked me up, but I'd been slapped with a curfew, branded with an ankle monitor, and didn't have a car anymore. So my older brother Doug, who's almost six-foot-four like me, drove through the storm. I made a few last phone calls to friends from the car, but mostly we sat there in tight-lipped silence, heading for an appointment that neither of us wanted to keep.

I knew this was going to be hard on Doug, maybe even more than on me. He was damn proud of me for what I'd done, blowing the top off the biggest banking and tax fraud conspiracy in history, and he was furious with the Department of Justice. Doug thought I deserved the Medal of Freedom instead of a pair of leg irons. I tried telling him it would be all right.

"Hey, dude, chill out," I said as I looked at his white-knuckled fingers gripping the wheel. "I can do three years in the slammer standing on my head."

But Doug wasn't buying it. He was outraged, bitter, and vengeful. And since there's no point in pretending otherwise, I was too.

I gave up on my phony bravado as the car entered a long curve through a forest of snow-slathered pines. The wheels suddenly lost traction and the car started to drift, but Doug handled the skid like a Formula One driver and he didn't slow down. He was hunched over the wheel, staring through the windshield where the wipers were on full and slapping at the snow. They sounded to me like a metronome, attached to a time bomb. Maybe that's a little dramatic, but they did.

"Take it easy, brother." I reached over and gripped his shoulder. "I'm in no rush."

Doug finally smiled, but it was more like a death's-head grin, and we both turned inward again.

I've heard that when you're about to die a violent death, your whole life flashes before your eyes. Luckily I've never experienced that, but I can say firsthand that when you're about to be locked up in prison, a similar phenomenon occurs. Yet my looking back felt more like some terminal disease, during which I had plenty of time to go over every joy and sorrow, plus all the perfect moves I'd made and a couple of dumbass screwups. My life didn't flash before my eyes; it unwound slowly like an old film on a rickety movie projector.

I had no regrets and I'm not a fan of pity parties. But there were things I sure as hell would've changed. For instance, I would *never* have trusted my Swiss bank bosses to have my back, when I knew deep down that traits like integrity were not in their bones. And I would definitely not have gone to the US Department of Justice, expecting them to protect me while I handed them, on a silver platter, the biggest tax fraud scheme in history. Even at the ripe old age of forty-four, I still had faith in the American justice system. Well, you live and learn.

What really occupied my mind as we drove were the things I'd miss: the lifestyle I'd worked my butt off to achieve, my parents and brothers, my friends, and my liberty. I knew that an hour from now I'd be faced with some very stark contrasts: the Disneyland of my life before today, and the Tower of London after.

I leaned back and closed my eyes, recalling my roller-coaster ride. Just two years ago I'd been living the kind of existence most men can only dream about, and the sights and smells and sensations of it all washed over me again like a warm Caribbean wave.

And there I was, back in Geneva, Switzerland, lounging on the veranda of my luxury third-floor flat overlooking Cours de Rive. Steam curled from a fine china cup of espresso and the orange pages of the Financial Times fluttered in the morning breeze. A mound of fresh strawberries from the farmers' market across the street glistened on my marble table, and the Swiss trams below were rolling back and forth like a Christmas morning train set. On Saturdays my lively Eaux-Vives neighborhood was quiet, the cabarets shuttered at dawn, and I could hear the clops of horseshoes on cobblestones from a tourist carriage in the distance. Sunlight glinted off the snow-capped Swiss Alps and Diana Krall jazz wafted through my tall French windows.

My exotic Brazilian girlfriend, Thais, was still inside, relaxing on a pile of Persian pillows. We were both hungover yet happily sated. I could still feel her skin, soft as Nepalese silk, and I could hear that provocative Portuguese accent calling out something that made me grin.

"*Bradleeee*, come back into bed, darling. And bring that thing I love *with* you."

It was one of those glorious weekends again, when we'd hop in my fire-red Ferrari 550 Maranello and take the drive to Zermatt, roaring through magnificent mountain passes, sunglasses glinting above our grins. My Swiss chalet was perched at the top of the picturesque town, where cars were forbidden, so we'd park at a small village near the base of the mountain range and take the cogwheel train up a long, steep valley to the summit. And finally after one last climb we'd arrive, standing breathless and thrilled before my picture-window view of the Matterhorn.

Maybe it wasn't so special, unless you're partial to magnums of Laurent-Perrier champagne, fresh beluga caviar, or boxes of Churchill cigars just flown in from Havana. I guess it was nice if you like Frigor Swiss chocolates, Audemars Piguet watches, Brioni suits, and gorgeous girls who care only about pleasing you and having a great time. But just imagine all that, and then—the best thing about it—it had all been paid for in *cash*.

After all, it was all about the money, right? That's why I'd gone into international banking, gotten a master's degree at the university in La Tour-de-Peilz, and put my nose to the grindstone in Geneva. That's why I was recruited for a coveted job at the Union Bank of Switzerland, UBS, the biggest and the best bank in the world. And once there, as the only American on an elite team of Swiss private bankers, I'd perfected my game, flying first-class all over the world, staying in five-star resort hotels, and seducing scores of One-Percenters into stashing their fortunes in secret Swiss numbered accounts, no questions asked. Armed with a big pair of *cojones*, financial smarts, and plenty of charm, I'd made millions of dollars for UBS, as well as for my clients, with a nice fat cut for myself.

But now, as I thought it over, I knew it hadn't been about the money at all. I'd lived the life of an Ian Fleming character, which was all about the thrill, and that's a hunger that can get you buried. I might have kept at it, except it turned out I had this annoying itch called a conscience, and I'd finally discovered that "The Firm" had no such thing at all. Those devious bastards at UBS, my nefarious Swiss bosses, had known all along that everything we were doing was in flagrant defiance of American tax laws and I could wind up in prison till my goatee turned white. They were setting me up for a fall, along with my clients and colleagues, so I'd checkmated the Swiss Mafiosi and jumped first.

Problem was, I'd landed in the wrong lap. The US Department of Justice was supposed to welcome me, protect me, *thank* me for being the first and only Swiss private banker to crack that impenetrable shell of Swiss secrecy and corruption, to ensure that American taxpayers would be cheated no more. But instead, the DOJ had reached out for my treasure trove with one slimy hand, and slapped cuffs on me with the other.

*Scumbags.* And that's being polite.

I opened my eyes as the fury of it all welled up again from my guts, but then the scenery outside snapped me out of myself. *You're not the only disgraced samurai around, Birkenfeld.* I was looking at coal country in middle America, with its run-down houses and farms, smoke curling from cracked chimneys, and rusty old cars perched on cinder blocks. I saw horses, the only mode of transport left when you can't afford overpriced gas, standing on snow-swept hills and nosing for scraps of green. I knew this had once been a place of American heroes, men who labored deep in the earth for that black stone their countrymen craved. Many had died in collapsing mines, and many more still would die from collapsing lungs. And now they were pariahs, cursed by the environmentalists, shunned by the politicians who'd sucked up their votes and tossed them away. Betrayed by their country, just like me. Except they'd never see a ski chalet in Zermatt.

We passed a road sign: "Minersville." Time to get my game face on. In short order, my ass would belong to the US government, payback for spilling the beans. *Thanks a lot, Uncle Sam.*

But I had a surprise for the federal goons; all that Swiss glitz didn't mean that much to me. I'd grown up without it and could live just fine under the harshest conditions. After all, I'd made it through Norwich University in Vermont, one of the oldest and toughest private military academies in the nation, where every day dawned with push-ups in the snow, ten-mile ruck marches, relentless drill sergeants barking orders, hours of mind-bending classes, and then studying like crazy till midnight. I knew nothing like that would be happening at Schuylkill. The Feds couldn't treat prisoners like

ROTC cadets, which was sort of ironic because it might've cut down on the recidivism rate.

Anyhow, I'd already decided that whatever they threw at me, I was going to beat them at their own game. I'd always been an avid fan of that old TV show *Hogan's Heroes*, a World War II comedy about a bunch of Allied prisoners turning the tables on their Nazi wardens. So, Schuylkill was going to be my "Stalag 13," and I was going to be Colonel Hogan. *Bring it on, baby.*

I looked over at Doug. He's a handsome dude, better looking than me or our older brother, Dave, with a full head of auburn hair and white teeth. Doug's a tough attorney and when his ire's up, he sticks his big chin out and lasers his target with those cold blue eyes. Right now his jaw was rippling.

"You're pissed," I said.

"Nah, I *love* taking my baby brother to prison. Maybe we can get Dave indicted on something so I can drive him too."

I laughed at that. The minute you can't laugh anymore, you're finished.

"Relax, dude," I said. "This'll all go by in a flash, you'll see."

"I feel like I want to kill somebody," he seethed. "Somebody like Kevin Downing."

I sure as hell agreed with Doug's urge. Kevin Downing was a senior prosecutor at the Tax Division of the Department of Justice, the one to whom I'd first brought my case. I'd handed him the keys to the kingdom, all the secrets of illicit Swiss banking, and he'd turned on me like a rabid dog. Doug, an attorney with impeccable ethics, viewed Kevin Downing as the profession's lowest life-form: petty, hypocritical, self-serving, and basically a spiteful prick.

"Anyone else on your list?" I asked.

"After Downing? Yeah, Olenicoff."

Ah, yes, Igor Olenicoff. Just the mention of his name made my blood boil too. Olenicoff was a Russian-born California real estate mogul, a multibillionaire, and he'd been my biggest client at UBS. We'd met at one of those yacht marinas where every boat costs as much as a mansion, the crews all look like Abercrombie & Fitch poster boys, and the yacht owners' mistresses flash their silicone boobs and diamond bracelets right in front of the wives. I'd met with Olenicoff again after that and had introduced him to my colleague in Liechtenstein, Mario Staggl, a wizard at making money and identities disappear.

Olenicoff was *big* money, and he wanted a large chunk of it stashed away for a rainy day from the prying eyes of the IRS. So Mario had created two Liechtenstein trusts with three underlying Danish shell companies, with Olenicoff as the ultimate beneficiary. Soon after that I had $200 million of his US real estate profits sitting in several UBS Swiss numbered accounts. The only thing identifying Olenicoff as the true account holder was an index card with his name on it, and his code name. That card was locked in a safe at our Geneva headquarters, and the only ones who could access it were me and my boss, Christian Bovay. No one else at UBS knew Olenicoff's identity.

Technically, nothing about this arrangement was illegal, unless Olenicoff "forgot" to declare his Swiss stash of cash on his US tax returns. I had plenty of wealthy American clients at UBS, and whether or not they filled out a W-9 was none of my business. But don't get me wrong. I wasn't a choirboy and I knew what I was doing. And UBS kept hounding us "hunters" to bring in more rich folks with cash, so I'd sent my conscience on sabbatical and played the game. It wasn't until I found out that my bosses were going to hang me out to dry that I took preemptive action and turned them in.

Then the US Department of Justice made me a deal I couldn't refuse. "Give us the names of your American account holders, Birkenfeld. *All* the names, or we're going to prosecute you, *too*." Didn't leave me much choice. If you're going to blow the whistle, you don't get to select who you'd like to protect.

At the time, Igor Olenicoff was the typical arrogant billionaire while being cheap as hell; I didn't feel bad about ratting him out because I figured he'd hire the best lawyers money could buy and wriggle out of it just fine. Igor even confided in me and told me he wished in his next life he could come back as a Newport Beach housewife. To this bizarre statement, I asked him why. He responded, "Because all they do is spend their husbands' money." What a great guy!

And I was right about that, but wrong about the Department of

Jackasses. Gratitude wasn't in their DNA. They charged Olenicoff with tax fraud and *me* along with him as a coconspirator! And just to make sure I went to prison, they claimed I hadn't turned his name over until *after* I was indicted.

It was unfuckingbelievable. I hadn't given the DOJ the name—and they knew why. But I'd already testified under oath after being subpoenaed before the US Senate, and detailed my extensive dealings with Olenicoff. But at my sentencing hearing, Kevin Downing looked the judge in the eye and said I'd held that name back. Poker-faced and sincere as Satan, Downing claimed I was covering up for a rich client and hoping to make a buck later for being a good boy.

*Bang* went the judge's gavel. Prison for Birkenfeld.

I'll never forget that feeling, or the sound of that gavel smacking mahogany. It was my Lee Harvey Oswald moment. Somebody just got killed, and guess what? *You're* the fall guy.

Olenicoff, on the other hand, had made a deal with the devil and gotten off with two years' probation and a fine for back taxes. The fine amounted to $52 million, which sounds like a lot, but it was pocket change for him. But what happened after that was the poisoned icing on the cake. Olenicoff then sued UBS, me, and more than *thirty* other individuals and business entities, claiming that *we* were responsible for his failure to pay his taxes! Talk about balls. You cheat on the government for decades, somebody turns you in, and *that's* the guy you go after, the one who's going to jail while you go back to your champagne orgies. By that time my legal fees had wiped me out and my lawyers had quit. I'd soon be in lockup, defenseless, while Olenicoff partied on and trashed me in court.

What a country, right? Land of the Free, if you can afford the price of liberty.

But stick with me for one last tagline on the whole affair. Olenicoff had a beloved son, Andrei, a guy I liked much more than his father. He was a classy young man, handsome and hardworking. I'd even attended his wedding in Newport Beach, California, to a sweet young woman named Kim. And then one day Andrei was driving his jeep on Route 1 along the coast, and for some reason the brakes failed and he wound up dead. I was shocked and genuinely saddened. Kim was devastated, and Igor Olenicoff has been forever heartbroken.

I guess the real moral of that story is no matter how much money you have, or how clever you think you are, you can't fix dead. As the old saying goes, nothing is certain except death and taxes; and ironically Igor got a big fat taste of both.

I turned my attention back to Doug, who now had a smirk on his lips. I could tell he'd been thinking about Olenicoff's twist of fate too.

That's the thing about us Birkenfeld Boys; we're a tough, fiercely competitive bunch, fighters by nature. Our dad is a well-known neurosurgeon, and the three of us brothers grew up playing hockey and football and working odd jobs from pretty much from the time we could walk. We were comfortable, but never spoiled. Our name means "field of birches" in German. That was us, tall and hard, sometimes bending in the wind, but *never* breaking. If you wanted to cut us down, you'd better show up with something bigger than a butter knife.

We turned a bend in the pounding storm, cruised down a long slim road, and then I saw it: Schuylkill (pronounced "school-kill," which made it sound like you wouldn't learn a damn thing there). It was out in the middle of nowhere, surrounded by forests and sprawled over an open pitch the size of ten football fields. The main entrance was a low concrete rectangle with smoked black windows and rows of razor wire coiling across the roof. An American flag whipped in the wind, its rope pulleys banging on the pole. My stomach tightened up. *Time to pay the piper*.

Outside on the street I saw a bunch of television news vans and a line of journalists' cars at the curb. Camera crews and reporters from all over the world were milling around in down jackets and slapping their arms in the cold. When they saw our car, they tossed their coffee cups away and flicked on their lights and microphones. They were there because they'd been tipped off, by me. I was determined to call a press conference and tell the US government just what I thought of their bullshit lies as they locked me up.

If you haven't gotten the gist of me yet, I'm a hammer, looking for nails.

"Here we go," Doug said as he parked at the back of the line. I got out and looked up at the sky, the snow coming down in big fat flakes, my last look at the free world before they put me away for three years. I was dressed like a regular dude, in a lumberjack flannel shirt, a red ski jacket, and a black baseball cap. Then I spotted one friendly face.

The only lawyer still on my side was Stephen Kohn, and he wasn't getting paid. A diminutive guy with wiry gray hair, glasses, and always an optimistic grin, he was as smart as they come and feisty as a pit bull. He was also chief counsel for the National Whistleblower Center in Washington, DC. Steve was convinced the government owed me a fat reward, and he was going to get it, or die trying. I loved the guy, but thought he was a dreamer. I gave him a nod as I started that long last walk, with Doug walking shotgun beside me.

The reporters crowded around and then I saw two prison guards in black parkas, slinging pistols and batons, stomping over from the main entrance. One of them waved his gloved hands in a panic.

"You can't have a press conference here!" he shouted. "This is private property!"

I shot my finger down at the road and gave him a blast of my New England accent. "This road belongs to the American people, not *you*. This is *federal* property. Are you going to deny me my First Amendment rights?"

The guards mumbled to each other, cursed, and backed off. A small female reporter looked up at me and stuck her microphone in my face.

"Mr. Birkenfeld, you're here to surrender yourself to federal authorities for conspiracy to commit tax fraud," she said as she posed for her cameraman. "Do you have anything to say?"

I gave her my best Clint Eastwood.

"I would like to say how proud I am to be courageous enough to come forward and do what I did to expose the largest tax fraud in the world." The reporters worked their recorders and scribbled notes. "And this is what I'm getting." I cocked my chin at the prison. "An indictment from the Department of Justice." Then I gave them all my steeliest stare. "You can draw your own conclusions."

A jumble of questions spat from the crowd, but I'd already fired my shot across the government's bow. Steve Kohn pushed past me and let his raw emotions fly.

"To take a whistle-blower who was responsible for the single largest recovery to American taxpayers and put him in jail? It's a travesty of justice! A *miscarriage* of justice! It's *grotesque*."

With that, I patted Steve on the shoulder, shook my brother's hand, broke from the crowd, and walked up the concrete slabs to the entrance. The two guards cranked my arms behind my back and slapped cuffs on me. *Claangg.*

They marched me inside and slammed the doors. The din of the reporters outside went dead; no sound but the snowmelt hitting my shoes. We walked through a reception area of whitewashed walls hung with portraits of jowly wardens. The linoleum floor smelled like a high school gymnasium, an odor I happen to like. At the end of it a portly blonde woman sat at a high desk, looking about as pleased as the Wizard of Oz. She already knew who I was, but I snapped to attention anyway.

"Birkenfeld, Bradley C.," I reported.

She didn't appreciate my snide side. "Miss-terr Birkenfeld, do you have anything on your person?"

I took off my watch, an Audemars Piguet Royal Oak Offshore T3, the same model worn by Arnold Schwarzenegger in *Terminator 3*.

"Just this," I said as I handed it to her. "Don't lose it. It's worth twenty-five thousand bucks."

She blinked at me, picked it up like it was a hissing cobra, and dropped it in a manila envelope.

The guards walked me into "Processing," an empty room with steel lockers that stank like dirty socks. They stood me up in front of a wall and took my prison photograph. I grinned as the camera flashed.

"Why the hell are you smiling?" one of them sneered.

"Because I'm here to have fun," I said.

The guards stiffened and shot each other a look. The other one jabbed a finger at my foot.

"Where's your ankle monitor?"

"I cut it off last night with a knife. Gave it back to probation."

After that, they took off my cuffs and watched me like a pair of kittens trapped in a cage with a jackal as I stripped and gave them my clothes.

A few minutes later, I was wearing tighty-whities, a gray T-shirt, an olive drab prison uniform, and lace-up work boots. The outfit didn't faze me; I'd done my research. I knew I was supposed to be going into the minimum-security wing, something like an army barracks where the white-collar perps did their time.

A doctor in a white lab coat came in, checked my blood pressure, and pronounced me fit to be tied. The guards cuffed me again and marched me back out to Ms. Happy Face. She was stamping down on some forms.

"So, where's the dormitory?" I asked her. "I'd hate to miss lunch."

She glared at me over her glasses. "You're not going there today, Mr. Birkenfeld."

"Oh? Where am I going?"

"Solitary." She pointed up at the ceiling. "Orders from upstairs."

I got it. The warden was probably pissed that I'd turned his prison into a public spectacle at the front gate. So, he'd decided to throw me in the cooler. But I knew if I asked for how long, it would come off as fear, so I just gave her my Birkenfeld grin.

"Works for me," I said. "I like my alone-time."

One of the guards wrenched my elbow and led me through a buzz-lock door. I heard the other one mutter to Ms. Happy Face, "First time I've ever heard *that*."

It was a long, silent corridor leading to one heavy door at the end with a small bulletproof window and a monster-sized lock. The guard pulled it open, took off my cuffs, shoved me inside, and slammed the door. I turned to the window as he was cranking the key, gave him a wink, and said, "Have a nice weekend."

He flinched a little and walked away, quickly.

I'd learned something important a long time ago, long before I got into business and banking. And I'd learned it on the ice, playing high school hockey in Massachusetts. Let folks know who you are right away: a guy who seems friendly, but totally unpredictable. Look down at them and give them that leopard smile that doesn't touch your eyes, and they'll know not to fuck with you.

Sure, throw me in prison. Pretend you're the law of the land, protector of the people, doing what's right and true. Invite me in with all my secrets that I'm giving up of my own accord, risking my entire career, not to mention my life. Then betray me, tell me I'm a dirtbag, while you make under-the-table deals with the Big Dogs and let all the real sharks swim away. Go ahead, toss me in solitary and throw away the key.

But just remember one thing, boys. I'll be out someday.

And you're going to *pay*.

# PART I

# CHAPTER 1

## MAKING THE CUT

*"Greed, for lack of a better word, is good."*
—*GORDON GEKKO, WALL STREET*

YOU DON'T REALLY WANT to know about my childhood. But I'm going to tell you anyway, so just hang in for a few pages while I wax poetic.

I grew up in a castle.

That probably got your attention, but it wasn't a real fortress of knights and damsels; it was just what everyone in our small town of Hingham, Massachusetts, called it—"The Castle" (Exhibit 1). The house was a sprawling six-bedroom edifice of stone with gables, turrets, and lead-paned glass windows, built in the early twentieth century by a wealthy industrial baron. It was perched on five acres of manicured lawns, surrounded by additional acres of undeveloped conservation land with a three hundred-foot driveway almost abutting the quaint Hingham harbor. If you drove by it today, you'd think, "rich folk, spoiled kids," but in truth it became "Schloss Birkenfeld" in the late 1960s for less than the current price of a Jeep Wrangler. And the reason I remember the acreage so well is that my brothers and I mowed the lawn, every week, every spring, summer, and fall.

As I mentioned previously, my dad was a well-respected neurosurgeon in Boston, a man who believed in studying hard, working harder, and only enjoying your downtime if you deserved it. He'd gone to a

Quaker boarding school in Pennsylvania as a child (which seemed a bit odd to me, since he hailed from Russian Jews), and that's where he acquired a "You're not going to learn much if your gums are flapping" viewpoint on education. My mom was a beautiful former fashion model and a registered nurse, raised as a Protestant, but she'd given up all that haute couture stuff to be a stay-at-home mother, which wasn't a disgrace back in the day, though some folks think so today.

The other figure in my young life was my mom's brother, Major General E. Donald Walsh, a man I respected and loved very much. We didn't see Uncle Don that often, because he was the Adjutant General of Connecticut, but his influence was powerful. The man was a legend, a highly decorated combat veteran of the Battles of Iwo Jima and Okinawa, and I suppose it was from him that I acquired a thirst for adrenaline and adventure.

So, when you've got a full-time mother with manners and class, a brilliant neurosurgeon father with an ironclad work ethic, and an Iwo Jima/Okinawa war hero uncle, you wind up with some interesting kids.

My older brothers, Dave and Doug, were good boys, with heads on their shoulders and senses of purpose. I was the one with a glint in my eye, which was good for me because the third child often gets more of a pass (Exhibit 2). But none of us were slackers. We had to mow that golf-course-sized lawn and shovel that runway-length driveway. In the summers we worked odd jobs, such as mowing other people's lawns and hauling furniture with the Teamsters union. Dad expected us to bring home good grades and encouraged us to play hockey and football to develop competitive spirits, which certainly worked in my case. We knew how to tie a tie, say "Ma'am" and "Sir" at Mom's cocktail parties, and get into trouble discreetly so Dad wouldn't find out. If he did, there'd be hell to pay.

When high school came, I begged my dad to let me go to a private academy. It wasn't a Harry Potter thing (those books hadn't been written back then), just something I thought would be cool. Dad's medical expertise was in high demand, so I knew the tuition wouldn't pinch his wallet. He sighed and complied, and I went off to Thayer Academy to don jackets and ties and snicker through chapel masses on Mondays. I got decent grades, knocked heads in hockey and football games, caroused with the girls on the weekends, and drank plenty of beer with my close cadre of friends.

By now you're getting the picture that I always had an itch for adventure and independence, despite the careful sculpting of my erstwhile elders. Nothing was ever enough for me. By eighteen, I was an avid marksman and had purchased my own Colt .45-caliber pistol, just like the one on Uncle Don's garrison belt. I was parachuting out of airplanes in New York and dragging my groaning buddies off to three-day treks in the Vermont mountains, where we'd camp, fish, hunt, and plot which girls we were going to bag next. Normal, lusty, Tom Sawyer–Huck Finn–type stuff.

However, I'd also gotten serious about my future. My oldest brother, Dave, was pursuing medicine, and Doug was going to be a lawyer. What about me? Well, I decided to explore a military career, and not just being some grunt with a rifle. I was going to be a fighter pilot and circle the globe as a "zipper-suited sun god." So, I filled out applications to military academies and landed a great one.

Norwich University in Northfield, Vermont, is the oldest private military academy in the nation. As you'd expect, it's nestled in a lush valley surrounded by mountains, and the buildings are solid brick and granite with a beautiful white chapel as a centerpiece and plenty of thick woods and rivers in which to play soldier. All branches of the service are represented at Norwich, so I came aboard as an Air Force ROTC candidate. But for the first full year, I was nothing but a "Rook," which basically means you're on probation until your advisor (a real military officer) decides you're worthy of the title "Cadet."

"Rook! That sun's been up for a full minute. Why the hell aren't *you*?!"

"Rook! Those boots should be shined like a mirror. If I can't use 'em to shave, then you can't use 'em to fight!"

"Rook! What the hell are you lookin' at? Get your ruck and your rifle and be back here in thirty seconds! We're going for a *walk*."

Needless to say, those "walks" were often in knee-deep snow, and nobody told us how long they would be, but they were rarely less than ten miles. We learned how to wear our uniforms, both combat fatigues and snappy dress grays, and how to shoot, move, navigate in the field, keep our living quarters spotless, and be ready to spit back regulations like robots on speed. The push-ups, sit-ups, and runs were endless, but that didn't faze me much. As a former high school athlete, I could do PT till the cows came home, which they never did.

The classes were challenging; there were some military subjects, but mostly the standards of math, English, history, and languages. All you had to do was to study hard, but that came with a caveat, a catch-22. You couldn't hit the books until all your soldierly duties were squared away, but you couldn't focus on your buckles and rifles if you weren't making the grades. So every day bled off past midnight, and then you were up again five hours later, no bitching allowed. "Hit the parade ground! Hit the books!"

Well, by the end of that first year, I had made Cadet, and then the real work began. I chose economics as my major, but as we swung into sophomore classes, guess what? I was already bored. The classes were interesting enough and I enjoyed learning about finance, statistics, the stock market, and so forth; but it was all just theory unless it was fun, and fun to me always means risk.

"Hey, Beeker," I said to my roommate Dave Burke one night while we were cramming for an exam in our quarters. "Let's start a business."

"What do you mean, a business?"

I sat up on my bed. We had a nice-sized room with a sitting area, although the place was as bleak as a highway tollbooth.

"This school's like a monastery, right? Nothing to do if you've got some downtime. Hell, with all this friggin' snow, you can't even get into town to catch a movie!"

"So, whatcha got in mind, Birkenfeld? A topless bar?"

I grinned and raised a finger. "A movie rental business."

"You're nuts."

"I'm serious! Lots of guys got TVs, but half the time all we can get is a weather report or *Mork and Mindy*. Now, if we had a bunch of VCRs and a pile of movies . . . "

Now Beeker sat up on his bed too. "But won't we get busted for that? What about the regulations?"

"I already checked the regs." I grinned. "Nothing against making money on campus."

"You're a wily bastard," said Beeker.

"I know."

That weekend, we pooled all our cash, drove down to Boston, and came back with four VCRs, thirty movie tapes, six movie posters, and a color TV. Then we measured our sitting room, went into Northfield, and bought wood paneling, hardware, wall-to-wall carpet, and three plush lounge chairs (we figured if cadets didn't have a TV, they could pay the fee and watch a flick in our "theater"). Before long, we had our place looking like a French cinema, and soon the word spread like wildfire from our Kilo Company barracks.

They came in droves! The guys were thrilled to be able to plop down a few bucks, take a VCR back to their rooms, and watch the latest Stallone flick. Some of them only rented the machines, so I figured they had a stash of porn somewhere. But if they got gigged for that (army parlance for "chewed out"), it was none of my business. And for the guys who wanted to just rent a film and watch it in our theater, of course we supplied popcorn at a very reasonable rate.

So pretty soon Dave and I were enjoying that ultimate goal of all businesses, Return on Investment, with which we paid for our books, extra-fancy military gear, off-campus beers, and weekend trips to Burlington, Vermont. It was all going smooth as silk, until one night when a big fist hammered on our door. I cracked it open.

*Shit! Colonel Carbone!*

Dave's eyes bugged out like a summer cicada, and as I pulled the door open we snapped to attention.

Carbone was a regular full-bird US Army colonel and our Commandant of Cadets advisor. His hair was high and tight, his buckles and brass like gold bullion, and he walked into our room and said nothing. We stood there like ice sculptures as his eyes scanned our wood paneling, the posters, the ordered stacks of VCRs, and a bookshelf lined with entertainment. He looked down at his spit-shined boots mashed in our high-pile carpet, and then at our fat leather loungers. Then he nodded.

"I'm impressed, gentlemen. This is considerably nicer than my own quarters." Something akin to a smile crossed his lips. "Carry on."

He spun on a heel and walked out. I turned to Dave and grinned.

"I told you there was nothing in the regs!"

"Jesus!" He laughed. "I almost pissed my pants!"

At the end of my sophomore year, I headed for home and applied for a few summer jobs in the Boston area. With a major in economics and a military bearing, I suppose I was attractive to the Human Resources folks, who were accustomed to rejecting long-haired college students with pot-pink eyes. I landed a job at one of Boston's finest and oldest financial institutions, State Street Bank and Trust Company. The pay was fantastic, about four thousand bucks for the summer, and during three months of fetching coffee for money managers and running stock reports back and forth to the trading floor, I learned more about the real world of high finance than anything my professors could offer.

Somewhere in the back of my mind I realized that if I'd really been serious about becoming a fighter pilot, I would have sought out a job in aerospace. But the money in banking was seductive and I did have a weakness for cash. As it turned out, the writing was on the wall.

By the end of my junior year I was a senior cadet and upperclassman, barking at the Rooks, strong as a bull and breezing through the training routines and business classes. That summer I worked at State Street again, and in the early autumn I was back at Norwich for my final year. I was standing on the parade field one fine foliage day, watching the newbies try to figure out left face from right face, when I felt a presence beside me. It was Colonel Carbone.

"Cadet Birkenfeld," he said as a drill instructor's cadence calls echoed across the field. "I've been meaning to have a talk with you."

"Sir?"

"You're a good troop; smart, disciplined, and determined. But I think you need to reconsider your future."

I turned and looked down at him. When you're my height, you pretty much have to look down at everybody. "How's that, Sir?"

Colonel Carbone gave it to me straight, no chaser. "You're never going to be a fighter pilot, Brad. Nowadays, all those guys are Air Force Academy graduates, engineering majors with four-point-oh scores. You're good, but you're a finance guy, and you've only got a three-point-oh." He shrugged, almost an apology. "And besides, you're just too damn big for an F-16 cockpit. They'd have to squeeze you in with butter and a shoehorn."

I wasn't really shocked. The cadets always talked about their realistic chances of getting what they wanted in the military, and I already knew my odds were slim. Carbone was just confirming my suspicions.

"Well, what do you recommend, Sir?"

"Adjust your sights," he said. "Think of something else you'll be happy with. If you carry on with this and join the air force, you're going to wind up as a fucking missile launch officer one mile underground in Nebraska."

And that was it. I took his remarks to heart, but I didn't whine or get depressed or think I'd wasted my college years. I thought about that Clint Eastwood line from *Dirty Harry*, "A man's got to know his limitations." So, maybe I'd never be a fighter jockey, but I already knew I could be an ace in banking and finance.

In the winter of 1987, I packed my bags and gave one last salute to Norwich University (Exhibit 3). I'd been accepted to complete my last senior semester overseas at Richmond College in South Kensington, England, and I was totally thrilled at the prospect of immersing myself in an international center of finance, making new foreign friends, and absorbing a wealth of European culture. I was fully formed now, sculpted, ready. I knew I would never be a war hero, but I was ready to conquer the world.

And that's how I embarked on that long road, which included a pit stop in a prison cell.

But if you'd told me back then that at the end of its twists and turns, pleasures, intrigues, and adventures, Schuylkill awaited, I would have said . . .

"You're out of your *mind*. Birkenfelds *never* do time."

# CHAPTER 2

## BOSTON MASSACRE

*"A superior man is modest in his speech,*
*but exceeds in his actions."*

—*CONFUCIUS, CHINESE PHILOSOPHER*

STATE STREET BANK AND Trust Company—1989
The first time I saw Nick Lopardo, the Chief Executive Officer of State Street Global Advisors, I thought he'd walked off the set of some *Godfather* sequel filming down the street and wandered into the wrong building.

He came barreling through the analysts' floor, six-foot-two and at least two-fifty, stuffed into a gleaming silver suit with a blood-red tie, and he was trailed by a beefy bodyguard with a prosthetic hook for a right hand. Lopardo had thick black hair, eyebrows like centipedes, a busted nose, and a jaw wider than his fullback neck. His face was red from some sort of meeting that had pissed him off, and as he stomped past the desks, making coffee mugs tremble, the first thing I ever heard him say was directed at some kid who wasn't quick enough to spot him.

"Get your feet off the goddamn desk! This ain't a dugout at Fenway!"

The kid jumped in his chair and snapped his feet down so fast I thought he'd wet himself, and as we watched Lopardo storm though a pair of glass doors for the elevator, my buddy Rick James leaned over and whispered, "That's the new boss."

Nicholas A. Lopardo. Not the very model of a stuffy Boston banker.

The son of a scrap-metal shop owner in Brooklyn, he'd played shortstop in baseball and fullback in football while at Susquehanna University in Pennsylvania. He'd only gotten a bachelor's degree in marketing and management, figured he didn't need any of that Wharton B-School crap, and had taken the mean streets of Little Italy out into the world of high finance. He'd spent eighteen years at Equitable Life marketing institutional pension plans, and everyone at State Street knew he was there to turn the firm's old-fashioned snobbery of catering to blue-blooded rich folk into something much, much bigger.

When Lopardo arrived at State Street in 1987, the money-management arm had $18 billion in assets. When he finally left in 2001, he'd grown it to over *$700 billion*. We were all in awe of him. We all wanted to be him. He was loyal to his employees and protective as a Doberman, but also demanding as hell. Nick Lopardo took no prisoners. You had to be careful around the guy. Whenever he boomed, "People, we're gonna make a *killing*," no one was ever sure if he was talking about profits or planning to garrote some goon like Al Capone.

So, Nick Lopardo set the tune, and the rest of us danced to it.

State Street Bank and Trust Company was my first landing on the shores of big-time finance. I'd been there before, working a summer job between college semesters, but I had pretty much been in the basement along with the other Warren Buffett wannabes. We were glorified messengers, hauling piles of files for bankers we only called "Sir," delivering sandwiches and sodas to meetings about subjects way over our heads, taking notes for quick-talking superiors, and then running them off to whoever needed them, fast. For the most part I'd felt like a kid running chits for bookies, but the pay was great and the summer weather in Boston was hot and steamy. There were more than seventy universities and colleges in and around Boston, and the girls who stayed on for summer internships wore practically nothing.

Now I was a full-time employee, and after that last semester in London I was puffed up. Like most fresh-out-of-college kids, I thought I was pretty damn slick and super knowledgeable about all this finance stuff. But this was the big time, the real deal. I was going to soak it all up like a sponge, work my butt off, and climb that ladder to riches.

State Street handled some big domestic and international pension funds, and under Lopardo's marketing genius the firm's fingers were reaching out and grabbing huge corporate accounts. I'll explain that banking business paradigm briefly.

For example, let's take a multibillion-dollar corporation like General Electric. A big company like that has a structure for making retirement payments, which start getting paid out when a loyal employee wraps up his twenty-five years, gets his gold watch, and goes home to fish. During that employee's tenure, the company puts a tiny part of its profits into his pension fund, and in some cases, the employee can also choose to put part of his salary in there, so on the back end he'll get more money for boats and poles.

Now, a company like GE has thousands of employees, so the pension fund is enormous—billions of dollars. But you don't just let all that money sit there earning a lousy street bank interest of three percent. You invest it, preferably in something with a much bigger return, like stocks and bonds. And that's where State Street would come in, taking over management of GE's pension fund and making a ton more money for everybody. And of course State would take a cut for all those management and custody transactions, which is how the bank made its nut.

So, that was the business we were in. And that's where I started, at twenty-three, working as an entry-level grunt for the international money managers, who had impressive resumes with MBA and CFA designations after their names, who worked for Nick Lopardo. I was so low on the totem pole that I had to look up to see the bottom, but that's how new kids learned.

"Birkenfeld, add up these numbers, check 'em three times, and don't fuck up!"

"Birkenfeld, run this purchase order over to Currency and make sure those clowns know which one's the buy rate. And move your ass! It's for deutsche marks and Europe's closing in half an hour!"

"Birkenfeld, if you walk out that door tonight before Chicago confirms that sale, they're gonna find you facedown in the aquarium tomorrow!"

I loved it. It was fast, raucous, profane, and nonstop. I was immersed in the company of investment professionals, an atmosphere I really enjoyed. Every day, no, every hour, I learned something new. We all worked on a trading floor, sort of a mini version of a Wall Street battle zone, with phones ringing off the walls, keyboards hammering, fax machines churning, papers flying, kids like me hustling up and down the stairwells, and plenty of practical jokes. Spitballs flew, whoopee cushions farted, desk drawers got superglued shut. At one point, one of the guys got a recording of Meg Ryan doing her orgasm deli scene from *When Harry Met Sally* and rigged it from his computer to the sound system. Somebody closed a big deal, Meg came like a freight train, and everybody yelled, "I'll have whatever she's having!" (That only happened once—a lady in the office, of Middle East extraction, complained.)

All this, of course, unless Nick Lopardo or one of his minions showed up on the floor, and then it instantly turned into a library: straightened tie knots, erect spines, and oh-so-professional demeanors. You had to look good for Lopardo. He made that clear when he paid off a bootblack across the street and put out a company-wide directive: "Show up in the morning with your shoes shined, or don't show up at all. It's paid for." One portfolio manager interpreted that as a "license to shine" and brought his entire shoe collection to work.

Lopardo, an ex-jock and huge Boston Bruins hockey fan, knew how to handle a team. He wanted us to win every game, but he didn't need to see the locker room antics. He expected *esprit de corps*, and that filtered down through our managers. You didn't *dare* shut down your computer at five o'clock and go home. You went out with the boys (and our few girls) to catch a Bruins game, or to some joint like Brandy Pete's, Tia's, or Clarke's just down the street, where we'd eat, raise a ruckus, drink till after midnight, go home, crash, get up six hours later, and be back at work, *on time*. If you didn't do that, you'd get the dreaded "Pink Pump" treatment, finding a lady's pink stiletto propped on your desk in the morning. Too many pink pumps and the guys would start looking at you like you had herpes.

Having come from the atmosphere of a military academy, this was just my style; work hard, play hard, and never miss an opportunity to have a few laughs. I earned a fearsome reputation as a "Pantser." Send some guy over to the bar to get beers for the ladies, and he comes back with his hands full, defenseless! I'd sneak up behind him and "pants" him right there, down around his ankles with his boxers flapping. I organized the State Street softball team (aptly named Liquid Assets), where we played other banks and sometimes the Boston PD, and I pantsed them all at one point or another. The guys started calling me "The Pantser Commander." Of course, I knew they were going to take revenge, so I tightened my own belt.

But back to the serious business at hand. As my time at State Street progressed, the firm was acquiring management contracts for more and more international and domestic institutional pension funds. We were handling the pension assets of multibillion-dollar corporations such as Amoco, IBM, General Electric, and NYNEX. In order to grow in value, those assets had to be invested in stocks, bonds, and currencies. My responsibilities began with corporate actions, working with portfolio managers to decide on actions to be taken relating to mergers, takeovers, rights issues, dividend reinvestments, and so forth. This also meant establishing relationships with brokerage houses and helping "pick the right horse" when the starting bell rang.

From there I moved over to the International Proxy group, where we applied firm guidelines to the voting of international corporate proxies to ensure such decisions would benefit our pension clients (basically advising on which way shareholders should vote on corporate actions, such as mergers and acquisitions). I voted the first-ever institutional proxy for a Japanese company. This was all part of the institutional investment arm of State Street, initially known as the Asset Management Division. But as it grew in importance, the division was rebranded State Street Global Advisors, or SSgA, and I finally wound up in the Currency department, which we created. The currency men and women were sophisticated, slick; some had multiple languages and they operated all over the world. Their stock in trade was foreign currency—establishing trading relationships with other banks, setting up credit facilities for our clients, and then executing foreign exchange transactions to settle foreign equity transactions and adjust currency hedge positions. I dove in headfirst to learn everything I possibly could.

To explain the foreign currency concept, you didn't want to merely invest in American securities. In the event of an economic downturn, diversification greatly reduced the risk. There were deals to be had all over the world, and often a foreign market could offer greater returns than the New York stock exchange. However, in order to purchase a foreign stock, you had to first own the proper foreign currency.

For example, if you wanted to buy the French pharmaceutical stock Sanofi, you had to do so using French francs (the European Union and its dreaded "euro" were not yet in play back then). But first you had to purchase those francs using US dollars, and since the buy and sell rates of foreign currencies fluctuated just like stocks, you had to know what you were doing, think fast and move fast, or wind up with Nick Lopardo's boot up your ass.

This newly created Currency department was where I flourished. It reminded me of a carnival, with lots of different rides spinning fast and bobbing up and down. You had to be quick, grabbing a ticket, jumping on a ride, then jumping off, cashing in, and catching another. There was a lot of attention to detail. We had ten different counterparty banks that we traded with, and for each bank we had to set up credit facilities and trading lines for about a hundred corporate customer accounts. And we had to have every major currency in the world on hand: French francs, Deutsche marks, Italian lira, Spanish pesetas, British pounds sterling, Dutch guilders, and so on. And then we quickly expanded into the emerging market currencies: Indian rupiahs, Korean won, Thai baht, Philippine pesos, etc. We had to have every bank's specific delivery and receiving instructions for all these currencies at our subcustodian banking network, being instantly ready to buy or sell foreign securities of just about every nation on earth.

Prior to the Currency department being set up, all our account managers had been executing their own currency trades. Now it was consolidated, with one group doing all the market research, buys, sells, and settlements. Instead of five different managers buying French francs at different times and for different values, we did it all in one shot, aggregating all of the firm's activity and placing trades out for competitive bidding. Then we worked with the IT department to set up an advanced computer system and made sure everything was automated, a sophisticated check-and-balance system. The effort dramatically streamlined the process and yielded savings for our clients as well as the bank, through reduced transaction costs, reduced failed deliveries, and improved executions.

Every day I was working with international money managers, and within a year I was handling spot and forward currency trading on ninety institutional accounts with more than $30 billion in assets. I thrived on the adrenaline rush and made good trades, while pulling down about $40K a year for myself. Back in the late 1980s, especially after the crash of 1987, that was fine money, but not quite enough. So, harkening back to my VCR business at Norwich, I started looking around for an extra buck.

I lived in a condo complex out in Weymouth, Massachusetts, three nice buildings, twelve stories high. Each condo had these towering picture windows overlooking the bay and the Boston skyline, and one Saturday I was out in the hallway picking up my morning newspaper when the nice elderly lady next door popped her head out.

"Good morning, young man!"

"Top of the morning to you, Mrs. Swanwick."

"Could you do me a great favor, Bradley? You are so tall, after all."

"And handsome?" I winked at her.

"Yes, of course." She blushed and fanned herself with a handkerchief.

Mrs. Swanwick's picture window was filthy and there was no way she could clean the top of it. So I went back to my place for a pail, a sponge mop, and a squeegee, and spent about half an hour making her window spotless. When I was done she reached up, pinched my cheek, and handed me fifty bucks!

Next thing you know, I had flyers slipped under all the condo doors, advertising my new window- and carpet-cleaning business. Every Saturday thereafter, I'd rent a steam cleaner at the local U-Haul store, haul my mop and pail around, and spend five hours cleaning, at one hundred bucks an hour! And then I started painting and installing outdoor carpet on balconies and made even more money. My side business never cramped my weekend style, because I partied so hard during the week after work.

Business at State Street Global Advisors was good, and getting even better as we swung into the 1990s. The bank's reputation and coffers grew, and Nick Lopardo was at the top of his game. It made us all proud when we heard he'd made an appearance before the Teamsters union in Boston, about the toughest crowd around. Lopardo basically told them they were pussies who didn't know how to handle their money, and they turned over their pension fund management to State Street. He got a big kick out of that coup and called it the "Jimmy Hoffa" fund.

My manager at SSgA, Joe Foster, was a stand-up guy and I really liked working for him. A Boston University MBA grad with a CFA distinction, he was fifteen years older than I, very bright, classy, and professional. Nothing escaped his detail-oriented eyes, everything was done on the up-and-up, and I learned from him that the smallest mistake could have massive repercussions. We never left work at the end of the day without double-checking every transaction, and only then could the beer flow freely as we bantered about sports.

I also had lots of friends at the bank, but Rick James was my best. Rick had a business degree and a CFA distinction, but never waved it around. He was a genius with numbers and could interpret a stock ticker like a heart surgeon reading an EKG. While I was tall, lanky, and loud, gesticulating a lot with my simian arms, Rick was shorter, compressed, darkly handsome, and quiet. He had a sweet, steady girlfriend, and it was clear she was going to someday be Mrs. James, and they'd wind up with a brood of kids and a Volvo. I was on the speed-dating gravy train, and though we kidded each other about our lifestyle choices, we never cramped one another's style. It was a yin–yang thing that works to this day.

But as for the bank, about three years into my tenure, the State

Street fairytale slowly began to turn grim. As the business of asset management and global custodianship grew exponentially, more people were being hired and our tight-knit family was encroached upon by "in-laws" we didn't know, or frankly did not trust. In the Currency department, my boss, Joe, an experienced trader, and I handled all the trading and back-office operations to perfection, but senior management decided to hire a pair of cowboys from New York and place them both above Joe. I wasn't shy about questioning the wisdom of "It ain't broke, so let's fix it."

"Why the hell do we need these guys?" I asked a glum-faced Joe.

"Well, management says they're going to expand Currency," he mumbled. "They want to offer it as a stand-alone product, sell it as an investment strategy."

That didn't pass the smell test, but I rolled my eyes and soldiered on.

So, to give it a subtle, descriptive flourish, these two cowboys from New York City were arrogant assholes. Real jackasses. And they started doing unorthodox things with trading. Up until then our currency activities had been limited to trading currencies to settle foreign bond and stock transactions, and to carefully managing exposures for clients seeking protection from the volatile foreign exchange prices. But the new kids on the block wanted to more aggressively manage currency exposure for our clients. Rather than follow the firm's valuation models to identify over- and undervalued currencies, they began shooting from the hip, taking aggressive positions, sometimes shifting these within a single trading day, across client portfolios. Such activity was contrary to our conservative long-term buy-and-hold investment philosophy, which was what our clients expected of us and we had a contractual obligation to live up to.

So, as losses began to pile up from these trades, the international portfolio managers who had the direct relationships with the clients were hung out to dry, left to defend actions they didn't condone or support, but were helpless to stop. The two amigos upstairs were treating our clients' portfolios as bottomless funding pits for their seat-of-the-pants views. These guys wanted instant profits and the bonuses to go along with them: bing-bang-boom. They thought they were in a fucking Las Vegas casino!

Those two clowns didn't care much for our equity portfolio managers, because the New York stiffs knew little about nothing, while the State Street veterans were very experienced and knowledgeable. Bullies always hate the smart kids. I, on the other hand, had gone through four years of military college. And while I hadn't pursued that career, I still had that culture in my bones: team player, support your troops, never leave a man behind. The equity portfolio managers liked me because I always made sure their currency trades settled on time and for good value while communicating market information to them in a timely manner, so in turn they could get the most bang for the buck when purchasing securities for pension fund clients. So, there I was, stuck between these new, green, know-it-all assholes and my battle-hardened buddies.

The first red flag whipped up the flagpole when the Manhattan morons brought in this new kid for the Currency desk, "Fresh out of Harvard, Dan." I tried to train him up the old SSgA way, but he'd just smirk at me over his bow tie. He made all kinds of mistakes, which I patiently corrected, but then one Friday something big went down behind our backs. Dan confirmed a major purchase order for Japanese yen, but instead of waiting to make absolutely certain that his counterpart in New York agreed with and confirmed the buy, he went home early to diddle with his girlfriend. The purchase went through.

Two months later, when the settlement date approached, my boss Joe's phone rang. Our New York counterpart was on the other end. Joe put it on speaker and I nearly shit an ostrich egg.

"Um, we've got a little problem here, Joe."

"What's the problem, Larry?"

"That purchase order for yen? Your guy Dan reversed it."

"*Reversed* it?" Joe was loosening his tie now, starting to sweat.

"That's right. He mistakenly confirmed it as a buy, not a sell. And we've got a loss here."

"A loss." (long pause) "How much?"

"Seven hundred and eighty thousand dollars."

*Holy shit!*

And that's when the snowball rolled off the summit and there was no way to stop it. Joe, of course, had to report this fiasco to the New York City cowboys upstairs. There was no way to bury a three-quarter-million-dollar loss, and to me it seemed the only way to make it up to the client was by SSgA writing a check. But those two slicks had another idea. Somebody upstairs called New York (Chemical Bank) and said something like this:

"Listen, we'll make that trade up to you guys. Going forward, for however long it takes, on future trades with us . . . just up the price a little bit, until you've made back from us what we lost for you."

*What?* When I heard that I nearly lost my mind! What those two clowns were saying was that if we, State Street, needed to purchase French francs for one of our clients—like Amoco, for example—Chemical Bank could sell the currency to us at an undisclosed mark-up and keep the difference! That practice was called "padding," and so illegal it would've made Tony Soprano blush. These clowns were basically telling Chemical, "You can still have our business, boys, as long as you shut up and play ball."

From there the snowball picked up more cow dung in its inexorable roll downhill. As I previously mentioned, our department had consolidated all the foreign currency purchases of portfolio managers throughout the bank. If there were ten portfolio managers who all needed Italian lira to buy Italian securities, we'd buy it all during a single business day to ensure a mean value across the board. However, if you were buying 100 million lira, you'd have to buy it in available tranches, and that might mean ten different buys from opening to closing bell. All those values would be slightly different; some better deals, some less so, and the fair thing to do was to spread the upsides and downsides evenly for all the managers.

Well, guess what? Those New York cowboys had their "favorites" at the bank. They liked some PMs (the ones who kissed their asses), and some not so much. So they ordered that all currency trade results be held until the end of the trading day, at which time they'd look them over and give the best deals to their favorites. That *really* pissed me off.

"Have you seen the shit that's going down with the client trade allocations?" I asked Rick one night over a couple of beers. I'd split him off from the regular herd and taken him down to a bar near Faneuil Hall, just the two of us alone.

"Yeah," he sighed into his mug of Sam Adams. "I've been wondering when you were going to bring it up."

"It's fucking unbelievable," I spat. "Like, if that ass-wipe Jack Tremont has a million bucks to buy Japanese yen, and Joe Foster has the same nut for the same thing, Joe winds up with 10,000 less yen! It's slimy as hell."

"And probably illegal," said Rick.

I leaned closer to him and whispered, "I'm gonna start keeping records on those fuckers upstairs."

"I figured you would." Rick clinked his mug to mine. "You're all balls, few brains."

So, for a long time thereafter, I kept my mouth shut and my eyes wide open. Whenever I spotted some squirrelly transaction, I made a copy and added it to the burgeoning pile back at my condo. But keeping quiet stuck in my craw. The hucksters upstairs got bolder and bolder, issuing false profit reports to pension fund clients to make themselves look good, while concealing losses so no one would know they'd screwed up. Then a very senior executive started strong-arming our managers, forcing them to donate big portions of their Christmas bonuses to the reelection campaigns of "friendly" state treasurers across the country. Lo and behold, those treasurers then signed contracts with State Street to manage their multibillion-dollar state pension funds. I was hardly surprised when I learned that a flat-out bribe was slipped to a senior Emirates officer, Dr. Bin Kharbash, and we got a $2 billion management contract for the Abu Dhabi Investment Authority. Apparently the SSgA team wasn't familiar with the Foreign Corrupt Practices Act.

By 1994, the firm was breaking more and more laws on the books. I'd been at State Street for five years, and while I'd never expected to stay there forever, my conscience was starting to nag me.

Then came the final nail in my coffin. The trading floor had purchased a used Dictaphone system and we were supposed to record all our telephone transactions. Well, that's all fine, as long as you advise the guy on the other end. "Mr. Jones, for your protection and ours, this transaction is being recorded." But our bosses didn't want our clients to know they were being taped, so they could cherry-pick tapes if they needed them later, while pretending the rest didn't exist. That's called *wiretapping* and it's illegal as hell. When it comes to recording conversations, Massachusetts was, and still is, a two-party state. That is, both parties to the conversation must consent to being recorded. Without all parties consenting to the recording, it becomes a criminal act.

"We can't do this shit, Joe!" I had stormed into my manager's office and was stomping around like a wild horse. "If the regulators find out about this, we're all fucked in banking forever!"

"I know, Brad, I know." He tried to calm me down. "But that's the way they want it."

"Fuck it. I'm going higher."

And I did, and it caused a shit storm, and Legal got involved and they all argued and sputtered and fussed. I, of course, was the bad boy with the big mouth. Managers started doing the "hair flip" whenever they saw me. But the results? The firm's legal beagles boldly issued a directive, *in writing*, that while this practice was technically outside the norm, we were to continue recording our one-sided taps. "I suggest we do something illegal," the memo seemed to say. "My view is we wouldn't be slapped too hard even if someone figured out what we are doing is illegal."

Well, I refused to use the Dictaphone. So they put me on probation. I *still* refused. And that's when two company security officers showed up on the trading floor, informed me that I was resigning from the bank, and asked me to pack up my "good-bye box" and get a move-on. I smiled at them, got right up on top of my chair, threw my arms out, and made an announcement to my coworkers, who all stared at me like stunned sheep.

"Ladies and gentlemen, my good compatriots, I would like to inform you that I am *not* voluntarily resigning from this institution!"

The company cops took my ID and escorted me out. Was I pissed off? That doesn't begin to describe how I felt. I hadn't done

one damn thing wrong, and the bank was sticking it to me long, hard, and without any lube. They wanted my resignation so they wouldn't have to pay me a dime in severance. Not happening.

The next day Rick James, risking his own career at the bank, snuck me back in by swiping his own ID twice at the elevator lobby. I plopped right back down on the seat at my desk. The company cops showed up again.

"What the hell are you doing here, Birkenfeld? You resigned yesterday!"

"I did *not* resign," I said. "I work here."

Then the big dogs showed up. "All right, wise guy. You're fired."

"Works for me," I said. I made my proper good-byes to all my buddies, who mumbled and cursed the powers upstairs, and I walked.

But in case you're wondering, I did not go gently into that good night. State Street offered me one year's salary as severance, as long as I'd sign a gag order. I told them to stuff it and hired a lawyer. We assembled a full dossier on all the dirty doings at the bank, and sent it to the chairman of the board, Marshall N. Carter. My lawyer's cover letter suggested that "Mr. Birkenfeld would consider a settlement of $500,000, since State Street has ruined his career." But Marshall N. Carter figured he could outsmart a pissant young banker and blew us off.

But I wasn't done yet with State Street. They'd broken my sword and branded me persona non grata, but I still had great friends at the bank, all pissed off that I'd been fired, and they were slipping me intel under the table. The bank was about to hold its annual shareholders' meeting, a five-star gala in the grand auditorium at State Street headquarters. I was still a bona fide stockholder, so I decided to exercise my shareholder rights.

It was a lovely affair, with more than 250 shareholders present and a host of local media. Marshall N. Carter was there on the dais. Nick Lopardo and the rest of their stuffed-shirt gurus were all in attendance. I sat there for an hour, letting them brag about the wonders of State Street's courage and coups, and then I stood up with a question.

"Mr. Chairman, I'm a shareholder and a former employee of SSgA. My lawyer recently submitted a detailed accounting of wide-ranging misconduct committed by officers of SSgA, much of it illegal. Could you tell us what you've done to rectify the situation and reprimand those responsible? And I'd like to know why the board has refused to respond to my myriad allegations concerning the bank's highly illegal practices and breaking of US laws."

Boom! Two hundred and fifty pairs of bulging eyes spun around to stare at me. "Who is this guy?" Carter's face turned purple and the master of ceremonies jumped up and announced, "Ladies and gentlemen, this meeting is adjourned for today. Please enjoy doughnuts and coffee in the adjoining room."

Well, I like doughnuts and coffee as much as anyone else. Needless to say, at that postmeeting party, everyone avoided me like kryptonite. Except for the media. The reporters were all over me as I smiled and accepted their business cards.

"Thank you for your concern," I said. "You will hear more from me shortly."

But they never did. It was the morning of April 19, 1995, and at that very moment, Timothy McVeigh was blowing up the Alfred P. Murrah Federal Building in Oklahoma City. The story of a quixotic young banker tilting at windmills wasn't going to make the news.

What did make the news a couple of months later was my last stab at State Street's heart. State Street had been sued by a female employee, Lisa Chui (my first boss), for unfair, prejudicial practices. She'd gone out on maternity leave with Nick Lopardo's blessing, then upon her return he'd demoted her, claiming her previous position was no longer open! This pained me because I'd so admired the guy back when, but I also held him responsible for my debacle; he should have bitch-slapped those cowboys upstairs (Nick retired in 2001 shortly after he clashed with his management over having given Ray Bourque, the Bruins hockey hero, a victory ride home with the Stanley Cup to Boston from Colorado on the company jet). Anyway, Lopardo had been subpoenaed to give testimony as part of Lisa's discrimination lawsuit. Somebody slipped me a copy of his deposition subpoena, from which I made five hundred printouts on thick pink stock paper. Then I hired two clowns, with bright orange hair, polka-dot dresses, red bulbous noses, and turned-up shoes. One fine summer afternoon, they were out there in front of State Street headquarters handing out copies of Lopardo's deposition subpoena, right in the heart of the financial district, at the height of the pedestrian lunch-hour crush (Exhibit 4). The local news stations had a field day. Who doesn't love clowns?

Still, that was all schoolyard stuff and I knew it. None of it was going to stop State Street from robbing its clients and snubbing the law. This was serious stuff and it was time to throw one last grenade in the bunker.

That summer, I walked into FBI headquarters at Government Center carrying a pile of documentation. At first, the agents were polite, solicitous, and curious. But they were also skeptical. After all, I was a twenty-nine-year-old unemployed banker with a beef, telling them that one of Boston's oldest and largest financial institutions was essentially running illegal bait-and-switch scams. However, I knew my shit, and over the course of six separate meetings, the agents finally began to nod and raise eyebrows. They wanted ironclad proof and it was obvious I had it.

The FBI opened a formal investigation into State Street, with Special Agent Ronald Keating of the Boston field office leading the charge. Somehow, word of the investigation leaked out to the media (how did that ever happen?). State Street struck back, claiming these were just "routine regulatory matters," but they were far from routine and everybody knew it. Lopardo presided over an internal meeting and he was on one hell of a rant. One participant told me he said, "They can't touch us! We have friends in the CIA and friends in the FBI!"

You'd expect those words to fly from the mouth of some Mafia don who'd ordered a hit and wasn't worried because he had the Feds on the payroll. But Lopardo was no Mafia don. He was a senior bank executive! And he was overseeing the pension funds of thousands of people around the globe, with billions of dollars in assets.

Well, as it turned out, they really *did* have friends in the CIA and the FBI—powerful friends. State Street CEO Marshall N. Carter's father had been Deputy Director of the CIA; the man who'd first shown President Kennedy surveillance photographs of the Soviet missile buildup in Cuba in 1962, launching the Cuban Missile Crisis. But what about the FBI? No problem. They had that covered as well.

Sitting on the Board of Trustees of State Street Bank was a lawyer named Truman Casner, a partner in the high-powered law firm of Ropes & Gray. State Street hired Ropes & Gray to spearhead the bank's defense against the FBI, and the first thing Ropes & Gray did was to hire a former special agent from the Boston field office to *counter* the FBI's investigation. When I heard that I said to myself, "So this is how things work. No wonder Lopardo was so full of himself at that meeting."

Now, you might be thinking I had a jaundiced view of the FBI's Boston field office. But history has revealed that, in 1995, it was the most corrupt FBI office in the nation's history. At the same time the FBI was supposed to be investigating State Street, they were also conspiring with the notorious gangster James "Whitey" Bulger. That's right. Boston's federal agents covered for Whitey and his gang, accepted bribes from him over many years, and turned a blind eye to his multiple murders of rival mobsters and innocent victims.

So, while the Boston FBI was supposed to be investigating State Street Bank, with plenty of supporting evidence and testimony from me, things went sideways, and then south. Despite corroborating evidence and the sworn affidavit of another eyewitness who still worked at the bank, the investigation started to flatline. It turned out that the former FBI agent hired by Ropes & Gray to kill the investigation was having sit-downs and lunches with Ronald Keating, the agent who was *leading* the investigation! Isn't that nice? I hope they enjoyed their sushi, pensioners around the world be damned.

Not long after these little get-togethers the investigation was dropped. So much for "truth, justice, and the American way." As for me, these were lessons learned . . . about banks . . . about the Feds . . . and about how to deal with them. Store it for later.

Finally, I decided to let it all go. It was time to get back to work and start making a living again. Two banking institutions in Boston had looked over my resume and offered me positions, and I was just about to settle and accept one of the offers when suddenly they were pulled. State Street had put out the word on me, all across Boston. I was blackballed, and that old Hollywood adage echoed in my head.

"You'll never work in this town again."

It was time to go, and far away. Somewhere out there, I knew I'd find a welcoming, gleaming shore, where a sharp young banker could make his name and fortune. I thought about it long and hard. Where oh where might that be?

Ah, yes.

*Switzerland.*

# CHAPTER 3

## CRACKING
## THE CODE

*"If you can't trust a Swiss banker,
then what's the world coming to?"*

—*JAMES BOND, THE WORLD
IS NOT ENOUGH*

SUMMER 1995

Switzerland was a banker's Disneyland, and I was thrilled to be there.

I stared out the window of the 747 as the rolling plains of Europe rose from the mist. I'd chosen a night flight without thinking much about it, but I realized now as the sun began to rise that it must have been a subconscious plan to embrace the dawn, a sign of rebirth, a quest to begin again. Boston was behind me, rolling away in the big jet's wash like so much flotsam in the churn of a navy frigate.

After burning my bridges in Boston and tossing a few hand grenades, I figured it was time for an expatriate sabbatical. If I could find someplace overseas to get a decent MBA, I'd be that much more marketable when I went on the hunt again. Plus, disappearing for a while would give me a clean slate. I'd found this small American university in a quaint Swiss town called La Tour-de-Peilz on the shores of Lake Geneva. The classes would be conducted in English, so I wouldn't have to dust off my rusty French. And who knew? Maybe when it was over somebody in Europe might offer me a job. I'd been to Lugano, Switzerland, in 1979 as a kid with my grandmother. It was beautiful, clean, safe, and there was no better place to ski, one of my favorite sports. If the job gambit didn't pay off, at least I'd have fun.

As the plane circled Zurich I thought about Boston, where I'd learned many things, but mostly about how my idealistic view of the world was sadly the detritus of childhood fantasies. Maybe if I'd stuck it out as a ROTC grad and become an air force officer, I would have thrived in a realm of real heroes, but I had my doubts about that fairytale too.

State Street had taught me that, at least in the world of big banking and mega-finance, heroes were as rare as Boy Scouts in a biker gang. If you bucked the system, you'd be a lonely outcast, never fully trusted or accepted, left in the garage to mop up the oil spills while the rest of the boys went off riding and carousing, getting all the hot girls and never getting caught. I wanted to ride with the big dogs somewhere, but without screwing the customers and feeling bad about myself. I'd picked up lots of tricks of the trade, but I wanted to use them to make my clients richer, and then reap the benefits. That's how I saw my role as a banker. Everybody goes home happy, right?

As the plane sank lower and the engines bled off, the twinkling landscape grew larger. There it was, the land of kings and billionaires, CEOs and priests, soft sweet chocolates and women to match. I'd had dealings with Swiss bankers while at State Street, and I knew that in Switzerland money talked and bullshit walked. You could do just about anything with secret accounts that the law allowed, and Swiss law allowed almost anything but homicide. I didn't know the system yet, but I'd be learning it all soon enough. At the moment I was squeezed into a cheap coach seat with my knees practically slamming my chin as we bounced on the runway. I smiled and said to myself, "Birkenfeld, if things work out, this is going to be one of your very last trips in coach class."

I'll skip the mundane details about my higher education. Let's just say that the next year went by like a rocket, as years seem to do when you're twenty-nine years old and off on the first great adventure of your life. I settled into a rental flat in La Tour-de-Peilz and threw myself into advanced studies in corporate finance, econometrics, business law, managerial accounting, and international marketing (Exhibit 7). My fellow students were wealthy, ambitious, and exotic, hailing from Dubai, Russia, Germany, and Finland. I made some great friendships that have lasted up through today, and we spent the weekends exploring Copenhagen, Barcelona, Prague, and Rome. I studied hard, partied harder, skied every mountain that had a chairlift, and discovered with great joy that European women use only one part of a bikini: the bottom. I met a beautiful girl, Charlotte, part Austrian and part Swedish, and we moved in together and enjoyed all the perks of lusty youth and boundless energy. As I neared graduation in the spring of 1996, I felt "well armed and financially dangerous," yet I still wasn't sure what would happen next. I'd come over to Switzerland to polish off my resume with an MBA, but without a Swiss work permit I didn't really think I'd get hired. But what the hell; I figured I'd interview anyway and take my best shot.

In late spring of 1996 I sent my curriculum vitae to Dr. Reto Callegari, head of French-speaking private banking for the vaunted mega-banking firm Credit Suisse. To my pleasant surprise, I was invited to interview with him. He was tall, slim, with gray hair and spectacles, had a PhD in finance from the University of Zurich and perfect English from an MBA at Stanford. I knew right away that here was a dude I had to impress.

Dr. Callegari asked me all sorts of professional finance questions, which I answered to a T. And then I turned the tables on him.

"Dr. Callegari," I said. "I have a question as well."

He raised an eyebrow. "Mr. Birkenfeld, you do realize that I am here to interview *you*."

"Yes, sir, that's true." I smiled warmly. "But I just need to ask you this question. I need to know where your top three problems are at the bank." Both eyebrows arched at that point, but I pressed on. "You see, I regard myself as somewhat of a problem solver. So, if you're considering taking me on and giving me a very good salary and a Swiss work permit, but I don't really know where the firm's problems are, then you shouldn't be hiring me."

That seemed to amuse him, and of course he didn't share any of his firm's delinquencies with me, but I didn't expect him to. We exchanged business cards and that was that.

Well, not quite. One of the things I'd learned in Boston was that smarts and talent are good to have, but friends are better, and you make friends in the business world not just by having two-martini lunches, but by delivering the goods. I'd serviced my clients as if every one of their requests were a life-and-death emergency. My work ethic was "Never wait. Do it *now*," and that's how I'd made friends with Joe Gelsomino, who worked at Credit Suisse First Boston as head currency trader in New York. I'd given tons of trades to Joe and naturally liked him, so right after my interview I called him up.

"Brad! What's up, buddy?"

"Hey, Joe. I need a small favor. I'm interviewing at Credit Suisse in Geneva, Switzerland, and wondering if you could put in a good word for me."

"Of course! Who's the guy? Gimme his name."

"Dr. Reto Callegari."

"Wow, he's a player! Leave it to me."

Ten minutes later, Joe sent Dr. Callegari an email from New York. I'm sure it was very polite and respectful, but the gist of it was "Bradley Birkenfeld is absolutely the best young banker I worked with at State Street."

One week later, before I'd even started my final exams, I got the offer from Credit Suisse: starting salary, 150,000 Swiss francs,[1] plus a Swiss work permit and four weeks of vacation. Holy crap! It was four times what I'd been making at State Street, and I'd be working directly for Dr. Callegari in Geneva. I thought maybe he wanted to keep an eye on me, but that was all good because I wasn't going to let him down.

The only melancholy part of that chapter was that Charlotte and I parted ways. She had a great job in Vevey with Nestlé and wasn't about to move, and I wasn't about to commute every day by bus and

---

1    As of July 2016, one Swiss franc (CHF 1) is worth approximately one US dollar (US $1).

train to Geneva. I wasn't too happy about it, but my buddy Luigi took me to lunch and straightened me out.

"Bradley, my friend, do you have any idea of the circles you will soon be traveling in? Or the types of women you are going to meet? You'll soon be over her, just you wait."

Seemed a bit callous to me, but I soon discovered he was right. My wounds were salved when Credit Suisse found me a gorgeous one-bedroom flat in central Geneva: second floor, parquet floors, marble fireplace, French doors out to the two balconies. Perfect place for a single guy, and only 1,200 Swiss francs a month! My troubled heart healed quickly.

At Credit Suisse, I quickly discovered that my new responsibilities as a highly paid American "guest worker" were essentially nil. The Europeans, bankers in particular, have an interesting work ethic: Show up at a respectable hour, dress well and absorb the ingrained culture, enjoy a two-hour gourmet lunch, leave at cocktail time; lather, rinse, repeat. Dr. Callegari wanted me to become an expert in private banking, which meant servicing and socializing with wealthy clients and suggesting creative ways in which they could make more money—invest in commodities, numismatics, artwork, securities, currencies, etc. Other than that, I was expected to write my dissertation for my MBA. "And if you don't mind, Bradley, make it a long and complimentary tone about the workings of *this* firm." Yessir! Why not?

So, basically I was being paid to learn the ropes. In the meantime, I also learned the history and machinations of "creative" Swiss private banking, which is something you should know too if you're reading this story. If you're already an international banking maven, skip it. Otherwise, pay attention; it's not a pretty tale.

The Swiss numbered accounts. You've heard all the stories. They're the stuff of legends and lore.

For nearly a century, secret bank accounts in Switzerland served as the treasure chests for the world's super-rich and all-powerful. They were the place to hide one's gold, jewels, bundles of cash, and bearer bonds—no names attached (Exhibit 5). They were the purview of the privileged few, and a subject of fascination for oh so many.

Oil barons loved them, spy novelists thrived on them. Dictators could always depend on the Swiss to look the other way as they raided a Third World country of its resources and delivered the spoils to Geneva by suitcase via private jet. Politicians could skim from their election coffers, make a quick stop in Zurich, and ensure their retirements for decades to come. A shipping magnate could sell off a hundred-foot yacht for cold hard cash, take a comfortable ride down a gleaming brass elevator to his safety deposit box in Basel, and never think twice about paying a single euro in taxes.

Those secrets were as safe as a whispered confession to the Pope. After all, who would tell? Certainly not the Swiss.

Switzerland, however, wasn't always known as a safe haven for rogues. The finer traditions of Swiss banking began with the Revocation of the Edict of Nantes in 1685 by Louis XIV, declaring Protestantism illegal in France. This led to the persecution and torture of Protestants and the eventual migration of hundreds of thousands to other countries, including Switzerland. Many private banks were established there to offer investment services to the wave of wealthy, newly arrived Protestant migrants. This wasn't a secret enterprise; simply a wealth management option for men of means. Later on, Switzerland became host to many respectable traditions, such as the establishment of the International Red Cross, the Geneva Convention governing the rules of warfare, and the League of Nations, later to evolve into the United Nations (or devolve, in my own jaundiced view). At any rate, there was nothing nefarious about any of these watershed traditions. They were accomplishments of which the Swiss could be proud.

Then, in 1934, the Swiss Banking Act was incorporated into the Swiss Constitution, Article 47, establishing Swiss bank secrecy. From that point on, no Swiss banker could reveal the details of a client's account, nor his or her identity, without risking prosecution and a life behind bars. Coincidentally, or not, this was just when the Nazis were reaching the pinnacle of power in Germany. Fascists throughout Europe were delighted at the prospect of depositing purloined property with stony-faced bankers who were now forbidden by law from revealing the source. Jews, who were already being persecuted and saw the writing on the wall, made haste to Geneva and Zurich, hoping their nest eggs would survive the coming cataclysm. Their savings did survive, but most of the account holders didn't, and billions disappeared into Swiss coffers, to the benefit of the banks. Throughout World War II, Switzerland reveled in its neutrality, with nary a banker's hair mussed. After all, everyone hid their fortunes in those vaults, Axis and Allies alike. The ongoing joke was that Switzerland would never be invaded. Who would be so stupid as to bomb their own bank?

By the early twenty-first century, there were more than 130 private banks in Geneva alone, a ratio of one bank for each city block. Private banking accounted for one-sixth of Switzerland's economy, and Swiss politicians regularly migrated from public service to the chairmanships of banks, trust companies, and law firms, guaranteeing the status quo. Rogues the world over benefited from Switzerland's corrupt banking practices. There were billions, no, trillions in hidden and pilfered assets.

The rich and famous, the bad and ugly, intelligence agents and Mafiosi used their numbered accounts to hide money from wives, husbands, and business partners; to embezzle company profits; to fund small wars and finance drug cartels. Movie stars loved the intrigue of it all, and mistresses clutched Swiss Black American Express cards in their Louis Vuitton purses. Never mind that if you held a numbered account, you actually *paid* the Swiss a flat fee for the privilege and never received a penny of interest. The balance was yours to dream about, tucked safely away under your steel Swiss mattress.

Best of all, money that no one knew about was *untaxable* money. For wealthy Americans who were less than forthright, it was a godsend. The American market was target-rich, and Swiss banks began assembling teams of private wealth managers who would travel to the United States, attending luxurious venues and soirées where potential clients were swimming in cash, and bring home the bacon.

So that's my brief lesson on the history of secret Swiss banking, and that's where I came in. I learned the whole story from inception to present practices and realized that the Swiss operated with a wink, a nod, and a big grin. Did I care that much if the money I'd be handling was from ill-gotten gains, or hidden away to deprive some government of its lust for taxes? Nope. Somebody much higher up the food chain had decided it was all perfectly legal. I wasn't about to start wearing a halo and going to confession.

Speaking of confession, Credit Suisse was also my first foray into the deeper intrigues of numbered accounts. One day I was covering for a colleague on vacation, Carol Hambleton-Moser, when two of her clients called up. They were coming in together and wanted to withdraw $100,000 each, from separate accounts. No problem. The building concierge sent them up the elevator to a second concierge, who escorted them to a private salon. I showed up, introduced myself, and explained that I was covering for Carol. They were Italians, clean-cut, wearing blazers and slacks and carrying briefcases. I asked for their passports and code names, and tapped the computer.

The system had multilevels of security to ensure that no impostor could just show up and withdraw someone else's money. Everything checked out: passport numbers, code names, matching photographs, ages, and physical descriptions. I called my assistant and she arrived with a cash box and a money-counting machine. Before long the two Italians each had $100K locked in their briefcases. They signed the withdrawal forms, knowing they'd be charged a fee for withdrawing their own cash, but they didn't seem to mind. We smiled and parted ways.

After they left, I scrolled farther down in their computer records. They were both Vatican priests! Why were they keeping their money in secret Swiss accounts? I never asked a soul. *Not my circus, not my monkeys.*

Anyway, about halfway through my overpaid education at Credit Suisse, Dr. Callegari suddenly announced that he was being transferred to Asia. The doc liked me and wanted to take me along with him, but I was having a helluva good time in Geneva and couldn't envision the same thing in Singapore, where if you spat a wad of gum on the sidewalk the cops gave you fifty lashes in the city square. So, for a while I was "homeless" at the firm, wandering around and looking for a new foster father. I found him in Olivier Chedel.

Olivier was a player, the guy in charge of all private banking for

North America, the UK, Israel, and all of English-speaking Africa. He was a classy-looking Swiss-German guy in his late forties, with swept-back dark hair, cool blue eyes, a strong jaw, and a cleft chin, and he spoke flawless English, German, French, and Spanish. He'd show up on a Monday all sunburned from skiing in the Alps, on Wednesday don a tuxedo on his way to the opera, and by Friday he'd hop in his BMW Z3 and take off for Saint-Tropez. I liked him right off the bat, and with our first handshake I knew we were kindred souls.

I spent my first days on the "Anglo" desk looking through all the account records, and noticed something strange. We had hundreds of millions of "English-speaking" money sitting in Credit Suisse vaults, but unless these rich dudes walked into the bank, nobody was seeing them face-to-face. Not *one* banker was out there visiting them. Really? To me, that was like owning an ice cream truck in summertime and never leaving the driveway.

"So, Mr. Chedel," I asked him one day over coffee (not Starbucks; the real Swiss stuff). "Who from our division services these clients?"

"Well, my boy." He gave it a dramatic pause and smirked under his Ray-Bans. "No one."

"No one goes out to visit them? Nobody schmoozes them or uses them to network and get more clients?"

"Schmoozes," he said. "An interesting colloquialism, but no. In case you haven't noticed, Bradley, Credit Suisse is a very conservative firm."

"But what about marketing trips? Someone should be out there pitching our products and services. It's a small investment for a potentially huge return."

"Well then, prove your point, Bradley." He smiled and clicked his cup to mine. "Show me what you can do. Set one up."

And so I did. I picked out three cities—Toronto, Boston, and Hamilton, Bermuda—and I got on the horn and called every contact I knew from my State Street days and told them my new boss at Credit Suisse wanted to wine and dine their favorite clients. I booked all the flights, five-star hotels, and then Olivier and I took off for two weeks of Chateaubriands, primo boxes at hockey games, operas, jazz clubs, and chats about secret accounts amid swirling cigar smoke and

Courvoisier. By the time it was over, six mega-money North Americans were frothing at the mouth to come to Geneva and hand over their fortunes to Olivier Chedel.

"Well, Bradley, that was quite a performance," he said to me as we sipped victory martinis on our hotel veranda in Bermuda. "You certainly delivered the goods. It's a shame I won't be able to use them."

"What do you mean, Olivier?" By this time we were on a first-name basis.

"I neglected to mention that I've just resigned from Credit Suisse."

"You . . . what?" I sat up in my lounge chair and spilled half my drink.

"Yes. I am going over to Barclays Bank in Geneva." He enjoyed my stupefied gape for a moment and grinned that impish grin at me. "But don't fret, my boy. You'll be going *with* me."

Good-bye Credit Suisse, hello Barclays, the powerhouse of British banking. My salary went up to $200,000, I stayed in my luxurious flat, and all I had to do was pick up my briefcase and swing over to Barclays headquarters a few blocks away. Having tested my talents, Olivier knew he had the perfect point man whom he could trust. He gave me an office and a beautiful young Swiss assistant, Valerie Dubuis, and he sat on his leather throne behind a mahogany door and called me in for assignments. It was like he was "M," Valerie was Ms. Moneypenny, and I was You-Know-Who.

"Bradley, have a seat. I believe you'll be stunned."

"What's on the menu, Boss?"

"Well, Barclays Zurich is closing operations and consolidating all of their accounts over here to Geneva, and that means all of their American and Canadian accounts."

"Why the hell are they doing that?"

"Because they are oh-so-English, my boy. No imagination. The Zurich branch is washing their hands of billions for the sake of clerical simplicity."

"Let me guess," I said. "No one services these North Americans."

"In your amusing parlance, 'Bingo.' You know what to do. Get on with it."

It was a license to make a killing. "Pleasure to meet you. I'm Birkenfeld . . . Bradley Birkenfeld, Agent 00$." I compiled a dossier of all our North American secret account holders, reached out to them (discreetly, of course), and filled up my planner with dinner engagements. Then I took off for Canada and the States and had a grand old time, staying in five-star hotels, riding around in limousines, and devouring fat steaks at Peter Luger's in Manhattan as I feted existing clients, proposed more investments, and charmed them into turning over the names of their mega-rich friends. Now, these folks weren't dummies. For the most part they were powerful, wealthy, successful men in their middle years, and we all understood they couldn't just hand me a briefcase stuffed with cash and have me smuggle it back to Europe. So, these dinners usually concluded with cigars, cognac, the flick of my business card, and a subtle suggestion.

"You know, Mr. X, Geneva is lovely at any time of the year. Maybe a man of your stature, with so many responsibilities and business pressures, should take a short break and enjoy its wonders. The magnificent mountains, gourmet restaurants, luxury shopping; it's almost too much at times. And the women . . . Good God! You know, I was actually stunned to discover that all that Swiss stiffness is merely a cover, sort of like the Japanese. The sex trade's booming and it's all perfectly legal. Not that you'd partake, of course, but it's an interesting cultural anomaly." (wink)

Naturally they showed up. I'd fly back to Geneva, exhausted, my jaw aching from smiles and sales pitches, and before I'd even unpacked, Valerie was pushing me out the door to welcome the folks I'd just met. Here we go again: fine dining, champagne, Swiss chocolates, and gorgeous Russian girls "charming" the pants off my clients at very reasonable rates. And then the handover: cash, jewelry, artwork. "A pleasure doing business with you, Mr. X." And I was off to do it all again, making CHF 200K, living the high life, all expenses paid, just putting on a suit and making sure people were very happy.

I was the only Swiss private banker at Barclays running this game—a total monopoly. I'd plop down in my first-class airline seat, humming my own version of "Ticket to Ride." "I think I'm gonna be glad, I think it's todaaay, yeah!"

It was *crazy*. Even my vacations were rarely just that. Business fell in my lap. Taking a short leave in St. Barts, I met a comely blonde woman who turned out to be an adult-film actress. She spent two days at my digs, which wasn't very restful, but she was fascinated with the prospects of a secret Swiss account, since she made most of her money in cash. A few weeks later she showed up at my flat in Geneva, carrying a pink suitcase and a giant teddy bear. She asked me for a serrated knife, decapitated the bear, and out poured $300,000 in cash. Barclays welcomed her money. Sometime later, US authorities welcomed her to a federal prison. She'd been convicted of insider trading, but I had nothing to do with that.

"Well, a bit of bad news, Bradley."

I was sitting in Olivier's office. He looked glum. "Is my phone bill too high?"

"No, it was only a thousand dollars last month. Quite reasonable. However, Barclays, in its infinite wisdom, has decided no more solicitations of North Americans. They're getting a bit nervous."

I knew what he meant. I was an avid reader of the *Financial Times* and closely tracked the regulatory agencies in the States, such as the Treasury Department and the IRS. We were heading toward the year 2000, the American economy was in flux, and whenever that happened there were big eyeballs on the rich folk—and tax-evaders in particular. I thought maybe my good days were done.

"Well," I sighed. "It was fun while it lasted."

"Don't be so hasty, my boy. I'm sending you over to London. Not permanently, just a couple of weeks here and there. We're giving you the three premier offices in the London branch network— Knightsbridge, Sloane Square, and Pall Mall. They've got bundles of money coming in from all sorts of wealthy customers and need an offshore home to house it."

My smile came back like a flashbulb. With the Brits, tax regulations were lax, to say the least. They didn't regard an English gentleman's overseas profits as depriving Whitehall of revenue. A British citizen could take his fortune, bring it over to Switzerland, and invest it in anything he wanted. Any profits he enjoyed, as long as he spent them outside the UK, were untaxable income. In fact, most civilized countries had similar regulations; don't ask, don't tell. Only the Americans and the Japanese were so tight-assed about taxes. But the Brits? "A gentleman never discusses his ailments or finances."

"So, Olivier," I said. "Another charm tour?"

"Just go make yourself comfortable on their couches, intercept a few million pounds, and bring it back here. There's a good fellow. Off with you."

On the way back to my office, Valerie was sitting at her desk, chin in hand, beaming at me with those beautiful brown eyes. She already knew all about my assignment.

"I like Rothmans," she said. She was a smoker with a taste for fine cuts. "And Hermès scarves, and sexy British rock-and-roll bad boys."

"I'll bring you the smokes and the silks," I said. "But I never smuggle musicians. And besides, you don't need me to match-make."

By the way, I never touched her. She was much too fine an assistant. We partied together on occasion, even skied a few times and teased here and there, but it was always hands-off.

The London gambit was ridiculously easy, and just as Olivier described it. I'd show up, check into the Royal Automobile Club, the English gentleman's club of preference in which I was a member, in Pall Mall near Piccadilly (it's an absurdly luxurious five-star hotel, with its own fine restaurant, breakfast cafe, ballroom, library, two bars, and a health spa; but hell, I couldn't look cheap), and then I'd make my rounds of the branches. The private banking managers at Knightsbridge, Sloane Square, and Pall Mall were relieved to see me, because they had all these mega-wealthy European tycoons selling off blocks of flats, container ships, and start-ups, and waltzing in with stacks of cash and expecting someone at Barclays to magically make it grow. And there I was, the Swiss concierge.

"Birkenfeld, old boy, so glad you're here. We've got this Romanian fellow, big real estate chap, with an extra million pounds sterling sitting here doing bollocks. We've suggested you'd be pleased to move it over to Geneva and have a go, and he's all aboard. Likes tennis, by the way. Here's his card."

So off I'd go to meet this Romanian dude and take him to dinner at Quaglino's, where I'd chat about everything *but* money: girls, racehorses, the Cannes Film Festival. Then I'd suddenly produce a pair of tickets from my suit pocket.

"Khosro, I heard somewhere that you're a tennis fan. I happen to have two very good seats for Wimbledon next week. Why don't we discuss elevating your fortune over a little excitement and sun?"

"Wonderful, Bradley!"

And it wasn't just one client. They never handed me less than three files at a time. I had several memberships at the best British gentlemen's clubs—East India, Royal Automobile—where I'd entertain them; stuff them with great food, scotch, and cigars; then whisk them off to their favorite passions: fashion shows, rugby scrums, cricket matches, football finals, horse races at Ascot. When a guy's favorite horse is two lengths ahead on the back stretch and he's on his feet screaming, that's the perfect time to pitch him hedge funds because he'll agree to just about anything.

At the end of every two-week stint, I'd head back to Geneva carrying three to six dossiers with transfer instructions for millions of pounds. London was just handing me money, like a courier service! It was so easy an orangutan could've done it, and I milked that Swiss cow like nobody's business.

I know what you're thinking. "This was his job?" Well, trust me, after a while it became exhausting. I mean, how many steaks au poivre and crèmes brûlée can you eat while stuffed in a suit before you're dying for a hot dog and a beer at Fenway Park? I was rocketing back and forth, bringing in millions hand over fist, busting my ass for the firm, and building an impressive Rolodex of VIP-connected clients. But when bonus time came, it was never performance-based. I mean $20,000 is nice at Christmas, but it didn't reflect my victories.

"I'm terribly sorry, Bradley," Olivier would say, and he meant it. "I'm afraid it's simply the British old-boy-network thing." Then he'd thrust a finger at the ceiling. "They're reaping your rewards upstairs." Olivier was Swiss-German. The old boys liked him, but probably called him Hermann Goering behind his back.

Meanwhile, the heat was being turned up by the American tax authorities, all over the world. Barclays was starting to divest itself of more and more North American offshore clients, which meant my clientele list in essence was frozen. One day I was sitting at my desk when Valerie popped her head in.

"It's Paul Major on the line, the relationship manager from Barclays Bank Bahamas." I took the call.

"Bradley Birkenfeld. How can I help you?"

"Afternoon, Bradley. Paul Major here, Bahamas branch. Tell me, who's the head of the US desk up there?"

"Well, technically I'm the head, but we don't travel there anymore. Why?"

"We're closing down all of our American accounts down here. Don't want to risk a dustup with Washington. We have an account here and want to know if we could transfer it to you."

"How big's the account, Paul?"

"Two hundred."

"Two hundred thousand? We don't take accounts that small."

He laughed. "Not two hundred thousand, Bradley. Two hundred million."

I sat up in my chair. "You've got a client with two hundred million and you're kicking him out of the bank?"

"No more Americans. We're done. No offense."

"None taken! Send him my way."

But it didn't work. This fat-cat client, a real estate tycoon from California, wanted to move his money to Geneva, but he wouldn't sign the Qualified Intermediary (QI) agreement. The QI is a contract between a foreign bank and the United States IRS, promising to provide information on revenues for the purpose of taxing the client, or not to hold US securities and still allow the client to remain anonymous. So, Barclays basically wanted this guy to fill out a W-9 and get creamed on his $200 million, which he wasn't willing to do. I thought about it for a while, and since I was about to take off to Hawaii for a friend's wedding, I figured I'd stop in California and have a chat with the guy. Maybe I could turn him around, or figure out some other creative way to get his money.

Before taking my vacation, I made another trip to London for the usual wining, dining, and lightening clients of their loads. While I was there, Harry Pilkington, a charming headhunter with Armstrong International, took me out to lunch and informed me that another Swiss bank, UBS, was very interested in hiring me away from Barclays Bank, with a substantial raise and benefits. UBS was huge, but I politely told Harry I wasn't interested in working for a big firm again; a boutique bank would be more my style, without all the bureaucratic bullshit. He asked me to think it over. I didn't.

It was April 2001 when I took off for Los Angeles. In the course of my wheelings and dealings, I'd made good friends with Martin Schuermann, the head of Bertelsmann CLT-UFA and financier of Don Johnson and Arnold Schwarzenegger movies, including *Terminator 3*. Martin was marrying "Downtown" Julie Brown, a beautiful British actress and former MTV VJ. They were lovely, warm, generous people, and I was looking forward to their wedding in Hawaii.

Weddings aren't much fun if you attend them solo, so I'd decided to take a companion along. Marketa was a bar hostess in Prague—tall, slim, pretty, and just turned twenty-two. She'd never been to the United States, so my invitation to fly business class, party in Hollywood, and then see some hot lava put a smile on her face. She was a sweet girl, innocent in many ways, and she gasped when I booked us into the Peninsula Hotel in Beverly Hills. Did we have a good time? Let's just say there's nothing quite like gratitude sex. I called her my "Czech Mate," which she didn't get, but I amused myself.

Just before the prewedding bash, Marketa and I were lounging out by the pool. She was in her nothing bikini, reading USA Today, while I perused the *Financial Times*.

"Bradley, who iss ziss fellow, Kato Kaelin?"

"He's a nobody, darling." I flicked my fingers. "Just some dude who was O. J. Simpson's houseguest who declined to give him an alibi for when he was out murdering his wife and a very nice waiter."

"Oh, I see."

Well, that night at the private party, which was held in a gorgeous mansion in Beverly Hills, who sits down next to us at our table? That's right, Kato, and the place was crawling with movie stars and famous athletes and I thought Marketa was going to faint from all the glitz. At one point she got up and went to the ladies' room, and I started to get concerned when it took her forever. Then she came back.

"Bradley, that was the strangest thing! I waited outside the bathroom for sooo long. And then, these two blonde ladies came out together, but they did *not* flush the toilet!"

I kissed her cheek and patted her hand. "You don't need to flush it," I said, "if you're only using the porcelain top." Her brows furrowed. Alice in Wonderland.

The next morning I rented a Porsche 911 convertible and we drove down the coast to Newport Beach, where I dropped Marketa off to do some shopping while I headed over to a modest bistro to meet Paul Major's now-stranded client, Igor Olenicoff (Exhibit 13). I was sitting there drinking coffee when Olenicoff walked in, and I knew right away this wasn't a guy who threw his money around. The first thing that came to my mind was "Goldfinger." He had silky white hair, cold blue eyes, thin lips, and one eyebrow permanently cocked. With him was a young man who turned out to be his beloved son and heir apparent, Andrei, who looked like a young Brad Pitt.

"So pleased to meet you, Bradley," Olenicoff said as he and Andrei faced me across a corner table. He'd immigrated to the States in the late 1950s, but he still had a hint of a Boris Yeltsin accent.

"The pleasure's all mine, Mr. Olenicoff. My apologizes about all this foolishness with Barclays."

"You may call me Igor, and no need to apologize." A waiter suddenly showed up with juice, waffles, strawberries, and a pot of coffee. Apparently the Olenicoffs were regulars. "I am sure that a more flexible institution will want to host my offspring." He meant his money, and his eyes crinkled. "I do not mind paying my fair share to the government. However, fair is a relative term. Perhaps you can think of a solution?"

"I believe I can indeed," I said.

After a few subtle inquiries about his financial status, I realized this guy was a multibillionaire, with scores of real estate properties and a healthy taste for fine motorcars and yachts.

"What I would propose," I said, "is a two-tiered strategy. First, I'll find you a bank in Geneva that's amenable to your preferred status." We all knew I meant *somebody who'll hide your money and doesn't give a shit if you pay taxes or not.* "Then, I'm going to refer you to a close friend of mine, a savvy CPA and trustee in Liechtenstein. That gentleman will set up company structures, trusts, foundations, and so forth. Your name won't appear on any of their records, but you'll be the ultimate beneficiary."

Olenicoff smiled and wagged a thick finger at me. "I had a good feeling about you, Bradley." He looked at his Rolex. "However, I'm afraid I have another appointment. We'll continue this discussion by phone?"

"Not by phone." I stood up to shake his hand and smiled as I held his grasp for a moment. "But we'll manage."

I picked up Marketa at the row of high-end shops in Newport Beach center. I'd given her five hundred bucks to spend, and she came out carrying just one small shopping bag with a sundress and a pair of sandals inside. I should have married her on the spot. We were already heading back up to LA when my cell phone buzzed. It was Andrei (Exhibit 14).

"My father liked you very much, Brad. Do you have time to meet me for lunch?"

Well, of course I did, and we turned the Porsche around again and Marketa and I had a fine lunch with Andrei at Las Brisas, a swanky Mexican place on the Newport coast. He was such a nice charming kid, and he said, "We're really happy to deal with you, Brad. My dad's ecstatic! He's really pleased you're going to help him find a new home to hide his money."

"That's my job," I said. "That's what I do." We all raised our margarita glasses and toasted. "Andrei, I think this is the beginning of a beautiful friendship." He didn't get the *Casablanca* reference. The kid was too young.

On the way back up to LA, my phone buzzed again. It was Harry Pilkington calling from London, trying to pitch me again on the

UBS job. Suddenly, a lightbulb went off in my head. Maybe, just maybe . . . "Harry," I said, "let's meet next week."

Martin and Julie's wedding in Hawaii was spectacular. It was held at the Paul Mitchell estate, there were more staff than wedding guests, and I hung out a lot with Don Johnson and his wife, Kelley Phleger, which was cool because I loved the television show *Miami Vice*. When we got back to Geneva, Marketa flew home to Prague and I went off to meet Harry.

"I might consider the UBS offer," I said over lunch. "But on one condition."

"What would that be, Bradley?" Pilkington looked like the actor Ralph Fiennes, but without the crazy eyes.

"A performance-based bonus is mandatory." What I meant was that any return on assets I produced from Net New Money I'd bring in would earn me a percentage, right off the top.

"That's rather unprecedented," Harry said. He was right. Most Swiss private bankers didn't have college degrees, and MBAs were extremely rare. They usually started off as tellers or clerks, worked their way up as interns, and even as managers made modest salaries rarely exceeding $100,000. Bonuses were modest; tips at Christmas of a few thousand Swiss francs. "How much do you have in mind?"

"Twenty percent."

"Good lord, Bradley!"

"Oh, and one more thing. My assistant, Valerie, comes with me."

"They'll never go for that!"

"Well, Harry, give it the old English try, or find someone else."

He did try, and UBS balked, but they kept nagging Harry to snag me on the cheap. In the meantime, I did my research, calling around and discreetly asking my contacts why UBS wanted me so badly. Harry met me again for lunch.

"Listen, Brad, they'll give you $250,000, a car lease, and a generous bonus. But this twenty percent? It's not on."

"Really?" I said. "That's interesting, because the reason they need me is that the guy who was doing my job got caught watching porn at his desk, so they had to can his ass. I happen to know that you also approached Fred Ruiz over at Credit Suisse, and he declined, so UBS is fresh out of options. Plus, they know I've got an MBA, hundreds of clients, and I've made money hand over fist for Barclays. Plus, I have a 'C' work permit. So it's twenty percent off the top, or nothing."

Next thing you know, I was walking into UBS headquarters for a meeting with Christian Bovay, head of all Anglo banking for the firm based in Geneva. Right off the bat I pegged him as a devious bastard, but I was no Boy Scout myself. Bovay was thin, fidgety, with thinning hair and a case of dandruff like snow in the Swiss Alps. He also had the weirdest set of crooked teeth. They reminded me of burglar tools. We jousted in his office for half an hour.

"Have no fear, Mr. Bovay," I said. "My bonus isn't going to break the bank. I just feel it's my due, given my past performance. And, should you have to pay it to me, it'll merely mean that I've been very successful for you. Isn't that about it?"

A week later, Harry called me, practically peeing his pants. "Come on in and sign the contract! They'll go for eighteen percent. They've caved!"

Well, that was good enough. But before I did that, I called Andrei in California.

"Hello, Andrei. It looks like I've found a chain store that likes your product. Are we still on board?"

"That's fabulous! You bet we are, Brad!"

On July 4, 2001, I walked into UBS, and as Christian Bovay and the head of Human Resources added their John Hancocks, I signed my new contract with UBS, including my eighteen percent performance-based bonus (Exhibit 6). Before the ink was dry, I mentioned to Bovay that I'd shortly be bringing him my first UBS client, along with $200 million in assets. Bovay's burglar-tool teeth gaped wide open.

Checkmate.

I was instantly the highest-paid UBS private banker in all of Switzerland.

# CHAPTER 4

## SPORTS CARS
## AND MODELS AND
## YACHTS, OH MY!

*"Banking establishments are more dangerous to our
liberties than standing armies."*

—*THOMAS JEFFERSON,
AMERICAN PRESIDENT*

AUTUMN 2001

There's nothing quite like a 2000 Ferrari 360 Modena spider convertible, especially one in candy-apple red (Exhibit 8). With the top down, the sun on your face, and your eyes behind a pair of Vuarnet sunglasses, you pop that six-speed manual transmission and the V-8 Dino engine growls like a crouching leopard, making you feel like a threat at Le Mans. From the outside, that car says *money, power, sex*.

But a Ferrari's even better when you haven't paid a dime for it. This one was the second I'd bought with my favorite kind of cash, "OPM," Other People's Money. I had overseas clients who just wanted a toy to play with in Europe; no need to ship one home and pay crazy taxes on the $250,000 price tag. So they'd tell me what model they craved and I'd buy the car, put Finnish tax-free plates on, and stow it in a luxury garage in Geneva. Whenever they showed up, I'd hand them the keys, and the rest of the time I tooled around whenever I felt like it. That was the deal. You can't leave a car like that sitting around getting rusty. Enzo Ferrari would turn in his grave.

It was early September, a beautiful time of year in Geneva, and I was cruising around the city in the early afternoon, looking for a nice outdoor lunch spot where I could park the car and keep my eye on it. I'd already resigned from Barclays and bid Olivier farewell, which was tough because he'd been such a classy boss and I knew I'd miss him. My new job at UBS was set to begin on October 2, so I'd already been on two months of "gardening leave." That's another weird European phenomenon; you resign from one gig and they pay you full salary for six months until the next one starts, maybe so you won't say anything bad about the one you just quit. I didn't have a garden, but I was happy enough to stay home; nurture my window boxes, liquor cabinet, and cigar humidor; and party with my friends. Marketa was back in Prague and our encounters had waned. She was looking for a husband. I was looking for fun.

The cell buzzed on the seat beside me and I picked it up. It was John Ross, a Canadian buddy I'd met at the Neuchâtel wine festival, *Fête des Vendanges*. He sounded breathless.

"Brad, have you heard?"

"Heard what, John?"

"A plane just crashed into the World Trade Center."

"Fucking impossible," I scoffed. "That's not even a flight pattern."

"I'm telling you, dude. A *big* plane."

"John, you're fucking dreaming. That can't happen."

But he insisted, and I just blew him off and said, "Okay, whatever. I'm driving right now. Give you a call a little later."

I hung up, annoyed, thinking people really should check their facts before doing this Chicken Little routine. The only such incident I could remember was back in the previous century, when something like an old Lockheed Electra had slammed into the Empire State Building. So maybe some dumbass flying a Cessna had hit the World Trade Center; no big deal. I was driving now on a cobblestone street and making sure not to scrape the undercarriage. The phone buzzed again.

"What is it *now*, John?"

"Another plane just hit the other tower."

"Oh . . . *fuck!*"

I pulled the car over. My heart was pounding.

Most everyone on the planet who watched that terrible event unfold that morning had the same reaction. One plane, it's an accident. Two planes, it's fucking terrorists. And certainly every American like me, wherever they were, felt the fury well up from their guts like poisonous bile. I drove the Ferrari right back to the garage and threw the keys to the valet. I didn't trust myself to drive anymore, and I wandered around, suddenly feeling very alone. Switzerland wasn't like the States, where you could storm into any sports bar and find three big TVs covering the news and scream at the screens while you drank and cursed with perfect strangers. I felt like I was on another planet, and home was burning.

Walking back to my flat, I picked up every paper I could find, but they were all yesterday's news. Then I sat up half the night in front of my big TV, drinking scotch and watching the towers fall—over and over—and the Pentagon burning, and that smoking smudge in a field in Pennsylvania. I knew lots of folks in Manhattan, many of them friends working in finance, and I called them all as I held my breath, and then my mom and dad and brothers Doug and Dave. Rick James was all right, though his voice sounded hollow and weary. No one I knew or loved had gone down in flames, but thousands of other innocents had.

The next morning was brutal. I bought all the papers again. The *International Tribune* headline screamed "Hijacked Jets Hit Trade Towers In N.Y. and Plow Into Pentagon." The European papers weren't censoring the images from New York and the TV reports were the same; people crushed to death on the sidewalks, body parts and smoking airplane wheels, long shots of screaming jumpers in flames taking that endless leap until they burst apart on the street. I felt infuriated and helpless, thinking about how if I'd stayed in the military, I'd probably be packing for Afghanistan to go kick some ass. But here I was, a thirty-five-year-old ex-pat banker in Switzerland, with not a damn thing to contribute. Then I watched the next colossus tumble—the stock market. *Well, I thought, at least maybe I can help some of those Americans secure their futures against the coming global financial hit.* It was small comfort, but all I could really do.

Every year at this time, I'd been taking three weeks off for a party tour with my friends. First we'd hit Saint-Tropez in the south of France, then drive up to Munich for Oktoberfest, and wrap it all up at the wine festival in Neuchâtel, an hour north of Geneva. I thought about canceling, but I knew Sevrine would be terribly disappointed. She was Swiss, gorgeous, and we'd only just started seeing each other. Selfishly, I thought she might provide the perfect distraction. Sitting around Geneva in mourning wouldn't help a soul, and dousing our Western freedoms and fun was exactly what those motherfuckers wanted.

Sevrine and I had a few forced laughs, and we sat on the Pampelonne beach talking about how screwed up the world was and drinking Laurent-Perrier rose champagne. She was topless of course, and magnificent, but my mind was preoccupied. In Munich, the Germans carried on as if nothing had happened, downing liters of beer, singing Bavarian dance songs, and staggering to the nearest train station. Maybe they figured New York was finally payback for Dresden. We stayed half in the bag for most of the trip, and the final leg at the wine festival was the sour icing on a melting cake. None of my American or Canadian buddies showed up, nor the Brits. I drove the Ferrari back to Geneva, put it away, and got ready to go back to work.

Oh, one more thing before I get to that. I had drinks with Osama bin Laden's sister. Seriously, no lie. Now, it's a fact that Mohammed bin Laden, Osama's randy father and billionaire Saudi construction king, had twenty-two wives and fifty-four kids, many of whom lived all over the world. So it wasn't as if Nadia had just come from cleaning her big brother's AK-47. She was in her late twenties, with classic Arabian features, long dark hair, and was always dressed to the nines. We moved in the same circles, so when I ran into her at La Centra bar I couldn't resist a chat. She had no aversion to alcohol and I don't think she'd ever worn a *hijab*.

It got pretty heated. She was defensive, which was understandable given that having the name Bin Laden was, at that moment, akin to being Ms. Hitler.

"You Americans shouldn't be so surprised at what's happened," she scoffed as she sipped her Courvoisier. "You are hated all over the world."

"Really?" That steamed me up. "Put the shoe on the other foot, Nadia." I was trying to be polite, but I'm sort of a chainsaw looking for trees and it's hard to keep it in check sometimes. "It would be like an American flying a plane into Mecca and killing three thousand innocent Muslims. That's what we're talking about here. *Understand?*"

Needless to say, we did not go dancing.

On October 2, I walked into 16 Rue de la Corraterie for my first day with UBS Private Wealth Management. It was a fine-looking four-hundred-year-old brownstone, five stories high, without a single plaque or anything else marking it as a bank. UBS headquarters, a much larger modern edifice, was a couple of blocks away and adorned with the blood-red UBS logo of three enormous skeleton keys. Our much smaller building said: "We're anonymous here, and you will be too."

Right away I understood this was going to be different from Credit Suisse or Barclays, where dealing with offshore clients had been done with aplomb and no overt indication that anything we did might be frowned upon elsewhere. These folks at UBS knew their profits were hauled in from the muddy waters between tax regulations and they weren't pretending otherwise. You needed multiple clearances to get past the front desk and up to the second floor, where thirty private bankers and their assistants worked at the "North American Desk," an open area much like the trading floor at State Street. Except this was no Boston frat-boy club; the bankers were dressed like GQ models, the desks were heavy and neat, chairs and couches plush, and stock market figures trickled down flat screens like something out of *The Matrix*. Rolling bars were stocked with liquor to keep the folks happy as they burned up the phone lines, and since the Swiss couldn't abide "no smoking" paranoids, cigar smoke curled through multilingual conversations about VIP clients, gourmet lunches, and Net New Money. You weren't getting anywhere *near* a computer without multitiered passwords. The place reminded me of a Cold War CIA spy cell. I liked it.

On my first day at work, I was given a list of names of secret account holders I'd been assigned to service. Some of them, corporate bigwigs, made me smile with pleasure. One of them made me blink; Abdullah bin Laden, half-brother of the now infamous Osama. Abdullah had $14 million in a secret account, but tracking him down to discuss his investments wouldn't be easy. He'd been residing in the Boston area along with other members of the OBL clan. Right after 9/11, while all commercial flights were grounded in the States, the Bush administration had whisked them all away on a private jet. My new clients were going to be *very* interesting.

For the first month, Valerie and I did the "Nice to meet you" and "So glad we'll be working together" routine. Naturally everyone loved her. She spoke perfect English, French, and Italian, smoked at her desk, and could practically get a client to unzip his pants by phone. Me, they weren't so sure about. I was the new Head of Business Development, a big American dude brought in from the outside. Thankfully, none of them knew about my performance-based bonus deal or it would have raised a major ruckus. But I just took my time charming them all, and after a few parties at my place and a few cheese fondue dinners, they warmed up.

Early in November I drove up to Ermatingen for a private banking "off-site." For those of you who aren't corporate types, an off-site is a meeting, usually held in some exclusive resort, where the company wines and dines its big earners, tells you how fabulous you are, and shows you how nice they can be if you do a lot more. But this place was over the top, the Wolfsberg Castle, a four-hundred-year-old sprawling fortress where Alexandre Dumas and Franz Liszt had once bedded down. I mean, the place looked like the Magic Kingdom and was valued at hundreds of millions, and since UBS was swimming in cash, they'd bought it. As I parked the Ferrari and looked up at its towers and parapets, I thought about our house in Hingham and laughed. "Now *that's* a fucking castle!"

About a hundred private bankers from all the branches in Zurich,

Geneva, and Lugano were there; no assistants. The senior bosses held sway over the meetings and five-course dinners: Christian Bovay, his counterpart in Zurich, Hansruedi Schumacher, and their superior, Martin Liechti, who knew of me because he'd had to sign off on my unprecedented bonus deal. But I didn't draw any special attention because I think none of them really believed I'd pull in some whale of a client. They all thought I'd been bluffing.

Surprise! In the middle of dinner in the castle's great hall, with waistcoated waiters bustling, champagne glasses clinking, and the stone fireplace roaring, a messenger whispered in Bovay's ear. He got up from his table and came over to mine, and I was just hoping his dandruff wouldn't salt up my chicken française.

"Bradley, we've just gotten word that this client of yours, Mr. Olenicoff, has wire-transferred his first tranche from the Bahamas into our accounts."

"Oh, really, Mr. Bovay? That's good news. How much was it?"

"Eighty-nine million dollars." He blinked a few times.

I grinned and tried not to fist-bump the air. "Well, don't worry. I'm sure the rest of the two-hundred mil will come along shortly."

Bovay staggered away and quickly came back with his boss, Martin Liechti, a slick-looking slim dude with oiled black hair and manicured fingers. I stood up as Liechti pumped my hand and congratulated me, and then word swept through the dinner like a brushfire.

"*How* much did he just bring in?"

"Ninety million!"

"From a *single* client??"

People were coming over to my table and slapping me on the back. From that point on at UBS, I was a rock star.

I started traveling on marketing trips for UBS almost right away, and eventually settled into a schedule of five or six a year to the States. But before setting the first one up, I went through the standard in-house training and familiarization that all new employees have to endure. With two years at Credit Suisse under my belt and another four years at Barclays, I figured there wasn't much they could teach me about private banking products. I was right about the products, such as the standard numbered accounts, stocks and bond offerings, hedge funds, currency transactions, gold and silver bullion, fine gems, and energy futures. However, it turned out that UBS also had a uniquely wicked and creative way in which to make money off clients. These guys were as slick as eels in an oil bath, something I discovered the first time Christian Bovay pulled five of us "newbies" into his boardroom for a lecture.

"Gentleman, it is natural that your first objective should be to acquire a client's money and secure it in one of our numbered accounts."

Bovay was a fidgety dude, pacing back and forth at the end of the table while the rest of us rocked back in plush leather chairs. I was already inwardly rolling my eyes, thinking they should rename this place the "bored room." Then he smiled through his burglar-tool teeth, a sort of creepy grimace that'd make a schoolgirl shiver.

"However, your second and most important objective is to make that money *unavailable* to the client, unless UBS benefits in multiple ways."

That made us all sit up and take notice. Bovay came up with a black marker and wrote "10 million" on a large white poster board propped on an easel.

"Let us say, for example, that your client is a cattle rancher from Texas and wishes to secure $10 million in a numbered account. We oblige him, of course." Another evil-looking smile. "He understands, from reading and signing our contract, that his $10 million will make no interest unless he instructs us to place the funds, and that we will be charging him a fee of three percent per annum, simply for managing his money, along with custody and transaction charges. However, our happy cowboy is pleased that he is paying no taxes on his nest egg, so such a minimal fee is attractive."

Well, no surprise there. That's how all the Swiss banks handled secret accounts. You paid them a fee for keeping your secrets safe and the tax authorities off your ass, but you didn't make a dime of interest unless you instructed the bank to invest it.

"But now, we get a bit creative," said Bovay. "You tell your client that it's a shame for his money to be sitting here in Geneva doing nothing, and you offer him a time deposit with a five percent return. 'Wonderful!' he says, and we lock his money away for a year, at the end of which it will accrue to $10,500,000." He jotted that new figure below the first one. "Doesn't that look attractive?"

It certainly did. The guy's making half-a-mil on tax-free cash for doing nothing.

"And now," Bovay said with a big flourish. "You simply wait until your cowboy suddenly needs to use that money, which most of our clients do at some point, and you *lend* it back to him, at a very reasonable interest rate."

Excuse me? By the end of that first training session my head was swimming. It was a helluva scam. You get your client to lock up his ten mil for a year or more, but suddenly he needs it to buy a real estate property somewhere, so you hit him with this.

"Mr. Earp, I'm afraid your $10 million can't be released until the time deposit matures. However, UBS can grant you a loan of ninety percent of your capital, $9 million. You understand that we *must* keep $1 million in the account as collateral, so very sorry. And of course a bank loan comes with payments and interest. But, it's an attractive rate and you'll have all the liquidity you need."

Are you getting this? UBS was making a fee for holding the guy's cash in the first place, then making *another* fee for loaning him his own damn money! And guess what? The guy's happy! He's getting his deal done, and he's still doing it with tax-free cash! I couldn't believe it, and you know what? It worked, over and over again.

My next set of training sessions shattered any notions I might have had that UBS wasn't up to speed on American tax regulations, or that they didn't exactly know what Americans could or could not do with their money overseas. In fact, UBS had hundreds of domestic branches all over the States, replete with lawyers and CPAs, so they knew the US banking laws and tax codes upside down and backwards. Only about thirty of us on the Americas Desk would actually be traveling over there to hunt for money, so they pulled us into the boardroom again.

This time the instructor wasn't Bovay, but a little bald dude from "Security and Compliance." After his lecture, I thought they should change his department's title to "Noncompliance and Ass-covering." His name was Hans; he had a thick Swiss-German accent and was dressed like a typical Swiss, wearing a trim black suit and white socks. I kept waiting for him to come up with a riding crop and slap it on his palm.

"Gentlemen! You vill lissen very carefully, please. At some juncture in your travels, zeh American customs agents vill no doubt stop you and ask you difficult questions. You must be prepared!"

I'm sitting there thinking, *This is too fucking weird. It's like some World War II movie with Otto Preminger, and we're the Nazi agents being sent to New York.*

"Und so," Hans went on, "you vill never keep zeh names or telephone numbers of your clients in your mobile devices." He tapped his bald skull. "You vill keep zem here, in your head. Und, if you absolutely *must* bring financial data sheets with you, you vill keep zem only on encrypted laptops which we vill supply. Undershtood?"

I was so tempted to snap my arm up and yell, "Heil, UBS!" I didn't, but I did decide right then and there that I'd *never* carry an encrypted laptop anywhere near the US, nor was I going to memorize a hundred client names and phone numbers. Maybe I wouldn't be handing out numbered account brochures, but I wasn't about to start sneaking around like some nuclear spy. If anything would raise a red flag, *that* would.

"So, gentlemen. Vat do you do if you are stopped by customs agents and qvestioned? Vell, zer are three scenarios. First, an agent vill ask you if you are here in zeh States for business or pleasure. Vat do you say?"

One of my mates raised his hand. "Business. You should never lie."

"Incorrect!" Hans slapped the table. "You are *always* traveling for pleasure!"

This went on for an hour, and I had to admit that some of Hans's points were well made. But all in all the guy gave me the creeps and I decided to come up with my own "security and compliance" plans, if for no other reason than they'd be different from everyone else's, lessening my chances of getting nailed. I was lucky because I was the only banker carrying a US passport. At the end of the session he announced that his next class would be "verry interesstink," and all about surveillance and shaking a tail. My conclusions? These UBS guys weren't fucking kidding.

As I immersed myself in the UBS culture, I discovered that the bank had a well-established program for hobnobbing with wealthy folks the world over, and it had been going on long before I came aboard. The firm seemed to be a great benefactor of worthwhile causes, a charitable supporter of artistic endeavors, and a sponsor of popular sports stars. But at every art exhibit, tennis match, charity event, yacht regatta, or Formula One race, UBS bankers were there to rub elbows with rich folk, so it was all about Net New Money and return on assets. One of the bank's big projects was the Verbier Music Festival, held at the Verbier ski resort in Switzerland. UBS footed the bill to stand an orchestra comprising young talent, then booked their appearances in New York, Washington, Chicago, Miami, and Los Angeles, wrapping it up in Sydney and Munich. The first gig was starting at Carnegie Hall.

"Would you care to go, Brad?" Bovay asked me one morning as he brandished a fistful of tickets.

"You bet your Swiss watch!" I said, which was sort of funny because the guy wore a cheap Hamilton, but I whipped out my Rolodex and packed my bags.

In New York I checked into my room at the Plaza, rented a tux, and showed up at Carnegie Hall for the gala, where I linked up with three guys I'd invited: an Upper East Side plastic surgeon, a cap-and-crown dentist from Queens, and a real estate dude from Jersey who looked like Tony Soprano. The orchestra played Strauss, I played it cool, and then I invited them all to a late dinner at the Russian Tea Room next door. At the time that place was like Lenin's wet dream, with red leather banquettes, paintings of charging Cossacks, and the best beluga caviar, vodka, and borscht. Per my usual style, I talked about everything but money, until they couldn't stand it anymore.

"So, Bradley," the Botox bandit finally asked me as he gobbled up his *Ptichye Moloko*. "What exactly can you do for us?"

I sipped my Anri XO brandy and smiled at him. "What I can do for you, Dr. Gold, is *zero*."

"Pardon me?" He looked a little stunned, and so did the mob-clone and the dentist.

"Actually," I said. "It's *three* zeros. Zero income tax, zero capital gains tax, and zero inheritance tax."

Well, that broke the ice, and once they stopped laughing I casually wandered into all the lush green fields of slushy money they could enjoy in my Swiss pastures.

"Gentlemen, let's just imagine a scenario," I proposed. "You're a professional who's worked very hard, and you've saved up $6 million. You're also a smart, cautious guy, so that money's not in the market, which is good 'cause Wall Street's currently in the shitter thanks to Mohamed Atta. With me so far?"

The three of them nodded, and I could tell from the gleam in the Soprano dude's eye that he had that much money. Maybe the doctors had a couple mil apiece.

"So," I went on, "that $6 million's sitting in Chase, making a lousy 1.3 percent, because interest rates currently suck. But then you decide to visit me in Geneva, and I take $5 million of your money and put it into a declared account."

"A *declared* account?" the dentist scoffed. "What good is that? I'll get killed on taxes."

"Patience, my good man." I raised a finger and gave him my "shut the fuck up and listen" smile. "We take the other $1 million and put it into an *undeclared* numbered account, which nobody knows about. You go home, and a month later, you take a loan of $4 million from your declared account and I add it to your numbered account, making that balance $5 million. Still with me?"

They nodded like the Three Stooges, but these guys were no dummies. I could almost hear the calculators clicking in their brains.

"So, now I look around for a very good investment. Ah, I've got it! Rheinmetall AG in Dusseldorf, which happens to make weapons systems and tons of ammunition. And since the Germans are already over in Kabul kicking Taliban ass, that stock's going to soar. Now, can you buy that stock with American dollars? No, you can't, so I take your five mil and buy euros, which sell dirt cheap, and then I buy your Rheinmetall stock. Six months later, I sell out for a twenty percent return, and now you've got $6 million in your numbered account."

"That's impressive, Brad," said the Botox bandit. "But it's undeclared money. I can't use it."

"There's a happy ending, Doc. Now you use that money to repay your loan." I didn't mention the UBS interest fees. Why spoil dessert? "Now you've got a total of seven mil; five declared and two undeclared. And guess what? There are no tax consequences for taking a loan, especially from yourself! You can use that legit five mil any way you want. And when you come over to merry old Europe, you can use the other two mil for vacations, partying, buying pretty baubles for your wives. Hell, you can buy a yacht if you want and park it in Cannes."

"I get it," said the Soprano dude. "If the Feds come nosing around, you've got open paperwork on a declared account. They can't look at anything else you might have 'cause you're protected by Swiss laws."

"Bingo," I said as I winked at him.

"You really know your stuff, Mr. Birkenfeld," the dentist said.

"That's my only talent, Doc." I grinned at them, lifted my cognac, and said, "You know, Geneva is beautiful this time of year." (With me, Geneva was beautiful at *any* time of the year.) "You really should consider a visit."

You've already guessed at what happened next. It happened after every one of my field trips.

A middle-aged American male, always wealthy, usually bored, shows up at Geneva airport, and from there he's on Mr. Birkenfeld's Magic Carpet Ride. There's a black Mercedes sedan with blacked-out windows waiting, which whisks him off to the Hotel Richemond, where there are fresh flowers and tropical fruit in his fabulous suite overlooking Lac Léman, along with a box of Frigor Swiss chocolates. I pick him up at seven p.m., expressing how sorry I am that his wife couldn't make it, and suggest he should buy her a nice present. First we have dinner at Le Comptoir, a five-star classy joint with amazing French cuisine. By nine he's had a few drinks, so I suggest just checking out the sexy girls at Velvet. It's a very upscale cabaret, which happens to have a "dance" stage off in one corner. There we're joined by my buddy from London, Ladjel Jafarli, an Algerian-born investment banker who looks like a young Omar Sharif and has a wicked sense of humor.

I also know lots of the girls at Velvet. All of them are "working girls," Russians, Czechs, Poles, a convenience I've taken advantage of on occasion—strictly business. Some of them are just "girls who wanna have fun," and they're all gorgeous. By midnight, there's this tall, blonde, friendly Czech chick standing behind Mr. Client's chair, massaging his shoulders and whispering God-knows-what in his ear. I wink at her. She winks back. That means I'll take care of her later. Ladjel yawns and says, "Bradley, your lifestyle is going to kill me, and so would my mother if she knew where I was!" I laugh and say, "I've got to get a move-on too, buddy." Both of us get up and I throw a thousand Swiss francs on the table. "Martina, darling," I say to the girl. "Will you please make sure Mr. Client gets back to la Paix all right?"

"Of course I will, Bradley!" By the time Ladjel and I are out the door, she's perched on this happy dude's lap. In about an hour she'll be giving him the ride of his life.

In the morning when I pick him up, Mr. Client looks like the proverbial canary-eating cat. He's in a dream state as we drive over to 16 Rue de la Corraterie in one of my Ferraris, where I escort him and his hefty briefcase into the lobby and across a polished marble floor, past towering pillars, tall windows girded with wrought-iron bars, and security cameras everywhere. We ride the elevator to a lovely private receiving room. A redheaded girl walks in with a silver tray piled with fresh croissants, fruit, and espresso. Another blonde girl shows up pushing a bill-counting machine on a rolling cart. She's wearing a tight silk blouse, a short gray skirt, and has endless legs ending in heels. Mr. Client opens his briefcase and hands her two fat stacks of hundred-dollar bills. She smiles and runs his money through the bill-counter like a manicured machine-gunner. Brrrraaaaap! "It is two hundred thousand," she says to me as she carefully stacks it all up and rolls away with the money. I then hand Mr. Client a small sheaf of forms and contracts, which he barely reads, but I make sure to get his signature in all the right places.

Then we walk down a long corridor to a desk at the end, perched on a plush Persian rug, where a security guard in a nice suit and tie smiles and opens a gleaming brass elevator, and we take a ride two stories underground. This next chamber looks like a VIP reception area at Fort Knox, with another Persian carpet, leather and chrome chairs, Ming vases, surveillance cameras, two female processing clerks behind a chest-high counter, a huge time-lock door, and past that, four subterranean floors of polished steel safe-deposit boxes. Some of those boxes are large enough to hold a framed Monet, while others are designed only for small gems of great value. The minimum annual rental fee for the smallest box is 500 Swiss francs, but that doesn't faze Mr. Client and he goes for a larger size. He produces his passport and fills out a small white card, which has the number of his account on it and his code name, randomly chosen by computer. He then signs the card and receives two silver safe-deposit keys. Another guard appears, locks buzz, keys jingle, and we're escorted into the vaults, where Mr. Client, his briefcase, and his large polished box have a private moment together in a sealed room. For all I know, he's got gold bars or bottles of Ecstasy to stash in his box. But who cares? He comes out with his briefcase empty. The clerks recover his safe-deposit key; that's the last thing he needs to be carrying around. If he wants access, he'll have to show up again.

I drop him off at the airport and promise I'll see him in the States next trip. He's got quite a spring in his step—probably still thinking about Martina and whatever the hell she did to him the night before. I grin, roar away, and take the rest of the day off. That two hundred thou was just a good-faith deposit. In a month he'll be wiring $3 million into his numbered account.

Score! Just another day in Swiss Paradise.

Over the course of my career as a Swiss private banker, I'll see all sorts of things that my clients trust I'll forget. Sometimes they show me what they've got, to get my advice on what to cash in or keep, but sometimes I think it's just to gauge my reaction. I see gold and silver ingots, grape-sized pearls, currency from every country on earth, rare stamps, fat emeralds, and bearer bonds. One guy has half a million bucks in cash and six different passports. He could be an intelligence operative, a drug dealer, or an assassin. I don't even blink. When a client has something large, like a priceless work of art, he doesn't come in through the front door. I call security; the painting arrives in an armored truck and is driven straight to an underground garage and whisked to the vaults. I have clients who, once they've signed on, never want to be seen at the bank again. I meet them at their hotels in Geneva, confirming they're my clients and it isn't a setup, and receive their withdrawal instructions. Then I show up later again with the cash. More than once I'm walking around Geneva with a million bucks in a briefcase.

I gain a reputation as a discreet, knowledgeable banker, a man to be trusted. One client calls and asks if I'll go to Italy to meet his close friend, a man who has questions about numbered accounts. When I agree, he gives me the guy's description and a password phrase, no name. I take the train and find the guy in a hotel lobby in Milan, sit down next to him, and say, "Weather's nice this time of year." He smiles and says, "Yes, but I always carry an umbrella." He's middle aged, well built, with an indiscernible accent. For an hour he asks me about Swiss secret account procedures, then he hands me an envelope. "For your troubles," he says, and he leaves. I open it on the way back to Geneva. It's 10,000 Swiss francs in cash, a "consulting" fee.

There were times when I pinched myself to make sure I wasn't dreaming.

By the end of that first year at UBS, most of Igor Olenicoff's cool $200 million had shown up in his numbered accounts and was getting structured through offshore companies and trusts per his request.

Just to be clear about that eighteen percent, it didn't mean I'd be getting that size a chunk off the top of any Net New Money I brought in. If that were the case, with Olenicoff's nut alone I'd have cleaned the table of $36 million and retired to buy myself a hockey team somewhere. What it did mean was that I'd be getting eighteen percent of any revenue made with that big figure. So, for example, UBS was charging Olenicoff three percent to manage his $200 million, which is $6 million, and I was getting $1,080,000 out of that. Whenever Olenicoff invested any of his nut and made a profit, which of course I encouraged, I got my cut for that too. On top of that, the combined portfolios of all my other clients amounted to another $200 million, so bottom line I was making eighteen percent on the fees, securities sales, loan interest, currency transactions, and profits on $400,000,000. My book was about double the size of most other bankers on the desk. In banking, as with other things, size does matter. And since you can't take it with you, I made sure to enjoy it.

I like fine watches. Hey, everybody's got an Achilles' heel. I was really craving an Audemars Piguet Royal Oak Offshore T-3, the same watch worn by Arnold Schwarzenegger in *Terminator 3*. So I went over to their showroom and plunked down $25,000. I also had a thing for good cigars, and since the Davidoff showroom was three blocks from my flat, I used it as my personal humidor and they'd call me up whenever they had fresh boxes of Romeo & Julieta Churchills or Partagas #4 Robustos flown in from Havana. I like fine clothing too, but I'm not a fanatic; just had to look the part. My suits were Italian Brionis, and the dress shirts Egyptian cotton from Jermyn Street in London. Got my custom-made alligator shoes with matching belts in Bangkok, so I guess I looked pretty slick. But the prices weren't outrageous, maybe $1,000 per outfit, and I only had ten.

But my flat at 20 Cours de Rive? That's where I put in some serious bucks. A guy's got to have his man cave; but if he's a private banker and entertains, he'd better look like a financial wizard who's not afraid to splurge. Just to set the tone, I had a porcelain sign custom-made for the front door, with a skull and crossbones and the words "Strong Ales and Loose Women." The place had fifteen-foot ceilings, with tall French glass doors leading out to two balconies. The floors were Hungarian-point parquet, I'd adorned the carved marble hearth on my fireplace with antique brass cherub andirons, and the living room was "guarded" by a pair of Indian sculptures I'd shipped back from Mumbai. My two sofas were the centerpieces; thick green leather softened with Persian pillows, very comfy for my female guests. They also seemed to enjoy the huge horse-trough tub in my bathroom, in which the water was always crystal blue because it was pure mountain water. The kitchen was Italian marble, modern, and all its appliances, plus my living room stereo and TV, were the best I could find in Geneva. You're probably wondering about the bedroom. It was big, with two high-paneled doors and a king-sized bed on steroids. I bought only satin sheets; girls don't like scratchy.

Which brings me to Thais, the girl I was seeing at the time, and for a long time after. She was Brazilian, worked in the fashion industry, and we'd met at a party somewhere in Geneva. Thais had long dark hair, a curvy figure, and a beautiful smile with brilliant white teeth. Like most sexy women in Geneva, she dressed provocatively, walked with incredible style, and she had this mixed Portuguese-French accent that drove me crazy, in a good way. Her skin was light brown and felt like a Gordal olive just plucked from a jar. She really appreciated those satin sheets.

Thais had boundless energy and was ready to party, anywhere, anytime. So, when I finally made my biggest purchase, without telling her exactly what it was, she showed up at my place dressed warmly, as I'd suggested; tight jeans, warm boots, a frothy sweater, and a mink jacket, packed for a weekend trip. At the time I was driving a Ferrari Maranello, a $250,000 twelve-cylinder beast I'd bought for a wealthy friend in Asia (yes, with cash), and we hopped in and roared off for Zermatt. Even after parking the car, taking the cogwheel train, and climbing a few hundred stone steps, she still wasn't sure what was up, until we got to the magnificent rustic Swiss chalet I'd just closed the deal on. I thought she was going to faint when we walked inside. Nothing was in there yet except for a high-pile carpet in front of the enormous picture window, with the stunning precipice of the Matterhorn framing it from top to bottom. She dropped her bag and gasped.

I'm a big fan of Austin Powers, and I smiled at her and said, "Does this make you *Matterhorny*, bay-bee?"

We wound up on the carpet.

Looking back on it, I think that day was the apex of my career in Swiss banking. I was making tons of money and my life was a 'round-the-clock party. My clients were mostly harmless, wealthy Americans who just thought the government was overtaxing them and then spending their hard-earned money on dumbass programs about which they had no say. Couldn't really argue with that, and these guys were very pleasant. On the very rare occasion when an investment went south, they'd just shrug and toss me more money. I was glad not to be working on the Russian or Chinese desks, where if you fucked up a trade you could wind up facedown in the Volga.

I slept very well at night, and, as I'd grown accustomed to, rarely alone.

# PART II

# CHAPTER 5

## BURNED IN BERN

*"You can't spend your whole life worrying about your mistakes. You fucked up, you trusted us."*

—*OTTER, ANIMAL HOUSE*

By my fourth year with UBS, I knew I was walking barefoot on the rim of a volcano.

Not that I wasn't enjoying myself, but I couldn't help looking down at my feet on occasion and swallowing a gasp. Up here in the rarefied air where I worked, the sun was bright and the feathery clouds were trimmed in gold. But way down there somewhere, chains rattled, dungeons reeked of sweat, and a pool of molten lava boiled and bubbled.

In Switzerland, where I lived and labored, not a damn thing I was doing was even slightly illegal. Hell, it was all encouraged. But over there in America, if the authorities discovered the high-stakes game I was playing, along with every other private banker at UBS, I knew they'd see me as a thief and a rogue. The balancing act was starting to take its toll.

And something was nagging at my conscience. The Global War on Terror and I had started our gigs together. Now we were engaged on two fronts, Afghanistan and Iraq, and the American body count was climbing. I had my doubts about Bush and his boys dropping the ball in the hunt for Osama bin Laden and going after Saddam Hussein instead, but I've never liked armchair generals so I figured they had their reasons. Yet many Americans at home were silently suffering, thousands of Moms and Pops sending their sons and daughters off to war and dutifully paying their taxes. In my long back-and-forths to the States I'd had lots of time to think about the people I was helping to *not* pay their share, while the tax man's axe fell on those who couldn't afford it. I knew that the largest corporations and most powerful people in the world were quarterbacking it all, making it happen, aiding and abetting their fellow fat cats. And here I was, helping those One-Percenters shirk their tax obligations while regular folks hefted the burden. It was starting to bug me. That's right; even a hard-ass, cynical, take-no-prisoners Boston banker like me.

Of course, my American clients loved me. Who says you can't buy love? I was making them richer with every tick of my Swiss cuckoo clock, as well as catering to every request, no matter how unusual, to ensure their happiness. And my clients comprised only a small percentage of American tax-evaders stashing their nuts in the UBS nest of secret numbered accounts. All in all, I had about 150 clients in Birkenfeld's Big Black Book, thirty of whom were North Americans. But across all the bank's branches in Zurich, Lugano, Geneva, and elsewhere, UBS had—hold on to your wallets—*19,000* American clients enjoying offshore secret numbered accounts. We're talking billions with a "B" here, folks. That's a lot of tax revenue *not* going for beans and bullets.

It wasn't pretty and it wasn't fair, but I still wasn't about to give it all up, join the priesthood, and go abstinent. God forbid. And yet, this Robert DeNiro line from a film called *Ronin* kept popping into my head.

"I never walk into a place I don't know how to walk out of."

Truth be told, I didn't know how to walk away from it all, and I wasn't quite ready.

Here's why . . .

I'm standing on the balcony of a seventh-floor luxury apartment, overlooking the undulating hills and twisting streets of Monte Carlo, Monaco. It's late May in the French Riviera, the sky's crystal blue and sunlight's glinting off pristine white sails tilting in the majestic harbor. That harbor's full of multimillion-dollar mega-yachts, packed gunnel to gunnel like gleaming white whales, their decks sporting pastel umbrellas like fancy summer cocktails and beauty queens in bikinis rubbing cheeks with Greek shipping tycoons, many of whom are old enough to be their fathers.

There's a ripping whine in the air like the sound of a squadron of fighter jets, and then a tight gaggle of 900-horsepower Formula One racing cars comes blasting through the tunnel right below the balcony, and the crowd of spectators in the stands comes to its feet as David Coulthard takes the lead in a McLaren Mercedes that looks like a blue and white *Star Wars* X-Wing spaceship. Coulthard's going to win this one, which is fantastic because I've got money on him, and so do lots of the folks in the flat.

I've rented these glorious digs using UBS money for the entire weekend leading up to Friday's race. And naturally I've invited a handful of clients and their very wealthy friends to enjoy the race from my spectacular view. Leaning on the balcony to my left is a young Italian movie starlet with flowing black hair and a Sophia Loren body. She's sipping Cristal and gripping my arm with excitement. To my right is Carlo Bandini, a big film producer from Rome and the girl's sugar daddy of the moment, who's grinning and enjoying a view that's much better from here than from his yacht in the harbor. Behind us in the flat and all along the balcony are the rest of my invited clients, past, present and future, plus a couple of my buddies who love fast cars, French nightclubs, and young pretty girls who crave the limelight. They're all bloated on the amazing gourmet cuisine prepared right there in the kitchen by a private chef I've hired for the weekend.

Down below, the spectators in the stands are here for the thrill of the race. But everyone else is here for the thrill of the money. Sponsors' banners hang from every building, stretch over the straight runs, and are splashed in bold on the barriers: *Bridgestone, Rolex, Foster's Lager, HSBC, Gauloises, Marlboro*. I know those images flash quickly by the TV cameras as they follow the rocketing cars, so I've been a little smarter and paid for a better spot for the bank.

Down at the back-end hairpin turn, where all the cars have to bunch up and slow before shooting back out on the straightaway, there's a stone circle garlanded with a belt of big UBS panels and a UBS flag above whipping in the breeze. It cost us thousands to get that spot and this flat, but it's all going to pay off. By the time this race is over, Bandini's going to make an appointment with me for the following week in Geneva, and he'll be dropping 10 million euros in a numbered account. Okay, so he's not an American client and technically not in my wheelhouse. But I'll tell the Italian Desk about it later—much later—after I've collected my eighteen percent.

I just *love* Formula One . . .

I'm wearing a black tuxedo, sitting at a $10,000 table in the grand ballroom of the Waldorf Astoria Hotel in New York, along with 1,100 other guests in black ties and gowns. It's the Hot Pink Party, the annual charity event for the Breast Cancer Research Foundation. I'm here on behalf of UBS, and I've got a nice fat check tucked behind my pink pocket handkerchief, which I'll shortly add to the $5.3 million that's going to be collected tonight.

This ballroom looks like the main-stage theater at the Metropolitan Opera, except that everything's in pink: pink bunting, pink tablecloths, pink dishware, and hot-pink flower arrangements. Hundreds of Broadway and movie stars are gossiping and applauding and clinking champagne glasses, many of the women wearing thousand-buck pink gowns. Mayor Bloomberg's at a table near mine, wearing a pink bow tie, and there's former Governor Pataki and his wife and half the George Soros clan. The Mistress of Ceremonies is movie star Elizabeth Hurley, which makes me grin hard because I'm such an Austin Powers fan. In just a few minutes, Elton John's going to take the stage.

Elton John doesn't just breeze through some number and leave. He does "Rocket Man," "Tiny Dancer," and by the time he slams into "The Bitch Is Back," the crowd's on its feet and rocking. When he rolls into "I Guess That's Why They Call It the Blues," the woman sitting next to me, a stately diamond-studded brunette, gets up and tugs at my elbow. Her husband's chair is empty. He's probably gone off to drum up some business. I remember the title of that Norman Mailer novel, *Tough Guys Don't Dance*. Well, maybe not, but bankers do, and I smile and take the woman in my arms and turn her to Elton's dreamy tune. I didn't suffer through all those white-gloved Friday-night ballroom lessons at prep school for nothing.

I ask my dance partner what she and her husband do.

"He's an aerospace guy, private jets." From the way her mouth turns down and her eyes roll up when she tells me about him, I figure he's got a mistress; an expensive one. "I just spend his money," she adds.

I laugh. "It's a tough job, but somebody's got to do it."

She grins. "What do you do?"

"I'm a private banker in Switzerland. I'd like to meet him."

"You'd be bored," she says.

"That's all right. I'm self-entertaining."

She laughs and presses herself against me. By the end of the night, I've got another client. I've also got his wife's cell number in my pocket, but I'll throw that away. No sense screwing up a good thing . . .

I'm in Carmel, California, on a hot day in August on the Pebble Beach golf course, watching Jay Leno hold court in front of his 1936 Cord Baby Duesenberg, which is worth about half a million bucks. Leno is just as I've seen him on TV—friendly, jovial, always happy to josh with the regular folks, and not remotely phony. Of course these "regular folks" are all high-end automobile collectors like him, which means they've got wads of cash in their pockets in case they have to make a down payment on some flashy new toy.

Leno's as rich as the prince of a small country and has about a hundred of these four-wheeled baubles in his private collection, which he calls his "Big Dog Garage." But I know he'll never be a UBS client. He's one of those dudes who feels blessed by what America's given him and doesn't mind a hard shave by the IRS. I respect that, but I'm here at the Concours d'Elegance car show to find the "other" type of guy—rich and rebellious.

Rolex is sponsoring the show this year, which means that the winner will be getting a $25,000 gold watch. But their giveaway's calculated and they've got a huge display of fine timepieces guarded by beefy plainclothes dudes wearing earpieces and belt bulges. Rolex is just like UBS, laying out cash on the bet they'll pick up a lot of slick customers here; and ultimately they will. The place is crawling with golf pros, top athletes, movie and TV producers. Famed race-car driver Jackie Stewart can't get far without drawing a crowd of photo and autograph-seekers, and I can see him trying to uncramp his shift hand.

I spot a beautiful classic 1954 BMW 502 convertible resting on a carpet of plush green grass, and I'm thinking the golf course groundskeepers must fucking hate this show. The car's magnificent crystal green with a tan canvas top that looks as soft as melted butter. The owner, a handsome guy in his sixties wearing linen golf trousers, a pink Polo, and pilot Ray-Bans, lounges in a beach chair reading *Hemmings Motor News*. I saunter over.

"Beautiful car," I offer. "Best specimen I've ever seen of this model."

He glances up. "Thanks."

"I'm a BMW guy myself. Just bought the new M5 in Finland."

"Good car." He lowers the magazine an inch and looks up at me. "Why Finland?"

"I live and work in Geneva. Private banking. Flew over to Helsinki and picked it up with tax-free Finnish plates." I look down and smile. "I'm allergic to taxes."

Now he drops the magazine on his lap. "Got that allergy myself, but I don't think there's a cure."

"You'd be surprised," I say as I extend my hand. "Bradley Birkenfeld."

"Thurston Whitegate," he says.

"Good to meet you, Thurston." I look around. "Mind if I join you? My feet hurt."

"Sure." He throws a thumb over his shoulder. "There's another chair under my awning."

Fifteen minutes later, we're sitting in the sun and sipping Manhattans. Whitegate's no fool. He knows I'm not here for the cars.

"So, Brad. What are you selling?"

"Zeros." I smile.

He smiles too. "You don't mean Japanese fighter planes, I assume."

"Nope." And I give him my "Three zeros" pitch, but it's done with a shrug as if I don't really give a shit if he's interested or not. Before long we're talking about numbered accounts, trust structures, and long-term capital gains with no tax consequences. By the bottom of our second round of drinks, Thurston's telling me how much he disdains the US government and its antiquated, fascist tax code, and I'm telling him that's why I live in Switzerland, the land of cheese, chocolates, and cash.

A month later, we're having drinks at *Perle du Lac* down by the shore of Lac Leman. I've just given him a countryside tour in the Ferrari at about 110 mph. He tells me he's moving $8 million over to UBS.

I tell him I'm moved by his friendship and trust in me . . .

And then I'm in St. Barths for a week while I sponsor, on behalf of UBS, the renowned St. Barths Bucket Regatta (Exhibit 10). *Ka-ching!* More clients. And then I'm in Miami for Art Basel, a fine arts exhibition also sponsored by UBS, which sort of bores me except that Miami's nightlife is always wild and who doesn't love drinking and dancing with all those Latina beauties? And then I'm in Newport, Rhode Island, for the Alinghi yacht trials where Ernesto Bertarelli is challenging for the America's Cup, again sponsored by UBS. His sloop wins it under the flag of the *Société Nautique de Genève*, so guess which banker cleans up when all those rich yachting fanatics are instantly huge fans of the Swiss?

Oh, and between all those high-end treasure hunts, and for three straight months, I organize an exclusive Rodin exhibit in the UBS "Artrium" in Geneva. George Gangebin, head of UBS Wealth Management, hosts the opening cocktail party for the event. I bring in fifty-four iconic bronze sculptures, the largest collection in a single place on the planet. Everybody who's anybody wants to see it, so naturally I spend a lot of time over there throwing more cocktail parties and handing out business cards. Does it pay off? I can't even remember how many of those art lovers wound up in our vaults.

Now a man's got to take a break from all that hard work, pitching, wining, and dining, right? I'm in the Philippines with my millionaire buddy, Mauro, and it's just before Christmas so we're having a nice family dinner at his mansion with his mom. She's a sweet lady, and I suggest that we should all reconvene in the morning and go to mass. Mauro kicks me under the table, while his mom claps her hands together, almost in prayer, so pleased that her son has some fine religious friends. We wake up at the crack of noon, and we never show up for church.

Instead, we join up with Calvin Ayre, the billionaire bad boy of Bodog fame. And third in our party is Jimmy Yang of the Chinese Secret Service, a guy who looks like he could eat Jackie Chan for lunch. Mauro can't go anywhere without his team of five bodyguards, each hefting three bulging handguns under their native shirts. One of them's a huge dude who looks like a snake eater and worked as a mercenary in Southeast Asia. I ask him how many people he's killed. He glowers at me. "With a gun or knife?" Question withdrawn!

Then we're off on Mauro's helicopter for a visit to Air Force One; not the president's ride, but the largest strip club I've ever seen, with three floors and a parking lot for six hundred cars. There's the usual bar and stage with its gleaming poles and glistening girls, but the floors are divided up into Coach, Business, and First Class. We ride the escalator to the top floor, which is lined with beautifully appointed, hotel-style "massage" rooms with hot tubs. We sprawl out on plush couches, drinks in hands, before a large billowy curtain that suddenly draws open like a Broadway stage. Ten girls are standing there, with comely smiles and manicured fingers on cocked hips. Mauro grins at me.

"Choose anyone you want, Bradley. It's all on me."

It's hard to choose. They're all gorgeous, and naked.

So that's why I couldn't just walk away from it all. It was too much fun, and way too profitable. For four years I was on a magic carpet ride, and the rug was made of fun and money. Whenever the weekends rolled around, I rarely hung out in Geneva to just chill in my flat and take a stroll in the park along the lake. I'd grab some buddies and we'd fly off to Marrakesh or Mykonos, or we'd swing down to Saint-Tropez or over to Budapest for some girls and goulash. If one of my pals like John Ross actually managed to catch me on a Saturday in my flat, he'd say, "Brad! You're visiting Geneva this weekend?" Sometimes I barely made it back to the office on Mondays, and more than once I had to sneak a nap in the bathroom.

My team on the Americas Desk at UBS called themselves the "hunter-gatherers," and we'd all coalesced into a tight-knit group of hard-charging, fun-loving, super moneymakers. I liked them all a lot and we helped one another, cheered for each other whenever someone scored, and had each other's backs in times of trouble.

Valerie had evolved from her role as "Ms. Moneypenny" to being more like Emma Peel in *The Avengers*. She looked out for me, never missed a pertinent detail, and could pull off any task I asked of her. When her twenty-fifth birthday was coming up, I asked her what she'd been dreaming of, as long as it was relatively legal. She put her chin in her palm and smiled.

"I've never been to Amsterdam. I hear it's pretty sexy."

"It is indeed, my dear." I grinned and snapped my fingers. "Poof! You're in Amsterdam."

We made a whole weekend of it, along with three other girls from the Desk and three male UBS banker buddies. I whipped out my Black American Express card and booked two suites at the Intercontinental Amstel Hotel, and we tore up the town, eating ethnic cuisine, drinking at jazz joints, laughing through an outrageous live sex show, and quality-testing some fine Dutch hashish while taking a midnight cruise on the canals in a classic wood boat. Whatever you're probably thinking, none of us wound up in bed with each other. We were all battle buddies. By Monday we were back at our desks, still half-toasted and giggling over our Hollandish adventures. Valerie beamed for a week. Happy Birthday!

I had so many friends in and out of the bank that I never lacked for a good-times partner. My Indian buddy Srinavansan Ramashanran ("Just call me Ram") was a fun-loving guy with a thing for vegetarian cuisine. He covered the Indian market for Barclays Bank, which was big in East Africa, where many of the wealthiest Indians immigrated to, lived, and worked, and I tagged along with him on money-hunting safaris. My buddy Cornel Vermaak was a nonsmoking, no-drinking, cyclist banker of Afrikaans origin, funny as hell and always looking to make trouble, so we were like two peas in a pod.

And then there was Mauro, my very close friend from Manila, for whom I'd bought a 550 Ferrari Maranello. Mauro was roly-poly, had a grin like the Cheshire cat, and was wealthy enough to own an Agusta helicopter. I'd swing down to Manila between hunter-gatherer trips and we'd jet over to Hong Kong, Singapore, or Bali and drink, dance, and flirt our way through exotic nightclubs and wild parties. It was nonstop craziness and I wallowed in it.

But there was method to my madness. Even though I had this hunger for fun, I never took my eye off the ball. I nurtured my big black Rolodex phone book, in which I recorded nothing more than people's names, where I'd met them, and their modes of contact. I took no notes because that's all I needed to remember who they were and what they did for a living. Then on my computer I created a master spreadsheet, and every year at Christmas I'd write a holiday letter, print it on high-grade paper, include a photo of myself on a white-sand beach in Asia, or in front of the Pyramids in Cairo, or on a majestic sailing yacht in Cannes, and send out two hundred via snail mail. And then I had another spreadsheet with all the annual high-end events taking place around the world—yacht regattas, tennis tournaments, film festivals, wine tastings, auto shows, and car races—and breakdowns of every country's best restaurants, bars, and hotels (Exhibit 9).

It got to the point where I was like the banker–travel agent–entertainment director. Clients and their friends would call me up and say, "Brad, I'm going to be in Brussels in May, and Harry said you're the guy to talk to." I'd say, "You bet!" and I'd click on Brussels and come up with festivals, hotels, restaurants, and the best nightlife spots. So, of course, after these folks got the skinny from me and had a wonderful time, they also turned to me for money matters or referred their wealthy friends. It was social engineering with a profit margin. I suppose anyone could have done it, but I made it my specialty. Bradley Birkenfeld, the "Go-To Guy." I was living the high life, traveling the world, making rich people happy, I had tons of friends, and I was raking in cash like a croupier at a craps table.

So, be honest. Could you have just walked out on all that? And why would you?

Well, the world was slowly changing and I knew it. First of all, the Patriot Act in the States had given all these federal bureaucratic agencies a license to rummage through everyone's drawers. The stated objective was to unravel a worldwide network of terrorist financing—to "follow the money," as the old gumshoe saying goes. Mohamed Atta and his 9/11 terror cohorts had purchased all their cell phones in Geneva, plus they'd had about half a million in cash, so it made sense for the FBI, CIA, DOJ, and IRS to start nosing around Switzerland. They were scrutinizing wire transfers, credit card transactions, offshore accounts, and business transactions. The Swiss, being oh-so-Swiss, would never cooperate. "Our reputation is built on discretion!" So that meant the spooks had to cast a wide net, with all sorts of fish being reeled in. However, whenever they came across a PEP (Politically Exposed Person), such as a congressman or big-time lobbyist, they'd pretend they hadn't seen the activity. But anyone else was fair game.

"This looks like money's being moved by Congressman So-and-so, so let's leave him alone. But *this* one looks like a rich guy who sells Beanie Babies. Let's shake him down."

My clients were more the Beanie Babies–type guys, rather than high-power politicians, and they were getting nervous.

International travel was being scrutinized as well. Guys like me and my fellow bankers zipping back and forth to the States from Geneva, Lugano, and Zurich were starting to raise some eyebrows. Never mind that the Department of Homeland Security and its absurdly incompetent and ineffective TSA were focused on all the wrong people, and still are; grandmas and toddlers being strip-searched at airports while a dude named Ahmed who's wearing a kaffiyeh can't be touched because that's "Islamophobic." But slick-looking Swiss bankers with big expense accounts? "Follow those men!"

And they did. Lots of my UBS colleagues were spending unusually long stretches at Customs being questioned and having their suitcases tossed. Some of the guys swore they were being tailed in the States, or approached by friendly, clean-cut, curious strangers while having drinks in luxury hotel bars. Personally, I never paid much attention to any of it. After my experience with the corrupt FBI clowns in Boston, I figured the Feds couldn't find their asses with both hands, and I wasn't going to start acting like Clyde Barrow on the lam with Bonnie Parker. I was a Swiss resident, working within the legal boundaries of Swiss law, and also paying my fair share of taxes. But don't get me wrong; I was careful, just not paranoid.

Paranoia, on the other hand, was starting to creep into my bosses' heads at UBS. I'd already seen it when I was privy to a panicky conversation between Hansruedi Schumacher and Martin Liechti, "senior capos" for our business in Zurich. Schumacher realized that because UBS had hundreds of branches in the United States (resulting from the 1999 UBS acquisition of Paine Webber), the bank was very vulnerable to American regulators; if things blew up, we could lose our license to operate there.

"Look, Martin," Schumacher said to Liechti, "we're getting into this regulatory environment, which is very dangerous. What we should do is close down the Americas Desk and move it outside the bank to a small Swiss entity that then books the business with UBS."

"Close it down, Hans?" Liechti was aghast. "Are you insane?"

"Just listen, Martin! Your people essentially resign from the bank and become independent asset managers for this private entity. Then they can take their existing business, plus refer any new business back to UBS, and book it with us. But now UBS will have plausible deniability. If the Americans come calling, we can say, 'It wasn't us! It was those people over there!'"

But Liechti was having none of it. He didn't want to lose his power base.

"Hans, you're fucking everything up I built over the last decade. Fuck you!"

Schumacher just sighed and said, "Well, we're going to get screwed one day and this is not good." Soon after the exchange Schumacher resigned from UBS and joined NZB, a boutique Swiss private bank. My Geneva colleague Hanno Huber and four senior Zurich private bankers followed their former boss's lead and also joined NZB, taking with them 1.5 billion Swiss francs in assets, including Ty Warner's, of Beanie Babies fame. That's when I started thinking: *This thing can't last forever. Huber's been in this business his whole life, and if he's thinking that way, we're heading for the falls. And I mean like Niagara Falls . . .*

Among my hunter-gatherer colleagues, the rumor mill was starting to grind, with folks whispering dark jokes about doom and gloom. My Swiss buddy Jacques Leuba cruised by my desk one day and dropped a comment with a wry smirk.

"Work harder, Bradley, faster. Bring in that cash, *mon ami!* Humpty Dumpty's about to fall!"

"Maybe we should shit-can all this traveling crap and just *print* money," I answered. "I'll bet somebody on the Russian desk knows an excellent counterfeiter."

Jacques laughed, but he was cynically responding to pressure from above, particularly from Martin Liechti. Our überboss was cranking out memos like the following to all of us private bankers:

Dear Colleagues,

The first five months of this year have been very challenging for our industry. The decline in investor confidence, the military conflict in the Middle East, and the ever-increasing regulatory scrutiny that has descended upon our business continue to present difficult challenges. We are, however, convinced that even in this difficult environment, we are well positioned to provide our clients with the best solutions for their financial needs.

Net New Money is, as you know, a key element for our success. This means that we all have to work hard to achieve our NNM goals for this year and the years to come . . .

I am already looking forward to awarding those of you who will achieve this goal!

Liechti didn't end his memo with love and kisses, but instead with a picture of a Breitling watch, which basically meant "Work your asses off for me and I'll throw you a bone." It was typical corporate pep-talk bullshit, and most of us scoffed and just carried on, because we were already working as hard as we could to meet Liechti's unrealistic Net New Money goals. And naturally every time we hit our annual expectations, let's say CHF 40 million per private banker, he'd raise the bar. "That's nice, but it's not enough! I want to see 60 million Swiss francs!" Besides enduring all this football coach crap, Security and Compliance and that Gestapo wannabe were constantly sending us watch-your-ass memos about properly encrypting the files on our laptops and making sure we knew how to lose a tail. It was pure Sicilian Mafia modus operandi, stuffed in a cheap corporate suit.

With all the pressure from above, risks bubbling up from below, and our sophisticated clients getting nervous with the stiffening regulations, it was starting to not be so much fun anymore. I took it in stride, because I knew no toga party lasts forever. The band gets tired, the food and drinks run out, the girls' makeup starts to run. The band played on, but the show was getting old.

Moreover, it was starting to get ugly, too. I hadn't much taken to Christian Bovay from the first day I met him, but serving under him for years had revealed all the sliminess of his character. Bovay was a typical Swiss bureaucrat, petty and spiteful. He didn't like going out in the field and risking his ass, but he resented the fact that his troops were out there living high on the hog. Often he'd try to take credit for someone else's Net New Money coup, which was absurd because all he'd done was rubber-stamp the paperwork. He benefited plenty from our hard work and successes, yet he was always sowing disharmony, whispering in people's ears about how one banker was better than the other or who was working less but getting bigger rewards. Almost from the moment I brought in Olenicoff's $200 million, Bovay regarded me as a wise guy who'd pulled a fast one and was getting an unfair cut of the nut. Most of the time I brushed him off.

And then he stole Valerie away from me.

He knew how much I liked her, and she liked me, so he targeted our bond because he couldn't touch my wallet. He had her transferred over to be *his* personal assistant, which was within his power as my boss. He knew there was nothing I could do about it except quit the bank. Valerie was pissed as hell.

"It'll be all right," I told her. "We'll still be on the Desk together and we'll still party and have fun."

"But Bradley, I can't *stand* him!" she whispered from her new desk just outside Bovay's office. "He drinks black coffee all the time and never chews gum! And those teeth!"

I laughed and squeezed her hand. "Put a bowl of mints on his desk. Maybe he'll take the hint."

But nothing cheered her up and she started talking about leaving. And Bovay, who could see how obviously upset she was about the change, instead of trying to win her over, screwed her on her annual bonus! When I brought her over from Barclays I'd promised her a big raise—20,000 Swiss francs. That was my deal with UBS and she'd gotten it. But bonuses were up to the boss's discretion, and Bovay was just being a spiteful prick. I found her one morning outside the bank, smoking a cigarette and crying. When she told me what was up, I nearly blew a gasket. I went upstairs and shouldered my way into Bovay's office. He was on the phone.

"What's with Valerie's bonus?" I was trying to keep from knocking him out.

"Not in the budget, Bradley." He tried not to grin through those tank-trap teeth.

"Not in the budget? Whose fucking budget?!"

"She's only been with me for three months. I haven't had time to evaluate her performance. Maybe next year. And I'm on the telephone. See?"

I stormed out and thought about it for a minute. I could fume and argue and fight it, but the holidays were only days away. So I took out my ATM card, went over to the main building and the machine in the lobby, withdrew ten 1,000 Swiss franc notes, and put them in an envelope. You can do that with a Swiss ATM. I took Valerie into one of the private client salons and placed the envelope in her hand. She only cried harder when she opened it up.

"You can't do this, Bradley. I can't accept it."

"You can't *not* accept it, Valerie," I said. "I told you when we came here together I'd take care of you, and I intend to keep my promise."

She hugged me, and I pulled away and went back up to my desk before the whole thing choked me up. But I was seething. *Cheap bastard.* This guy wouldn't even pay to fix his own horrific dentition. Turns out that when it came to money, Bovay was so tight you couldn't pull a needle out of his ass with a tow truck. Ugly, spiteful, and cheap is a bad combination, eight days a week.

It wasn't long after that, early in 2005, that Bovay tried to pull the same thing on me. My annual bonuses represented eighteen percent of the revenues generated by my client accounts, as had been negotiated to lure me to UBS. I tracked the revenues carefully, down to the penny, knowing full well that Swiss bankers had never cheated anyone! So bonus day arrived, but the extra quarter million did not. I waited two days, until a few of my colleagues confirmed that their performance payoffs had come through. Then I sauntered into Bovay's corner office, and I was cold as death.

"Christian, I believe we've got an accounting issue." I took out a slip of paper and squinted at it. "According to my calculations, there should be an additional 247,890 Swiss francs in my personal account. My bonus appears to be AWOL."

He scrunched his rat-like nose at me. "What does that mean?"

"Absent Without Leave. In other words, missing."

"Let's not make a fuss of it, Bradley." He waved a dismissive hand. "I think you're making quite enough."

I barely raised an eyebrow.

"You know, Christian, you're right. No need to fuss. You can either fix it right now, or discuss it with my attorney." I pulled one of his business cards from the silver holder on his desk. "I'll just give him your card so he knows how to reach you. In the meantime, you might want to pull out my contract."

And I left. Lo and behold, the very next morning my bonus was sitting in my account. But after that, and the thing with Valerie, the atmosphere around the Desk was sour as the stench of low tide. I found out that Bovay was screwing with everyone, not just me. It felt like our big happy family was starting to splinter under an abusive father. When that happens, it's not long before folks get cannibalistic.

One early evening in April 2005 I was sitting at my desk, thinking happily about doing a little clubbing after work with some friends. Then I felt someone's presence at my shoulder. It was my buddy James Woods, a tall, bald Scottish guy with merry eyes and always a kind word for everyone. His brows were furrowed and he was creasing a sheet of paper in his fingers. He bent to me and dropped his voice.

"Bradley, I think ya should have a bit of a look at this," he said in his brogue. "It's the top page of a three-page memo, internal."

I took the paper and looked at the title. "Cross-Border Business Banking." It only took a few lines of reading for me to get the gist (Document 2). It was a ticking time bomb to all of us on the Desk. "Private Wealth Management personnel will *not* engage in the following activities." Then the page had a list of activities that it was warning us *not* to do, though they were everything we were being paid *to* do! Excuse me? I snapped the sheet in the air like a whip.

"Where the fuck did you get this, James?"

"Found the bloody thing on the intranet."

"Show me! I've never seen this, and I sure as hell was never trained on it!"

So he did. Now you can only imagine the size of the UBS intranet. For products alone you could go through a thousand pages, then all kinds of training materials, compliance forms, PowerPoint presentations, internal memoranda, worksheets, accounting records, and the annual report. You could have stuck *War and Peace* in there and no one would have found it! James took my mouse and guided me through his excavation, clicking on "International Private Banking," then "Americas," then "USA," and finally, "Country Paper: New."

I took the mouse back and clicked. There it was, the whole Three-Page Memo, paragraph after paragraph in tight single space. Every word of it was a dire warning to all Private Wealth Managers on the Americas Desk:

"PWMs shall *not* travel to the Continental United States for the purposes of seeking out American clients. . . . PWMs shall *not* propose products which fall outside the legal parameters of US tax regulations. . . . PWMs shall *not* engage in subterfuge while soliciting clients with marketing proposals in order to acquire Net New Money."

*WTF?*

In other words, "Private Wealth Managers for UBS shall *not* do all the things we've been telling you and paying you to do for years, over and fucking over!"

My hands were actually trembling as I read it. The firm we had worked for all these years and trusted with our futures was prepared to sell us down the river!

"Shit!" I hissed. "I've never fucking *ever* seen this. Why didn't they tell us they put this on there!?"

James took the paper back from me. "*That's* why I'm bringing it to your attention, lad."

"Okay," I said. "Go back to your desk and we'll talk about this later."

He left, and I sat there blinking at my computer monitor like some wife who'd just found a condom in her husband's wallet. This couldn't be right. It had to be some sort of "burn bag" draft, drummed up by the lawyers long before UBS had even thought of sending us out to be first-class pickpockets, and meant to be destroyed. Or it had to be some "watch your asses, boys," warning they were going to issue, but decided it might curb our enthusiasm and had just filed it away. And then they'd decided to just go balls to the walls, train us all up on crypto and shaking tails and using pay phones and never, ever overtly breaking a law when we could just bend it a little and bring home the bacon. Right? James had just misunderstood the intent of this thing. Right? They wouldn't sell us all down the river. *Right?*

My gleaming blue eyeballs crawled up to the letterhead. But there was none. Almost always with such directives the blood-red UBS logo with its three skeleton keys was prominently displayed. This memo had nothing but "Legal and Compliance Department" on the header. That cleft between my eyebrows deepened like a fresh stiletto gash as

I focused on the date. November 24, 2004. *Two-fucking-thousand-and-FOUR*. Long, long *after* we'd first started winging our way off to yacht races and golf tournaments, and almost half a year *earlier* than today's date flicking at me from my monitor like some New England lighthouse. Right in the middle of the war, boys. Right in the middle of the bloody hunts for untaxable millions, the company's lawyers had come up with this cover-your-ass document and buried it deep in their tight Swiss assholes where no one could ever find it!

I read through it again, fast, while my cheeks burned and my nice white shirt collar squeezed my throat like a boa constrictor. I tore my tie knot open. Three whole pages of single-spaced legalese bullshit.

"Don't you dare do *this*, boys. Don't you dare do *that*, boys. This kind of behavior is nothing that this upright, forthright, oh-so-squeaky-clean establishment would ever allow. And if you get caught doing any of it (even though we taught you exactly how to do it and pushed you out the door without a parachute), the Secretary will disavow any knowledge of your actions."

Just like Mission Fucking Impossible. I balled my fist and slammed it on my desk and a secretary jumped in her chair. I heard her say something to me but I didn't even glance at her. My eyeballs were melting the monitor.

Christian Bovay. That fucking slimy, rotten-toothed, dandruff-flinging scumbag. This was all him, all the way, and I cursed myself for not having tossed his office one night after he'd gone home. Who knew what else I'd have found in that asshole's rat hole? Cocaine? A handgun and three forged passports? A thick Birkenfeld dossier with my mug shot and records of all the schemes I'd pulled off for him? Right now I was ready to bet every Swiss franc in my bank account that the fucker had a file on every one of us, just in case the Americans or Canadians came calling. And then he'd grin through that jail-door mouth of his and hand us all over, claiming he'd been running some internal corruption investigation all along. And then you know what? He'd whip out this Three-Page Benedict Arnold shit and wave it around as proof that we'd all been warned to never flout the laws!

That bastard Bovay was like Satan. And what did that make me? A trusting, naive dupe. Nothing more than Lucifer's fucking banker.

I snapped my head around to his office. Empty. Dark. Door locked. The lucky fool had already gone home, because if he'd still been in there, I would have taken his Swarovski-crystal ashtray and buried it in his head. I was breathing like a marathon runner as I stabbed my keyboard and the printer spat out the three pages of doom. Then I folded the printout, stuffed it inside my suit jacket, shut down the computer, got up, threw my scarf around my neck, and shoved my chair against the desk, where it banged like a car bumper. The chatter in the room had frozen, I could feel the eyes on me, but all I could see was a tunnel of red and that big glass door at the end of the corridor. All I heard as I smashed it open and stormed into the night was my own curdled voice hissing.

*Motherfuckers!*

# CHAPTER 6
## COUNTERPUNCH

*"I don't know what's going to happen, man,
but I just want to get my kicks before the whole
shithouse goes up in flames."*
—*JIM MORRISON, THE DOORS*

I KNEW THE VULTURES had finally come home to roost.

My head was reeling as I stormed out onto Rue du Rhône, and I suddenly stopped, not knowing which way to turn or where to go. I flipped open my cell phone and blew off my drinks and dinner partners, although God knows I needed at least three stiff belts of one hundred-proof something. But I decided to walk it off instead. I needed to think, and think clearly. It was a cool spring evening, the lights flickering from the roof gardens of the luxury hotels across the lake and some sort of classical concert wafting over from the water-side promenade. I didn't really see or hear any of it. I just walked the cobblestone streets, passing through crowds of spring revelers as if they were ghosts while I smoked, pondered my ugly twist of fate, and tried to cool down.

"Take it easy, Birkenfeld," I said to myself. "Let's logic this one out."

But I hadn't gotten to be a globe-trotting, high-risk-taking, extremely successful private banker by being as sweet and naive as Mary Poppins. Something was rotten at UBS, and though I'd had a gut feeling about it for some time now, I'd suddenly bitten down on a nauseating chunk. But could the whole secret memo thing be a simple mistake? Was I jumping the gun? Maybe in fact that memo had just been a draft of something, an idea cooked up by some young legal intern and mistakenly dropped into the computer system. Or maybe it had been drummed up by some pissed-off, underpaid employee who just wanted to stir up trouble. Planted like an anti-tank mine until someone like me ran over it and . . . "Boom!" I mean, would Christian Bovay and Martin Liechti really set us all up like that? We were all making a fucking fortune for the firm. Would they throw their best moneymakers under not merely a bus, but a bullet train?

"Yes they *would*." The ugly conclusion suddenly escaped from my mouth. "In a fucking heartbeat." The heat was on, the United States and Western European "Feds" nosing around and applying pressure all over the world. It could all blow up any minute, and the Swiss Mafia at UBS wanted their asses thoroughly covered. What did they care about us? All of us bankers on the Americas Desk could get hanged by our thumbs and they'd still be making their comfy Swiss salaries. I knew there were very few honorable men in banking, and no heroes. If you think otherwise, just have lunch sometime with your local mortgage loan officer.

It started to rain. I tossed my cigarette in a puddle and it hissed like a snake. Those were the kinds of people I was dealing with, pit vipers, so I walked on home to plan how to cut their heads off.

It was cool enough in my flat for a fire. I stoked up the hearth, kicked off my shoes, poured myself a huge tumbler of Johnnie Walker, and hunkered down on my green leather couch, watching the dancing flames. I thought about calling my brother in Boston, but I knew Doug would tell me to fold up my tent and get the hell out of Switzerland. He'd probably have been right, but running wasn't my style. I'd worked too hard to build a career in Geneva, and if I was going to leave UBS, it would be as General Sherman in the Civil War blazing a path to Atlanta.

But it had to be calculated, carefully planned, no shots from the hip. I hadn't studied all the great military tacticians in college like

Patton and Rommel for nothing, and I'd learned plenty of business law maneuvers in graduate school. My execution would have to be precise, like a master chess player, with every response anticipated if I was going to save my own skin and those of my colleagues. After a couple of hours of drinking, and two fat Cohibas burned down to the nubs, I'd eliminated all the harmless theories about that memo and arrived at that stop called "Hard Truth." At any minute, my two-faced bosses might turn my colleagues and me in to the American authorities, while claiming they'd forbidden our practices all along. *That's* what that Three-Page Memo meant.

Finally, I went to bed. Some people don't sleep well on the cusp of a life-altering confrontation. But I slept like a sniper, refueling my strength, locked and loaded.

---

The next morning at nine sharp I came barreling into Christian Bovay's office like a steaming bull. He jerked back in his chair as I slammed the door, slapped my copy of the Three-Page Memo on his desk, and bent over, knuckling the gleaming wood.

"What the fuck is *this*, Christian?"

He raised one hand as if to ward off some demon, craned his neck, and squinted down at it. Then he nodded, sat back, and smiled with those burglar-tool teeth.

"It's nothing that should concern you, Bradley."

"Nothing that should concern me?" I leaned in further. "Really?!"

"Yes, really." He was trying to avoid my eyes, which were probably gleaming like charcoal briquettes. "There's no need to make a stink. It's not that big of a deal."

And that's when I reached out, grabbed him by the collar, and yanked him right out of his chair. We were nose to nose and my other hand was cocked in a fist.

"Fuck *you*, Christian!" I hissed in his face. "It's not a big deal? It's a *huge* fucking deal!" I jabbed my finger at the memo. "You're exposing all of us to this shit. And we're *all* exposed. Not just me, but my colleagues, the clients, and all our fucking shareholders! Right?"

I could feel him trembling in my tight grip. I was a lot bigger than him and he knew I could just pick him up and throw him right through his fancy picture window. He mumbled something about not getting all emotional over standard office procedures and practices, but the blood was pounding so loud in my ears I could barely hear him. My assault had been calculated, but my fury was all too real.

"You know what, Christian?" I said as gripped him close enough to bite off his nose. "Go fuck yourself."

I dropped him, swiped the memo from his desk, stormed out, and slammed his door behind me. The first pair of eyes I saw were Valerie's, staring at me from behind her desk as if she'd just heard a lion ripping her boss into deli slices. Then I realized the entire floor was deathly quiet and all the bankers and assistants had frozen in the exact same pose. I straightened my tie, grinned at them, and said, "*Bonjour, mes amis*. It's a lovely day today!"

Then I weaved my way over to my own desk, sat down, took off my suit jacket, and lit up a cigarette. Jacques Leuba appeared with a steaming mug of coffee and set it down in front of me.

"I should probably have poured a shot of bourbon in that, but it's early," he said. Then he perched on the desk corner. "Do tell, Bradley."

"Thanks, *mon ami*." I took a long sip and handed him the pages. "Take a look at this."

It didn't take long for Jacques's eyes to widen, and then he was flipping back and forth through the pages, as if trying to figure out if the thing was some sort of a prank. Then James Woods showed up, who'd discovered the dastardly thing and already knew what it was all about. He cocked an eyebrow at Jacques.

"That's a bit of prickly shit, isn't it, Jacques? Found the bloody thing on the intranet."

Then my buddies Angel Gomez and Stephan Mundwiller showed up, each of them taking a read and glancing at each other and whispering, "What *is* this shit?"

"It's our death sentence, boys, you better get measured for your coffins," I said.

"When did this go up, Bradley?" Jacques asked.

"It says November," I said. "But who the fuck knows? It could have been up there for years. And it just says 'November 2004 version,' which implies it's gone through who-the-fuck-knows-how-many iterations. Notice there's no letterhead? Notice our UBS 'Three Keys of Corruption' logo isn't anywhere on it? It's a UBS cover-their-asses document for a rainy day. We all drown, while they stay nice and dry under their gold bullion umbrella."

"So what does this mean, Brad?" Angel's dark brows were scrunched up together like a pair of crow wings. In just two weeks, he and Stephan were supposed to be taking off together on one of their hunter-gatherer excursions, to Dallas and Miami, respectively.

"It means, amigo . . . that we're all fucked. The party's over."

The guys wandered off, back to their desks, shaking their heads and muttering to each other. James was the last to go, and before he did I grabbed his elbow.

"Listen, dude," I said. "You need to get off the Americas Desk. Transfer out to something else, like maybe South Africa. And I mean like ASAP. Got me?"

He nodded solemnly. James didn't need to be warned twice.

"And where are you going, Brad?"

"Nowhere, for now," I said. "I've got some studying to do."

"Sun Tzu, perhaps?"

I smiled at him. "That's right. *The Art of War.*"

James smiled back and left, but I could see he was shaken up. And me? I was stirred, but not shaken. I knew what I had to do next. I wasn't going to just walk off the job. If I did that, and suddenly the whole thing went belly-up, any investigators looking into UBS's nefarious practices could still find me complicit, and I'd have no proof that I'd ever protested or done a damn thing about it. I'd have to make a stink, all right. However, first rule of discovering a corporate crime: Gather the evidence and store it safely.

So, over the next couple of weeks, I acted like I'd gotten over the "memo incident." I went through all the motions of seeking Net New Money clients and servicing the ones in my book. I made my slews of phone calls, propped my feet on my desk, smoked and drank in the office like everyone else, and cracked the requisite number of

Birkenfeld off-color jokes. I even treated Bovay with courtesy, letting him think I'd just had a temporary tantrum.

Meanwhile, I was quietly collecting evidence in order of priority for my plan of attack. First thing I did was to gather up copies of all of our in-house Security and Compliance training modules; basically the UBS handbooks on how to discreetly solicit North American clients while making sure the US authorities got left in the dust. After that, I went through years of my computer records and email, saving all the "Push harder! Bring in more Net New Money!" memos from Liechti, Guignard, Bovay, and even the higher-ups like Raoul Weil. Then I assembled my own clients' records, as well as a few big fish handled personally by Bovay, which I managed to get access to in his safe, and made sure the enormous amounts of secret account holdings were tagged to each record. All of these things I made copies of and walked them out of the bank. I took them home and spent long nights drinking, smoking, and listening to my favorite jazz as I reviewed the extensive documentation of UBS's illicit practices.

I didn't party much during those few weeks, just here and there to keep up appearances. And although I knew that my days at UBS were numbered, I planned to leave on my own terms when the time was right. I'd already decided that I was done with private banking forever. It had all been a fun, wild ride, but how many times can you woo some client into investing in stocks, bonds, currencies, or gold bullion before you eventually lose your enthusiasm? I was ready to progress into private equity, using all the contacts I'd made over the years to put big moneymakers together for partnerships and then take my cut of whatever that new endeavor might be. I knew plenty of people with great ideas for start-ups, such as new energy or biotech firms, or proposals for constructing resort hotels in prominent locations. I also knew plenty of others looking for such investments. I'd put them together, and get my cut for the matchmaking plus stock options in the new entities. Do that just a few times successfully and you're set for life. I knew I'd be successful, and I'd no longer be reporting to corporate ingrates.

It was mid-May 2005, just as I was feeling pretty good about the amount of backup material I'd gathered, when Igor Olenicoff got busted in California. That was definitely an "oh shit" moment. I had called him up from a public pay phone, standard practice with those "types" of clients, just to consult with him about a particular investment.

"I cannot speak to you now," he said in a low, guarded tone, and he didn't use my name. "The IRS is here in my office . . . with a SWAT team."

The phone went dead and I looked at it as if it had suddenly turned into a shrunken head. Did he actually say "SWAT team"? *Holy shit.* The wolves were at the door, and Olenicoff had just been first-bitten. The odd thing was, he'd pretty much predicted it would happen.

A few years prior, Olenicoff had acquired a 120-foot yacht that he christened *Rusalka* (Exhibit 12). Some Japanese power players had built this beautiful vessel in the hopes of taking it to the America's Cup and using it as the flagship for the festivities; that venture had failed, maybe because the Japanese haven't sailed very well since the Battle of Midway. At any rate, Olenicoff saw it sitting in Tokyo harbor, paid hard cash for it, and had his boat captain drive her to California and then through the Panama Canal to Florida, where I'd had drinks on the yacht with Igor and a bunch of pretty people at the Palm Beach Boat Show. In the spring of 2004 he'd called me up and said, "Bradley, I am taking the *Rusalka* for a wonderful cruise to Guatemala, Honduras, and Belize. Why don't you and Mario come along?"

"Lovely!" I'd said, and I called up Mario Staggl, who'd arranged for all of Olenicoff's offshore structures, and we flew off to LA and then all went to Central America together. By that time Mario and I had become more than just business acquaintances. His Liechtenstein trust company was at the top of its game, and on multiple occasions I'd delivered my clients and their money into his hands for safekeeping. Every time Mario formed a trust structure for one of my clients, he and his partner, Dr. Klaus Biederman, who'd actually written the comprehensive book on the trust laws for Liechtenstein, got very well paid for their services. I, in turn, was rewarded by Mario with gifts of appreciation, often fat envelopes containing 50,000 Swiss francs (they were untaxable, by the way). In between deals we'd partied together, gone skiing in Zermatt, strategized in London, and attended the Venice Film Festival and other high-roller events all over Europe. Mario was a brilliant CPA, fashionable and funny. He looked a little like Eddie Munster and belly-laughed like Buddy Hackett.

So we were down in Central America, having a great time on Olenicoff's yacht, until one evening off the coast of Belize the "Mad Russian" took us aside.

"Gentlemen," he said in his Boris Yeltsin lilt, "I must tell you that these ventures of ours may be drawing to a close."

"What makes you say that, Igor?" Mario asked.

"Let us just say that I believe I am being looked at."

"Little gray tax men?" I asked as I sipped my scotch. The breeze was beautiful and the fragrance of the sea permeated the air.

"I am a billionaire, Bradley." Olenicoff smiled and shrugged. "Men who make pennies as government employees are not enamored of men with yachts. We should consider moving my money out of UBS."

"Well, that's easy enough to do," I said. "Right, Mario?"

"Child's play," said Mario.

"Whenever you like, Igor," I said. Although truthfully, I was hoping the heat would cool down and he'd change his mind. If he moved his $200 million out of UBS, my own bonuses would take a nosedive. However, keeping clients safe and happy was always the prime objective. If you gave them bad advice, you'd soon be clientless.

"I shall let you know." Olenicoff smiled and waved at his other guests, a gaggle of old fraternity brothers having drinks near the wheelhouse. "Let's go watch the sunset."

But he hadn't pulled the trigger back then, and now the trigger was being pulled on him—by dudes with big guns and helmets. I could just picture them rifling through his office, walking out with computers and reams of paperwork, and I wondered if my name would pop up anywhere as they pored over all of it back in Washington. But I wasn't too worried. I was just the go-between, and a protected Swiss banking employee at that. Olenicoff was the money guy, responsible alone for his taxes. Whether or not he paid them was not in my wheelhouse, or so I thought at the time. It didn't cross my mind that if the Feds hit him with some sort of indictment, he might panic and start finger-pointing . . . at *me*.

Anyway, after that phone call with Olenicoff I rang up Mario and warned him. "Stand by for action, buddy. Igor's getting some serious heat in California."

But it didn't faze Mario. He was successful, wily, had scores of super-rich clients like Olenicoff, and was perfectly safe and comfortable in Liechtenstein, where the banking laws were even more covert and rock solid than in Switzerland. Then I told him about the Three-Page Memo, and that he should keep it under his hat.

"I've never cared much for the Swiss," he said.

"I'm learning to hate them myself."

"Well, you'll always have a home here in Liechtenstein, Bradley."

"Thanks, but I've still got irons in the fire."

"Of course." Mario knew I wasn't the type to just turn the other cheek.

As the month of June rolled around, it was time for the second phase of my tactical gambit. I didn't know whether Christian Bovay had passed on my concerns to his superiors, but given the slimy bastard's nature, I figured he'd kept it to himself so that nothing would impact his moneymaking fiefdom. It would be up to me now to undertake an in-house protest. "I know what you guys have been pulling here, and now you know that I know. So come clean."

I sat down at my desk and wrote a memo to the UBS Head of Legal, Rene Wuethrich, and the UBS Head of Compliance, Philip Frey. With it I attached a copy of the Three-Page Memo.

Dear Rene,

I am contacting you regarding a **very** serious matter that has a variety of negative consequences and I wanted to ensure that I made you aware of this, as well as ensuring I am in total compliance with the policies and procedures of UBS as a Director.

I was on the UBS intranet website (Wealth Management International, Americas International, QI–deemed sales, Country Paper USA new) and read a very lengthy and legal document (please see attached), covering the market I presently cover—the United States of America.

Please respond back to me, as I feel this should be given immediate and top priority, not just for me, but for my colleagues in Geneva and Zurich too! Thank you for your expertise and time in this matter.

Best regards,
Bradley C. Birkenfeld
Director

I hit the "send" button and waited. And then I waited some more. Honestly, I expected some sort of reply, at the very least a summons to a quiet consultation during which Wuethrich and Frey would try to assuage my concerns. Nothing. *Nada.* After a week I realized they were going to just blow me off. "Okay, boys. Wanna play the stonewall game? I'll hit you again, just when you think I've given it up."

Meanwhile, Olenicoff called me up and told me he had decided to move his money out of UBS over to a much smaller bank in Liechtenstein. I had to admit the guy had balls, calling me on an open line like that after the Feds had already tossed his offices and were most likely tapping his phones. Or maybe he figured the jig was up anyway and he wasn't going to be able to hide his assets, so he might as well move them to somewhere even safer than Switzerland. The Liechtensteinians were even tougher than the Swiss when it came to outsiders screwing with their private business, and Mario knew bankers who'd die before talking to American tax authorities. Mario, as the trustee, told Olenicoff that he'd give him a full accounting of his assets and wire the goods on his orders.

In fact, it was a stroke of good fortune. I knew I'd be getting out sooner rather than later; and with Olenicoff's money leaving my portfolio, it was a good excuse to exit stage left. Not that I really needed an excuse, but in Europe a resignation comes with many benefits, and if the reasoning for it seems sound, the whole thing goes down easily. You get your gardening leave for six months, your base salary, and by law any bonuses owed you still have to be paid.

Over at the Desk the working atmosphere was growing ever more foul, like those oil refineries in New Jersey spewing crap in the air while the governor keeps touting "the Garden State." For the time being, I wasn't traveling anywhere outside of Europe, yet many of my colleagues still had to make those hunter-gatherer trips. Incredibly, Martin Liechti was sending out more and more of his "Go get 'em!" memos, while my banker buddies had grown as nervous as cows in the minutes before an earthquake. I felt bad for them all, but over the course of numerous dinners, late-evening drinks, and soirees, I'd been waving my red hurricane flag and warning them to batten down the hatches and prepare for the worst. That was about all I could do.

In July, having heard nothing but crickets from Wuethrich or Frey, I fired off my email again and also sent it by interoffice mail, Three-Page Memo attached. But my in-box remained empty of any replies, naughty or nice, and believe me I was checking it twice. When August rolled around I hit them again. The silence was deafening. "All right, you fuckers," I said to them via brain waves. "I gave you a total of six chances and you're treating me like some girl in grade school who wipes her snot under her desk. Watch what happens next."

With four years under my belt at UBS, I knew scores of private wealth managers like me at all the other branches: Geneva, Zurich, and Lugano. So guess who got copies of the Three-Page Memo, generously shared by Yours Truly? I knew what I was doing, spreading fear and uncertainty like the Black Plague, yet with a definite purpose in mind. I wanted to see how their superiors would react when their loyal bankers protested the knife in their ribs. Well, all my friends reported back to me that their managers danced jigs of excuses and lies, pretending ignorance of the Legal and Compliance warnings, which further confirmed my suspicions. They were closing ranks, leaving all of us out in the cold. Not a damn thing changed; it was business as usual at UBS. None of the offshore antics of any of the desks were modified or dismantled. The bastards wanted their money, and if their soldiers were "killed in action," so be it.

That did it. I wasn't going to be carried off the field in a coffin draped with a Swiss flag. In mid-September I met with two different employment law firms in Geneva and told the attorneys my tale. Neither firm knew I was consulting with the other, which I kept in my pocket because I wanted to compare their reactions. Both sets of lawyers said the exact same thing.

"Mr. Birkenfeld, resign from this bank immediately!"

Well, I don't need to be shot at twice to get the message. Still, it wasn't an easy thing to do, saying good-bye to the most successful and lucrative years of my professional life. But I took a deep breath and, on October 5, 2005, almost exactly four years to the day of my start date at UBS, I typed up a short letter of resignation and walked it in to Christian Bovay.

"I am shocked, Bradley!" he said. "You've done so well with us. I don't understand."

I just shook my head at that little weasel, thinking how I wouldn't miss his raccoon teeth and dandruff.

"I'm sure you'll figure it out, Christian," I sneered, and I walked out.

They kept me in my chair for a week while they did all the post-mortem paperwork. I took Valerie out to lunch right away because I didn't want her to hear it from anyone else.

"It's all so terrible," she sniffed. "I don't want to be there any-more. It won't be the same without you."

"Hey, cheer up." I smiled and touched her tear-stained cheek. "We'll always have Geneva. And besides, I'm not dying. We'll still party, just not on a UBS expense account."

But she wasn't really consolable, and it wasn't long after that she left as well. I still miss her. She was a sweet kid, a great friend, and the perfect Ms. Moneypenny.

At the end of that week, they summoned me over to the main UBS building for a little sit-down exit interview with Human Resources. The head of HR, Monica Boesch, was in the room, along with this dude known only as "Juerg." This guy was the intermediary between Christian Bovay and Michel Guignard in Zurich, so I knew the big dogs were concerned. I was pissed before I even sat down.

"Bradley, why are you resigning?" Monica said with phony concern. "We don't understand."

I rolled my eyes. "Let's cut the crap, Monica. I've been asking you all for three months now why the hell this Three-Page Memo exists, and no one has answered me."

Juerg puffed himself up. "Well, you are not going to get an answer." He looked like a Swiss Shrek, with oversized hands, a pumpkin for a head, and a cheap suit with white socks.

That *really* pissed me off. I pulled a Birkenfeld on them, got up, and leaned over their desk. They both shrank back in their chairs.

"You are fucking wrong. I *will* get an answer. I *guarantee* you I'll get an answer. But I'm not going to deal with this shit anymore." I took out my wallet and flipped it open. "Here's my UBS card and all my credit cards." I splayed them on the desk like a full house. "And I'm done here."

I walked back over to our building. When the guard saw my face, he didn't dare ask for my ID. I went upstairs, shook hands all around, gave a couple of hugs to James Woods and Jacques, winked at Valerie, and took exactly one minute to check over my desk. I didn't need to take a single piece of paper; I already had everything secretly and safely stored away. I left the bank with only two items—my favorite ashtray and a UBS coffee cup.

I wanted that "Three Red Keys of Corruption" logo sitting above my fireplace like the severed head of a dragon.

---

I am definitely a big fan of the gardening-leave concept. There's a time to kill, and a time to chill, and this was going to be six months of the latter. I was forty-four years old and had been hustling a living in high finance around the world for half my life, a high-speed existence of super stress with my internal springs wound tight. During all those years, even when I'd take a vacation, I was always on the lookout for potential clients. Now, for the first time in forever, I was unemployed yet still drawing a salary of about fifteen grand a month, with bonuses still accruing. Technically, all of my clients at UBS were still locked in the Birkenfeld Book until the date of my final paycheck, six months down the road. As long as UBS earned revenues from my accounts, eighteen percent of that would drop into my Swiss piggy bank.

I rang up Thais and suggested a week together in Saint-Tropez, which four years before had been doomy and gloomy with Sevrine on the heels of 9/11. Ever ready to party, Thais informed her bosses that the world of high fashion would have to survive without her talents for a week. She packed up her slinkiest outfits and bikinis and we jumped in my M5 and roared off to Saint-Tropez. Our first day at the beach, my fingers kept twitching toward my cell phone with the urge to call the office and check on my clients. She took it away from me, buried it deep in her beach bag, and dragged me into the ocean. Then she plied me with champagne, dancing, and romance until I finally realized that I was something other than just a Swiss private banker.

It was tough going back to Geneva after that. Winter was coming and even though I love to ski, I wasn't yet in the mood to freeze. So I turned around and took off for the Philippines and spent the holidays with Mauro, hopping all over the islands in his Agusta helicopter, one party after another. Then I came back for a breather, but that didn't last long either. Off again, this time to Morocco and a boatload of beauties with my buddy Ladjel. By the time that little jaunt was over, I was trying to figure out how to just retire and spend the rest of my life as a wandering financial philosopher. That wasn't a profession I'd ever heard of, but maybe it was time to invent it.

Reality, however, is one of those beasts that can't be held at bay for long. In February I was back in Geneva, relaxing in the flat I hadn't seen much of lately, when I checked my bank account, expecting to see my well-deserved, substantial bonus. It wasn't there. *Fuck. Here we go again.*

I fired off an email to Bovay, no frills.

"Where's my bonus, Christian? It didn't hit my bank account."

In reply, I got a long email back from Human Resources, with lots of curly language and Monica's signature. But her basic message was no frills either.

"Mr. Birkenfeld, I am sorry to inform you that you are not entitled to this period's bonus, nor any thereafter. You have chosen to resign from the bank, and these are the consequences."

Oh, really? I fired back with both barrels.

"Dear Ms. Boesch, apparently you are misinformed. According to Swiss banking law, which I have studied and researched in depth, the contractual obligations between a financial firm and an employee survive the current status of his employment. The fact that UBS has been paying my annual bonuses without hesitancy or complaint is an irrefutable indication that my performance, from which the bank continues to reap benefits, is still deserving of reward. Therefore, the fact of my resignation does not release the bank of this contractual obligation."

She didn't answer me. No big surprise there. But after a day, Bovay sent me one curt line, and I could almost see him sneering like a crazed Swiss leprechaun as he did it.

"You're not getting your bonus, Bradley. Forget about it."

I actually laughed. After all these years, you'd think the little weasel would have known me by now. But he probably figured that I wanted to go on living in Switzerland, maybe make a career move to some other bank or financial-type firm. He probably thought that the last thing I would do was take radical action, without giving a shit if I burned every bridge from the Thames to the Somme. He didn't know me at all. I called up Olivier Chedel.

"Bradley, old boy! How are you? Barclays has never been the same without you, you know. I heard that you and UBS parted ways."

"We did indeed, Olivier," I said. "And I'm fine. Enjoying my gardening leave."

"Very good. And what can I do for you? Are you looking for another position?"

"No, Olivier. Actually, I'm looking for an attorney, the best litigator money can buy."

"Ahh, blood sport," he said. "Sounds like a fray's coming up." He paused for a moment, then said, "It would be unseemly of me, of course, to recommend someone who'd help you dismember a fine sister institution, if that's what you have in mind."

"That's exactly what I have in mind, Olivier."

He laughed. "Dr. Charles Poncet. *Juris Doctor*, that is. You'll find him easily. And tell him I sent you."

"I always loved working with you, Olivier."

"I miss you as well, my friend."

It took me about five minutes to dig up Dr. Charles Poncet, who had a reputation as a hard-ass attorney and corporate lion-killer. I made an appointment, took along a copy of my UBS contract, plus records of all my salaries, bonuses, and the killings I'd made for the bank. I found him ensconced in a luxurious office of French antique furniture, an impeccably dressed elderly gent with a balding peak, fine wings of gray hair swept over his ears, and a pair of rose-colored glasses perched on the tip of his nose. I told him that UBS owed me a bonus of 600,000 Swiss francs. He smiled like a jackal.

One week later, I sued UBS for a million Swiss francs.

I like round numbers.

# CHAPTER 7

## TARANTULA

*"Let them hate, so long as they fear."*
—*CALIGULA, ROMAN EMPEROR*

SWISS BANKERS DON'T TALK.

If they do, they can wind up in a cold stone prison for a very long time, until all their clients are dead and there's nothing left to talk about.

After being sandbagged by that UBS Three-Page Memo and then stonewalled over and over, I was sorely tempted to scream to high heaven and let the whole world know what those bastards were up to. But Swiss banking laws strictly prevented me from taking it public. I knew I'd barely get out a peep before some Swiss Vatican Guard–type goons showed up and dragged me off to jail, where the only ones I'd be able to talk to would be some French-speaking janitor and my attorney. This wasn't like Boston, just a matter of hiring a couple of clowns. These guys were deadly serious about crushing anyone who fucked with their money.

The other thing Swiss bankers don't do is sue Swiss banks. It's not something you do if you're thinking about ever working in corporate finance or private banking again. In my case, I didn't give a damn about that; I knew I could still make a living in six different ways. But news of my lawsuit spread through UBS like a California wildfire. A couple of days after Dr. Poncet filed in court in Geneva, James Woods called me up.

"Bradley, you're suing the bank? Are you out of your bloody mind?"

"Which question do you want answered first, James? It's 'yes' to the first one, and 'maybe' to the second."

"Seriously, sport. You know you'll never work in this town again!"

"I've heard that before. Besides, the bartender over at the Pussy Cat's a good friend of mine. I'm sure he'll give me a job."

"Oh, please!" Then James dropped his voice. "I'm telling you, Brad, the steam's coming out of their ears over here."

"Good. Then they'll pay up."

"Bollocks! They'll die first."

I laughed. "That's one funeral I'll really enjoy."

I could imagine him shaking his head as he hung up. He was right; no one would dare sue a multibillion-dollar worldwide mega-power bank like UBS, the largest financial institution in the world, and think he could get away with it. No one except me.

The thing about suing a major corporation is that with battalions of lawyers they can make the proceedings drag on forever. I knew they'd stall, file for postponements, pull me into endless depositions, and object to every motion. Dr. Poncet had warned me about that, but it was exactly what I expected and had already planned for, and I was looking forward to it. If they thought being sued was my last surprise, they had another think coming. It was time for Phase Three of my assault. It was time to become the scourge of every great financial institution: a pissed-off, dangerous internal whistle-blower.

Yank my tail, you get the horns.

Every major corporation in the Western world has a set of internal whistle-blowing policies. Now, you might think those are designed so that any employee who discovers something amiss can complain to his or her superiors and remain confidential, still hold on to his job, and make sure the company stays on the straight and narrow, right? Well, the reality is that usually when an employee finds himself between a rock and a hard place, with no choice but to whistle-blow, everyone nods their heads and says, "Thank you *sooo* much." But after that the guy's a pariah; might as well have a "T" for Traitor tattooed on his forehead. Folks who whistle-blow internally know their careers within that firm are essentially fucked, which is why such action is as rare as virgins in Paris. Most whistle-blowers never get any kind of reward. They're treated like snitches: They're intimidated, threatened, retaliated against, and blackballed. They lose their jobs, lose their finances, their families are devastated and their lives destroyed. Almost nobody does it unless their backs are against the wall.

I, on the other hand, was in a very rare and advantageous position. Technically I was still employed by UBS, out on gardening leave yet still drawing a substantial salary. But I'd already resigned, so what could they do to me? Deny me my bonus? They'd already done that and we were battling it out in court, so they were fucking with a dude who had nothing to lose. Talk about stupid. With all those big-shot finance businessmen at the top of the UBS pyramid, there wasn't one functioning brain in the bunch.

One of them, a gentleman named Peter Kurer, was a Managing Director and also General Counsel for UBS worldwide. He had personally authored the UBS internal whistle-blowing policies. There were three long documents, about ten or fifteen pages each: Group Policy, Corporate Policy, and Private Banking Policy. Within those policy documents the procedures for bringing misdeeds to attention and seeking redress were carefully enumerated. Unlike the Three-Page Memo, these things had the UBS logo and letterheads all over them, and they were signed by Kurer himself.

Well, guess who had very nice digital and hard copies of the policies? I wrote a long letter to Kurer, invoking my rights as a UBS employee, shareholder, and internal whistle-blower, and of course I told him exactly why. To make sure he got the message loud and clear, I attached his own policy documents and a copy of the infamous Three-Pager. Now you're probably thinking he stonewalled me, just like Human Resources had, but I made damn sure he couldn't. This time I acquired the mailing addresses of every member of the UBS Board of Directors and sent each one a hard copy of the letter and attachments I'd just sent to Kurer—registered mail, return receipts requested. By the way, the Swiss postal system runs flawlessly; their main distribution center just outside Geneva looks like a NASA rocket facility and the postal employees are obsessed with good mail. No one on the board could pretend they hadn't received their poison-pen letter.

Three days later . . . Boom! It was like I'd hit them with a nuclear bomb. My friends inside the bank started emailing me from their personal email accounts.

"Brad, you have no idea what's going on in this bank now!"

"I think I might have some idea."

"They're shitting themselves!"

"Good. I'll send over a pallet of toilet paper."

Then I got an email from Peter Kurer. "Mr. Birkenfeld, a pair of internal investigators from Zurich headquarters would like to interview you tomorrow. Are you available?"

"I'll clear my calendar," I replied.

Then I took Dr. Poncet out to lunch at the Hotel des Bergues, just across the footbridge on the other side of the lake. We had lobster risotto in the same bar where Ian Fleming used to hang out when he was studying for a year in Geneva. It was the perfect place for conspiratorial conversation: dark chestnut wood, royal blue brocade chairs, rich Persian carpets, and discreet waiters who kept their distance.

"Listen, Doc," I said. "These goons are going to try to snow me, get me to back off, and make it all go away."

"That will not happen, Bradley," said Poncet. "Because I shall be there with you. We're in the middle of legal proceedings and you should not be there without your 'gunslinger,' like in one of those westerns you Americans like so much."

I smiled. "Like *Unforgiven*?"

"I haven't seen that film, but the title sounds apropos."

The next morning Dr. Poncet and I appeared at the same UBS headquarters building where I'd met with Monica and Juerg. By this time my name and face had been flashed to all the UBS security desks like some sort of BOLO ("Be on the Lookout"), so we got ourselves a wary escort up to the designated floor and into a small sterile conference room. Inside, the two internal investigators from Zurich were standing on the other side of the table, Mssrs. Schmidt and deCourton. They looked like a pair of skinny twins from *Men in Black*. Dr. Poncet took out his business card and placed it on the table. Their eyes glowed.

"What is your attorney doing here, Mr. Birkenfeld?" one of them demanded.

Before I could answer, Poncet pushed me aside and snapped, "Number one, Mr. Birkenfeld does not trust this firm. Number two, he certainly does not trust either of *you*. So, if you have an objection to my presence, we can leave right now."

"No, no, no." The other one waved his hands. "We've got to report back to Zurich!"

"Then I suggest you sit down and shut up," Poncet snapped. "And let's simply do this."

The whole thing was like a boxing match, with me reiterating everything I'd done and why I'd done it, and those two clowns dodging and weaving. Dr. Poncet didn't interrupt much or whisper cautions in my ear, because I'd already briefed him on my plan. I was going to feed these dudes some accurate information, and some stuff I'd just made up, because after this I was going to use my friends in the bank and "backdoor" these guys. If they were going to conduct a serious internal inquiry, they'd look into all of my documented claims. If not, the whole thing would be just a sham dog-and-pony show, as I expected.

After an hour, they packed up their notebooks and briefcases.

"We are going to conduct a very thorough investigation," one of them promised while the other nodded.

"I'm sure you are, gentlemen," I said. "Have fun."

Well, I was right again. Peter Kurer called for a full and formal internal review. It took about a month, but he and his little gray men whitewashed the entire scandal. Out of the thirty-plus people on the Americas Desk in Geneva, they briefly interviewed only twelve. And up in Zurich, where an identical Net New Money operation was still in full swing, they didn't speak to a single soul! None of the "creative" accusations I'd made were even mentioned. My backdoor intel was just too good. Sometimes I hate being right.

Finally I got an email from Kurer, in which he hopped around like a ballerina on a bed of hot coals.

> "We have conducted a most thorough investigation, and I am pleased to say that all of your concerns have been resolved. Apparently some small missteps were made in the past, and it is understandable that you misinterpreted some old emails and communications which, over time, have become irrelevant . . . "

Blah, blah, blah, blah. He didn't address a single slab of the Swiss cow dung that was smeared all over everyone's shoes. I was furious. Treat me like a loose cannon and a traitor, fine. But call me a liar? Now you're playing with fire. His letter ended with a tag line, and then I understood its prime objective.

> "Given that the investigation is now concluded, we would like to reach a settlement with you regarding your bonus. Please do get back to me on this at your earliest convenience."

I faxed the letter over to Dr. Poncet. He called Peter Kurer direct.

"I see that you'd like to settle with Mr. Birkenfeld," Poncet said. "We're amenable to that. You owe him 600,000 Swiss francs. Write him a check for that amount and we'll go away."

Boom! Broadside with all cannons firing. UBS Legal went nuts and their team of lawyers streamed into court for preliminary hearings, hopping and fuming and yelling "Foul!" while Poncet and I sat there and yawned. But the judge wasn't buying their bullshit and he gave them the option to settle it amicably, or risk a full-blown trial, with all the horrors of bad press and publicity. I went home again to wait it out. James Woods called me up and we went out drinking at La Clémence, a trendy bar-cafe in the Old Town with big green umbrellas and fresh draft.

"You should just see what's going on at the Desk," he told me as he swigged his St. Andrew's Ale. "Your name spits from their mouths like they're talking about Osama bin Laden."

"That's pretty funny, James, since they're probably his bankers."

"No, seriously, Brad. I think they might be ordering up custom-made dartboards with your face on them. You've got a big set of bollocks doing this."

"Well, what else does a man have but his balls?"

The bank made one more stab at a pathetic settlement, which was another dumbass tactical error. They called up Dr. Poncet and offered me CHF 100,000; *one-sixth* of what they owed me. I was pissed enough, but I thought Poncet was going to bust a gut.

"We shall see you at trial!" he yelled through the phone.

But as that date grew closer, everyone at UBS headquarters knew they were going to lose. The Swiss laws and regulations regarding employment status were completely inflexible and they knew the judge was going to rip them a new one. For that one moment in time, I admired the whole Swiss "pole up your ass" thing. That judge wasn't going to budge. So, apparently the day before the trial, Zurich headquarters called Bovay in Geneva and said, "Christian, just pay him his fucking money!"

And so it was. We all gathered outside the courtroom in counsels' chambers, where the UBS lead attorney, from the prestigious law firm of Lenz & Staehelin, who looked like he'd been through a train wreck, muttered his offer.

"Mr. Birkenfeld, we are prepared to wire you 575,000 Swiss francs first thing tomorrow morning. Will you agree to that?"

I walked around the table, clapped him on the shoulder, and smiled.

"That'll do just fine," I said. Just to stick the knife in deeper, I added, "And you're going to pay me *offshore*, right?"

The guy snapped his pencil and turned so red I thought he was having a stroke. Dr. Poncet took my elbow and dragged me out of there. We went to a local bar and celebrated my historic win over champagne. I had sued the largest bank in the world, in their own backyard, and won!

I partied pretty hard for the next ten days. After all, I'd just trumped one of the most powerful banking institutions on earth at their own dirty card game and gone home the winner. The Pussy Cat Club, another old Ian Fleming haunt, was just around the corner and up the hill from my Eaux-Vives flat. I'd been a regular there for years and the Russian and Ukrainian dancers were always happy to see me, especially now as I bought them rounds of overpriced champagne and got girl-handled by a pair of stunning blondes named Natascha and Svetlana. But pretty soon the blush was off the rose. For the first time in my life, I wasn't sleeping well at night.

You might think that a sudden injection of half-a-million-plus would be an effective relaxer, but I already had plenty of money, and winning my bonus wasn't doing the trick. One morning, after having finally crashed at four a.m., I sat straight up in my bed at seven to the sounds of the trams starting to roll. My sheets were rumpled, a fire still smoldered in the hearth, an empty bottle of champagne bobbed in a bucket of melted ice, and my bathroom mirror was adorned with a big pair of red lips crafted in lipstick. Nothing about the night before was very clear, but one thing was: I wasn't done with UBS.

That's when I realized that I hadn't won a damn thing. *UBS* had. The whole corrupt Swiss banking monstrosity had. I'd been working with and for that system for a decade, made them tons of money, and built up their whole North American cash-sucking game into an exquisite art form. And even with all of that, they were ready to screw me, my colleagues, and their shareholders without a shred of integrity or a hint of regret. Even after I'd caught them red-handed, they'd lied and connived and tried to ream me one more time for good measure. Sure, they'd cried and fussed and fought me over my bonus, but it was all just a sham. Six hundred thousand bucks? That was lunch money to UBS! They could have been smart and apologized, doubled my bonus, bought me a new car, and thrown me a farewell party. The expense wouldn't have fazed them, and maybe if they'd made such gestures, I might have just walked away.

But not this way. Not with the metallic taste of betrayal still in my mouth. My bank account was flush; I could do anything I wanted. I could start my own private equity business or just tool around Europe or go home and visit my family and friends. But the whole thing was still stuck in my craw like a rotten apple core. They doubted my determination and resourcefulness. They thought they could just pay up and continue doing their dirty business, while I rode off into the sunset like some dumbass American rodeo clown. *Wrong.* I wasn't half done with them, not by a long shot. Too many regular folks who could barely afford their overblown tax bills had been harmed by this whole Swiss scam, and during my career I'd been one of their top enablers. And the idea that those UBS bastards would just carry on fronting for worldwide fat cats and bad actors, while not giving a damn about anyone else's laws, or the guys like me who'd pay the price, made me furious. There had to be some way to end it all.

I couldn't talk about my roiling inner conflict with any of my friends in Geneva; they were mostly bankers like me, shackled to Swiss regulations about discretion and secrecy. But I had one very close friend I could trust, Sanjay Kumar. He was a quiet professional, a trust expert born in India and raised in Switzerland, and we'd done some business deals together but had never worked for the same people. Sanjay was all class, tall and lanky, happily married and calm as Lake Geneva in July. His only "peccadilloes" were fine art and classic old cars. "Trust" was his calling card.

I arranged to meet him for dinner at La Favola, a quiet little Italian restaurant in the Old Town where cash was the only accepted payment. It was a weeknight and no one was in there but us, the waiters, and ten empty tables of fine linens, gleaming silverware, and antique wood paneling. I pushed my pasta l'arrabiata around with a fork.

"I can't seem to let it go, Sanjay."

"But you won, Brad," he said in his Indian-British lilt. "I heard you were *brilliant*." Sanjay used that word sparingly.

"I haven't won anything but the money. I think I need to take this further."

"What exactly does 'further' mean?"

"The Americans."

He stopped eating, sat back, and sipped his Pinot Noir. "You do realize, my friend, that you'd not only be risking prosecution here in Switzerland, but perhaps more. You might be risking your life."

"Not if I can get protection from the US government."

Sanjay shrugged. "Well, Brad, you know I shall support you in whatever course you decide to take."

"I know," I said with a smile. "That's why we're having this dinner."

He smiled back. "And that's why you're picking up the tab."

We parted and I walked on home, past the glowing windows of Davidoff's cigars, Auer's fine chocolates, and Bally's butter-soft leathers, recalling how once I'd been so enthralled by all those treats and toys. Now all that stuff was suddenly meaningless. My conversation with Sanjay had been as close as I'd come to consulting a shrink. But I didn't need one. I knew what I had to do and was determined that my strategy would succeed.

I'd had lots of time to think about the things I'd done, and I wasn't happy about them. American taxpayers were always struggling to make ends meet, while the rich got richer, squirreled away their money, and duped the IRS. The same thing was happening all over the world, and the sneaky Swiss were the banking pirates making it all happen. I was going to take it to the US government. I was pretty damn certain the Internal Revenue Service or the Department of Treasury would be fascinated by the secrets only someone like me could reveal, and only powerful law enforcement bodies such as they could topple the moribund Swiss banking castles. Hell, maybe they'd even be grateful. But getting some kind of big reward for my revelations didn't even cross my mind. Besides, at that time no such whistle-blower law existed.

However, I wasn't going to just show up in Washington, DC, with a smile and a pile of secrets. I was still a Swiss resident, and unless someone in the United States issued me a subpoena, I wouldn't be able to name names. I'd have to tread carefully.

Back at my flat I sat down at my computer and looked at my overpriced watch. It was six hours earlier in the States, still the middle of the business day in Washington. If I was going to whistle-blow to the US

**Exhibit 1:** The Birkenfeld "Castle" in Massachusetts, where Brad and his two brothers were raised. *Photo Credit: the Birkenfeld family*

**Exhibit 2:** Brad and his brother Doug playing at the beach during a summer in the early 1970s on Cape Cod, Massachusetts. *Photo Credit: the Birkenfeld family*

**Exhibit 3:** Brad graduated from Norwich University in 1988. This private military academy instilled a deep code of honor in him, and taught him to "never leave a man behind." *Photo Credit: the Birkenfeld family*

**Exhibit 4:** Brad left State Street Bank and Trust Company in 1994. To show the Boston bank what he thought of their dubious practices, he hired clowns to pass out information about their activities during the busy lunch hour. *Photo Credit: Bradley C. Birkenfeld*

**Exhibit 5:** These are actual UBS safe deposit box keys. Clients could stash practically anything in these boxes with the guarantee of strict Swiss confidentiality. *Photo Credit: Bradley C. Birkenfeld*

**Exhibit 6:** As a Director of KEY Clients at UBS in Geneva, this was Brad's nametag for special functions. *Photo Credit: Bradley C. Birkenfeld*

**Exhibit 7:** After earning his International MBA, Brad began his work in the lucrative, secret world of Swiss private banking, starting with Credit Suisse, Barclays Bank, and then UBS in Geneva. He resided in Zermatt. *Photo Credit: Bradley C. Birkenfeld*

**Exhibit 8:** Brad purchased a Ferrari 360 Modena spider convertible for 265,500 Swiss francs; he paid for it in 1,000-Swiss-franc notes. *Photo Credit: Bradley C. Birkenfeld*

**Exhibit 9 (right):** In 2002, Brad attended the private jet event in Nassau, Bahamas sponsored by UBS. *Photo Credit: Bradley C. Birkenfeld*

**Exhibit 10 (left):** In 2003, Brad was sailing on the yacht, Destination, as the main UBS sponsor of the St. Barth's Bucket Regatta. *Photo Credit: Bradley C. Birkenfeld*

**Exhibit 11:** Jack Manning, the billionaire real estate businessman, and his second wife, Lyle Howland, on the island of Nantucket. *Photo Credit: Bradley C. Birkenfeld*

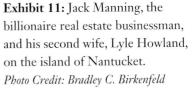

**Exhibit 12:** Igor Olenicoff's 120-foot yacht *Rusalka*. In 2004, Olenicoff invited Mario Staggl and Brad along with a host of his college friends on a one-week tour of Central America.

**Exhibit 13:** Igor Olenicoff's business card. *Photo Credit: Bradley C. Birkenfeld*

**Exhibit 14:** Igor Olenicoff and his son, Andrei, are all smiles in front of his mega-yacht in Florida. *Photo Credit: Bradley C. Birkenfeld*

**Exhibit 15:** On June 19, 2007, Brad wowed the Department of Justice with privileged information on Abdul Aziz Abbas, a UBS private client with over $400,000,000 in secret numbered accounts. *Photo Credit: Bradley C. Birkenfeld*

Abdulaziz Abbas TJS performance NETTE CONFIDENTIAL BB ①
6-19-07

| | | | |
|---|---|---|---|
| Titulaire: | 0279/C0-099'790-C.B. | Titres UBS N | |
| NZ | 0279/C0-259'518-B.N. | Cpte. Paiements | |
| NZ | 0279/C0-617'500-T.B. | APS (fee à 0,8 %) | |
| | 0240/535.075-K.F. | APS (fee à 0,5 %) | Indivi. |
| Signature Autorisées: | 0240/584.954-F.K. | APS (fee à 0,5 %) | Aresco |
| | 0240/588.541-Z.W. | UBS Capital | Ch & A |
| pas considéré | 0240/584.955-F.L. | | Emeco |
| | 0240/562152- R.W. | 2nd cpte Emeco New York Ltd. | |
| Compte Garantie: | 0240/541.596-R.C. | ~~Emeco N.Y.~~ Abdulaziz Abbas | |

Coffre No 8170 lié au Co-259.518-B.N.
Asra Abdulaziz a pouvoir sur le coffre

AMEXCO MOT DE PASSE:
ROSE AND EAGLE

YR 320327 Emeco LLC nouveau, NY

72 Bld Maurice Barrès
92 200 Neuilly-sur-Seine

NY (212) 230'1500

46/47 th floor Olympic Tower
641, 5th Av. NY 10022

CONFIDENTIAL

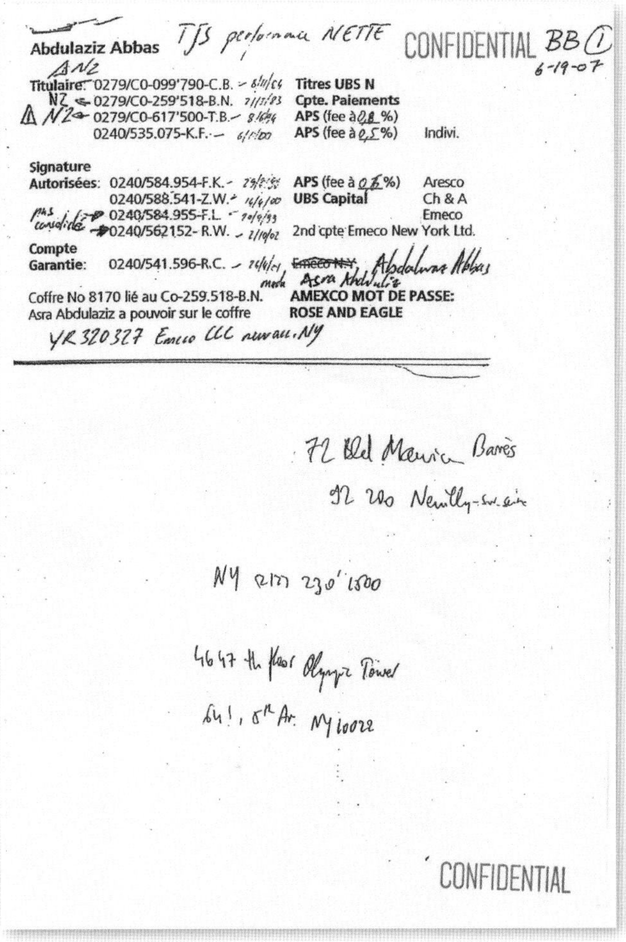

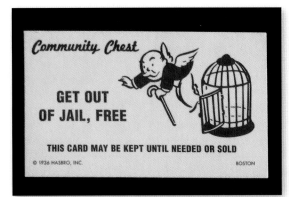

**Exhibit 16:** Never a man to lose his sense of humor, Brad presented the Department of Justice with its own Monopoly "Get Out of Jail Free Card" after he was arrested. *Photo Credit: Bradley C. Birkenfeld*

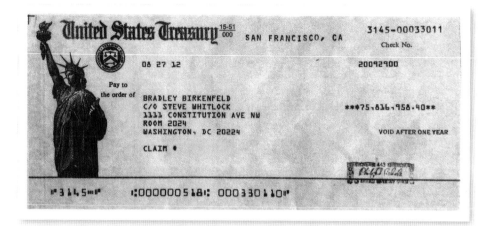

**Exhibit 17 (top):** On August 27, 2012 the IRS Whistleblower Office awarded Brad $104 million, the largest payout in history. After he paid his federal income taxes, Brad took home almost $76 million. *Photo Credit: Bradley C. Birkenfeld*

**Exhibit 18 (middle):** Brad was honored with the international Guinness World Record certificate, which required the establishment of an entirely new category: whistleblowing.
*Credit: Bradley C. Birkenfeld*

**Exhibit 19 (bottom):** On February 28, 2007 Igor Olenicoff paid the government $52,018,460, dated two days after Brad's birthday.
*Photo Credit: Bradley C. Birkenfeld*

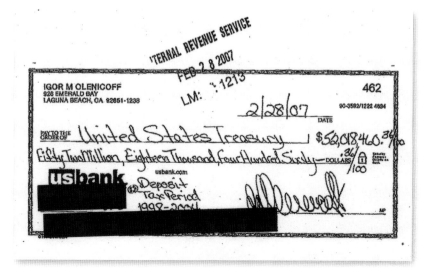

**Exhibit 20:** Jeff Bauman as Brad's guest in his skybox at TD Banknorth Garden during a Boston Bruins hockey game. Jeff Bauman was a hero of the Boston Marathon who lost both legs in the attack but managed to positively identify the bombers to the police, giving law enforcement authorities an enormous early break in solving the case. Most of those surrounding Jeff in the photo are members of the Boston Police Department. Brad is at his side, wearing his #40 Boston Bruins jersey. *Photo Credit: Douglas Birkenfeld*

authorities, I knew I'd need a pack of high-powered attorneys backing me up. I had no illusions about a government welcoming committee with party balloons and a cake. There was a chance they might view me as complicit, and it could turn into a brawl—with me on the ropes. I wasn't going in naked, armed with only a gold Montblanc pen.

I started trolling the Internet, picking out the names of the big firms I knew: Williams & Connolly, LLP; Hogan Lovells, LLP; Arnold & Porter, LLP; Covington & Burling, LLP. They were all rated as top litigators with experts in finance and tax law. I thought about my pitch and how to pose it without revealing too much, and made my first call to Williams & Connolly, asking for a top litigator who'd represent a client in matters of tax-evasion revelations. One of the partners got on the line.

"Please pardon my need for discretion, sir," I said. "But for the moment, my name is John Smith."

"Yes, Mr. Smith?"

"I am an American citizen, currently a Swiss resident. I'm looking for representation in a matter involving a Swiss banking institution."

"I see. And which institution might that be, Mr. Smith?"

"UBS, AG."

"Mmmm." He paused for a moment and I could hear some papers rattling. "I'm afraid that might pose a problem."

"How so?"

"Well, UBS Americas has this firm on retainer. That would be a conflict of interest. My apologies, but you'll have to try someone else. Good luck to you."

And he hung up. Fuck! "Dumbass," I said to myself. "You just blew your cover to some dude who might just pick up the phone, call UBS, find out who you are, and blow the whistle on *you!*" Then I thought it over and calmed down. The fact that UBS had Williams & Connolly on retainer didn't mean they were all drinking buddies; it just meant the bank could keep the firm in their back pocket in case they ever needed their advice or services, or a political "fix."

But then I got careful and started digging for the rest of the law firms' brags about who they represented. Sure enough, every major firm was retained by UBS! Those Swiss fuckers were smart;

throw your money around and lock down every major law firm in Washington, just in case somebody like me wanted to take you on at some point. My last stab was at Covington & Burling, where Eric Holder was a partner. I knew he'd been Assistant US Attorney under Bill Clinton and had approved Clinton's highly unorthodox pardon request for Marc Rich, the billionaire oil king residing in Zug, Switzerland, on the very last day of the Clinton administration. A guy like that who knew all the ins and outs of worldwide mega-financing might be just the type to take up my cause. Then I scrolled through Holder's client list. Christ! UBS!

Okay, I was striking out big-time. This wasn't going to be so easy. Then I remembered that I'd once met Bob Bennett, the legendary litigator from Skadden Arps, in Washington. Bennett had represented Casper Weinberger during the Iran–Contra scandal and Bill Clinton during the Monica Lewinsky affair. This dude was a serious big dog, in both girth and reputation, and I had his personal number in my black book. I called him up, but this time I didn't give him any details, just that I was looking for a kick-ass litigator.

"We're pretty pricey, Brad," he warned me.

"Well, I happen to be flush."

He laughed. "In that case, why don't you come on in for a sit-down. Are you in the States?"

"Not at the moment, but all I need is a few days' notice."

"I'll switch you over to my secretary. Happy to have a chat."

Things were looking up. Bob Bennett. Big gun! I called my travel agent, started packing, and didn't tell a soul where I was going, not even my cleaning lady.

———

It was springtime 2006. The cherry blossoms had already fallen and were littering the Washington wading pools like bloody flamingo feathers when I landed at Reagan National Airport. The first of May had come and gone, which meant my gardening leave was up and I was no longer a UBS employee. I wasn't shackled by a contract anymore, and any sense of loyalty to the firm was long dead. Usually in my previous trips to the States I'd stopped off in Boston to see the family, but this time I hadn't even told Doug I was coming. No one I cared for could be forced to tell about things of which they knew nothing. For the time being, I was keeping the whole thing compartmentalized. I checked into the Four Seasons—for the first time in a long time on my own dime.

Skadden, Arps, Slate, Meagher & Flom, LLP, had offices in every major city across the country. I'd arranged to meet Bob Bennett at their second largest enclave, in the nation's capital on New York Avenue NW, a fine old building that took up half the block, ironically overlooking the US Treasury. Both of us knew the score when it came to attorney–client confidentiality; even though I hadn't formally retained him yet, whatever I said would remain in his office. But still, I was careful. Turns out it didn't matter much anyway. As soon as I revealed that my case would involve going up hard against UBS, he tilted back in his big leather chair.

"That's a game-changer, Brad. I thought you were interested in litigating some sort of dispute with a displeased customer."

"Don't tell me, Bob. They're your client."

"They're *everyone's* client." He shrugged and fingered his suspenders. "That's what all the major financial firms do, especially if they've got big interests and lobbyists here in Wonderland. They put everyone on retainer. It's like buying lawsuit insurance."

"I know." I sighed heavily. "I thought maybe they hadn't gotten to you yet."

"Well, I wouldn't put it quite that way, but in essence . . . "

"Okay, so who the hell can I go to? I need some kick-ass attorneys who can hold my coat."

Bennett rummaged through his Rolodex and plucked out a card. "I think you should try these fellows. Good guys, and they're both former Department of Justice attorneys. I have an instinct you're angling that way, so you'll need folks who know the ropes. I'll give them a call."

He did, and the next day I went over to a small building on 7th Street NW, where Paul Hector and Rick Moran ran a boutique law firm of which they were founding partners. Hector & Moran, LLP, wasn't exactly a powerhouse like the ones I'd wanted, but Bennett had assured me they were clean of any conflicts and had great reputations in corporate internal investigations, agency enforcement matters, and white-collar criminal defense. That last bit was one of their talents I hoped I wouldn't need.

With a recommendation from a big dog like Bennett, Paul and Rick welcomed me warmly in their modest shared office. They looked so much alike they could have been brothers; both about forty, short dark hair, clean jaws, white button-downs, slim ties, and stovepipe suits. They could have been actors on the set of *Mad Men*, if that show featured federal prosecutors.

"So, Mr. Birkenfeld," Paul said as Rick poured coffee all around. "What's the essence of your case?"

"It's Brad," I said, "and the essence is that I have inside information on a worldwide conspiracy, and I'd like you to represent me and help me take it to the US government."

They looked at each other, took out their yellow legal pads, and clicked their pens.

"What sort of worldwide conspiracy?" Rick asked.

I leaned back in the chair across from their double desks and laced my fingers in my lap.

"I'm an American citizen, residing in Geneva, Switzerland. For the past ten years I've been working there as a private banker. The last four years were for a firm called UBS, AG, the Union Bank of Switzerland, from which I've now resigned. During my tenure there I was a director and head of business development for the Americas Desk. My job was to come over here, solicit wealthy American clients, and move large portions of their fortunes into secret Swiss numbered accounts."

Hector and Moran were now scribbling furiously, glancing up at me and nodding for me to go on.

"The objective of all this," I continued, "was to help these American citizens hide their money, avoid paying taxes, deceive spouses and business partners, and in effect defraud the US government. In my personal portfolio alone, I acquired about 150 clients, including thirty North Americans, and was very well compensated for it. At my branch of UBS in Geneva, we held approximately 7,000 such accounts. Throughout the three UBS branches in Switzerland that conducted offshore private banking business, the total number is about 19,000 American clients." I paused for effect. "UBS encouraged these practices. In fact, they trained us all on the methods of secret solicitation, as well as on how to dupe American federal authorities. For all these years, I went right along with it, but now I've had a change of heart. The Swiss have been running this scam for almost a hundred years, hiding fortunes for drug lords, dictators, Mafiosi, politicians, movie stars, and plain old tax cheats. UBS is at the top of the great pyramid, and I happen to know where all the pharaohs are buried."

The partners had stopped writing and were staring at me like some alien who'd just landed in their office in a flying saucer.

"I think it's time somebody blew the whistle," I said. "I think it's high time somebody brought those bastards to their knees. Don't you?"

I smiled at them. I thought they were going to fall off their chairs.

---

I hung around Washington for a few more days, most of which I spent with Hector and Moran in their office. I was lying pretty low because I knew people all over the world, and chances were high that I'd run into some client, consultant, or banker who might spot me walking into a law firm and say, "Brad! What the hell are you doing here in Lobbyland?" At any rate, I wasn't there to party, and I had lots of work to do.

It took about two full days for me to lay out the details to Paul and Rick. We'd signed an agreement for my representation, which included strict confidentiality, so I held nothing back. After a day their heads were swimming and their fingers were blistered from scribbling like stenographers. I regaled them with very true tales about how UBS whipped us into bringing in Net New Money, as if we were oarsmen on a Roman galleon, and how the bank prepped us to lie, cheat, and—for want of a prettier term—steal. I gave them client names and account holdings that made their eyes pop: Igor Olenicoff, celebrities, corporate titans, Abdul Aziz Abbas (a shady character with direct ties to Saddam Hussein), porn stars, prominent physicians, and one of Osama bin Laden's biological brothers. I'd brought along just enough documentation to prove my claims, but made it clear that they could not show any of those to US officials without my first getting immunity and a subpoena for protection from Swiss prosecution.

When our final session was done, Paul looked at Rick and gave me their tactical plan.

"Brad, we've decided to take this to the Department of Justice."

"Okay," I said, "but just tell me what informs that decision."

"Well," Rick said, "we're both former federal prosecutors, so we'll have common language, and we know how that system works."

"You're sure that's the right move, guys?" I asked. "Not the IRS or the SEC?"

"We're sure," said Paul. "We're going to put together a brief, about five pages, which'll lay out the case without specifying exactly who you are or where you are. We'll call you something like, 'John Fortune, the Oil Trader,' just to keep them off the scent. The brief will say that you're ready to blow the whistle on Swiss private banking, and that you've got lists of American tax-evaders and lots of supporting documentation."

"Sounds all right," I said. "Just get me immunity and a subpoena from those Feds and I'll be ready to spill the real beans."

"We'll get it," said Paul. "Don't worry, I have lots of friends over there at the DOJ. I used to work there."

So we shook hands and I packed up and flew back to Geneva. Over the next few months, I assembled more supporting evidence to go along with Hector and Moran's work-up for the DOJ. Then in August I came back to Washington to meet with them again, and flew back to Switzerland. I was feeling pretty positive about the whole thing. After all, Bob Bennett had convinced me that these two guys were slick, smart, and could thread the proverbial legal needle.

I had no idea that they'd just made a major tactical error that would change the course of my life.

It took another four months before Hector and Moran felt they were ready. Back in Geneva I cooled my heels and waited for word. Just after New Year's Day 2007, they finally called up the Department of Justice and tossed their first hook in the water.

As bad luck would have it, the first fish that sniffed at it was a bottom-feeder named Kevin Downing, one of the lead prosecutors for the Tax Enforcement Division. Apparently Downing wasn't in the best of moods, because he was in the midst of prosecuting the biggest tax fraud case in US history against a huge accounting firm called KPMG, LLP (162,000 employees worldwide). KPMG was accused of creating fraudulent tax shelters to help their richest clients skirt $2.5 billion in taxes. Sound familiar? Well, the DOJ had won the case back in 2005, but now it was on appeal and looking pretty bad for the Feds. And guess who was defending KPMG? Skadden Arps! So Bob Bennett of Skadden Arps, at that time the government's worst nemesis, sends me over to lawyers who decide that the DOJ's in the perfect frame of mind to receive me. I'm walking into a meat grinder.

Hector and Moran set up their first meeting over at the DOJ with Kevin Downing and another assistant tax prosecutor, Karen E. Kelly. Downing skimmed through their "John Fortune, the Oil Trader," brief and flicked it on the conference table.

"I'll need a lot more than this fairytale," he scoffed. "Who is this guy?"

"Can't tell you that yet," said Paul. "He'll need some assurances."

"Show me some evidence and we'll talk again."

Paul and Rick called me up, asking my permission to show Downing some of the supporting documentation I'd left in their office.

"Sure," I said. "Just make sure you redact anything that points to UBS, client names, or my identity."

"Will do."

As the spring of 2007 grew breezy in Geneva, my attorneys prepared for their next big sit-down. Prior to that, they sent Karen Kelly a warm-up email. "We're telling you, this is a once-in-a-lifetime case!"

"That's just what I need," she shot back. "Another once-in-a-life-time case!"

Uh-oh. When they told me about the cool reception they were getting, I started to wonder if they'd made a mistake. Maybe they were barking up the wrong tree. Maybe they should have gone right to the IRS, which probably would have protected me as a confidential informant. I found out that back in December 2006, the IRS had instituted a program for whistle-blower rewards, something on a much larger scale than anything since Abraham Lincoln, who'd effected such programs to root out scofflaws during the Civil War. "Well," I thought, "Bob Bennett recommended them, so they must be all right."

Downing and Kelly looked over my documents, which included some client lists with the names redacted, but clearly laid out the huge amounts of untaxed holdings. Also in there were some redacted UBS memos about hunting-gathering all over the States. It wasn't enough.

"You're telling us this is potentially the biggest tax fraud case in the world?" Downing sneered. "And this is all you've got? Bring me some serious paperwork and we'll talk."

Paul and Rick begged me for a substantial pile that would make it impossible for Downing to reject our pleas any longer. I was already working for a friend of mine on some big private equity projects, but I put those aside and started assembling the mother lode: selecting, copying, redacting, yet highlighting the points that would just blow these guys away. This time I revealed the identity of the bank involved. But I wasn't going to risk shipping the stuff off by FedEx. Who knew if the Swiss were already suspicious and might be intercepting my mail? So I got on a plane again, flew to Washington via a diversionary stop in Boston, handed the stuff off in person to Hector and Moran, and told them they'd better hit a home run.

I went back home to Geneva. Hector and Moran went back over to the DOJ. Kevin Downing and Karen Kelly took the fat portfolio of my evidence and said to my lawyers, "Don't call us. We'll call you."

Late spring rolled around. A whole fucking year had passed since I'd first shown up in Washington. I decided on a "destresser," spending a week with Mauro in the Philippines. As usual, we had lots of fun flying around in his helicopter and chasing women, and I was feeling pretty optimistic. With all the stuff that Paul and Rick had now laid in the laps of the DOJ, they couldn't refuse me any longer, right?

"We're not issuing any sort of subpoena for an anonymous snitch." Downing had called Hector soon after May Day, which seemed appropriate since that's what a pilot yells when he's about to crash and burn.

"Well, how about immunity from prosecution?" Paul asked.

"No promises. He's getting nothing till I meet this guy face-to-face."

My two legal eagles sounded like they'd had all their feathers plucked when they called me up and gave me the news.

"What the hell do these people want?" I fumed. "A blood test and a urine sample?"

I told them I'd get back to them, and I thought about it long and hard. In fact, I pondered it for a month. I knew that once I made this move, there'd be no going back. In late May I made my decision. This was it. Game time. Balls to the wall. At that point, it would have been much easier to just let it all go; stay in my beautiful digs in Europe's Candy Land, keep making money, forget about the screwing by UBS, and just chalk it all up to a sour experience. But as I've said before, I'm not built that way. Hammer looking for nails.

"I'm coming in," I told Paul and Rick on the phone. "Get out your flak jackets."

But just before I packed up every single UBS disc and document I had, I came up with an insurance policy. I knew that from the moment I stepped into the Department of Justice, I'd be in a black hole, possibly never to come out whole. But, if somehow my story were already out there, headlines blazing and with shocking revelations about Swiss secret banking, it would be that much harder to shove me off into some witness protection program, which would definitely *not* match my lifestyle.

Before going anywhere near American federal agents, I needed to whet their appetites and make it impossible for them to turn me away. I was sure that once they heard my story, they'd welcome me as an American patriot, a virtual Paul Revere.

I'd been reading the *Financial Times* for years, and there was this one investigative journalist on the paper who couldn't be bought or swayed from a story: Haig Simonian, an old-school reporter and highly respected expert in financial funny business. I put on my coat and walked down Eaux-Vives in a driving rainstorm to the tram-switching circle, where a bank of pay phones perched outside a warm cafe. I popped a phone card in the slot and called the Times. Simonian got on the line.

"Yes? Who is this, please? And how can I help you?"

"Mr. Simonian, you are going to know me only as 'Tarantula,'" I said. "And I've got a story that will blow you away and end Swiss banking secrecy forever."

I stood there with the rain soaking my hat and shoulders, and in twenty minutes of rapid fire gave him a scoop that would turn out to be the out-of-the-park grand slam of his career. I could hear his keyboard hammering away like a machine gun.

Just as had happened with my attorneys, Simonian nearly fell off his chair.

# CHAPTER 8

## THE MEXICO SETUP

*"The world is a dangerous place, not because
of those who do evil, but because of those
who look on and do nothing."*
—*ALBERT EINSTEIN, GERMAN PHYSICIST*

AT THE DEPARTMENT OF Justice in Washington, DC, this anonymous Swiss private banker was already becoming a major problem.

Kevin Downing, a senior prosecutor for the department's Tax Division, had approached his superiors with the case, and they were less than happy. First of all, this guy whom they hadn't yet actually met was a "walk-in," an informant, which meant the DOJ hadn't initiated the case based upon its own detective work. And if what this informant's lawyers were claiming was true, it could turn out to be the biggest tax fraud case in US history.

Now that might seem to be a good thing, but this anonymous banker was promising lists of names, American names, rich folk who'd hidden their money in Swiss accounts. Plus, he apparently had lists of Swiss banking officials who'd orchestrated this whole shell game themselves and had partied with American bankers and politicians who knew exactly what was going on.

From Downing's point of view, this Benedict Arnold in Switzerland appeared ready to come over and hand him a roster of

PEPs, or Politically Exposed Persons. Who knew who'd be on that list? Downing still worked for the Bush administration, but it was already in its waning days. An election was looming and powerful people were throwing millions in campaign contributions at Obama, Clinton, Giuliani, and McCain. Who knew which way the winds would blow? Normally with a switch in administrations, a new Attorney General took the helm and civil-servant lifers like Downing remained at their desks. But if this case broke open and somebody high up the food chain got burned, he and his colleagues might all be out on the street.

It might get even uglier. Obama had already picked out Eric Holder as his candidate for Attorney General. Holder was a partner over at Covington & Burling, one of the most powerful law firms in DC. And guess what? One of Holder's biggest clients was UBS.

Kevin Downing didn't want this case. His head was still reeling from the KPMG case, which had just gone into the shitter. The DOJ had won the case back in 2005 by strong-arming KPMG into not contributing funds to their employees' defense. But a judge had just ruled that tactic outrageous and unconstitutional, a violation of the defendants' Sixth Amendment right to legal counsel, and thirteen of them had walked, a huge loss for the DOJ. In his stunning rebuke of Kevin Downing and the entire prosecution team from the DOJ in Washington, Judge Kaplan stated in his written ruling: "The government has let its zeal get in the way of its judgment. It has violated the Constitution it is sworn to defend." The next case up had to be a home run, or it might mean Downing's ass. If he had to take it on, he would, but only if he could hijack it and get all the credit.

He preferred not to come near what this Swiss turncoat had. He didn't even want to *meet* him. So he'd denied the turncoat immunity and even a subpoena, hoping he would get cold feet and just disappear. But it turned out the mysterious banker didn't give a shit. He was coming in anyway, full speed ahead. The fucking idiot was a pit bull.

Okay, full stop.

I know I wrote that stuff above as if I knew exactly what this guy Downing was thinking. Pretty arrogant of me, you might opine. But on the other hand, I've been studying this dude for nearly ten years and by now I know him pretty damn well. Full disclosure: I also hate the guy's guts, and I relish the fact that he hates me right back. But that's a side issue.

Back to the above. How did I conclude what Kevin Downing was thinking when my lawyers called him up and told him they had a client who was ready to turn over all the secrets of illicit Swiss banking? Process of elimination. Nothing else made sense to me.

One way to look at what happened is to parallel the whole thing to a spy story. Just imagine you're a guy like Kevin Downing, working for a big government intelligence agency. You're a mid-level career guy, not the big boss, but not just some street agent either. Along come these two attorneys acting as go-betweens for a guy who says he's very high up in the Russian FSB (what they now call the KGB spy agency in Moscow). And this spy-client of theirs says he knows all the Russians' deep dark secrets and he's prepared to go turncoat on his own intelligence agency and give you everything. Jesus, this could be the thing that makes your entire career! You'll be a hero, get a medal! Hell, the president will congratulate you . . .

*If* the spy is the real deal, of course. So what do you do? If you've got half a brain in your head, you welcome him. You tell his go-betweens that you'd very much like to meet him and see what he has to say. You encourage them, you set up a meeting. Of course you're cautious, but very courteous, very respectful. You don't want to scare this guy off 'cause he just might be bringing you the secret launch codes for the whole Russian nuclear arsenal. You want to seduce him, make him feel good, get everything out of him that you possibly can. Hell, you might even send him back into Russia to get you more information!

Cautiously, before you meet him the very first time, you ask his go-betweens what he wants in return. You're stunned when they tell you, "Nothing. He just wants to make things right and make sure the Kremlin pays for their crimes."

Really? Sounds too good to be true. But hell, you go for it. That's your job. Truth, Justice, and the American Way. Right?

Unless the biggest thing you fear, your worst nightmare, is that this Russian traitor is going to spill all kinds of secrets that might come back around and bite you in the ass. What if he tells the ugly truth about some very powerful people in your government, who happen to be very good friends of your boss? What if some of this Russian agent's secrets are nasty things about some of your mentors, friends, or the powerful people upstairs who cut your paychecks? What if whatever he reveals to you, you know you'll have to report on, and it'll cost you your job? What if you suspect that many of the people who rule over you are in fact colluding with the Russians, because they care only about money and power, and not so much about Mom and apple pie?

So basically, instead of being thrilled about this turncoat spy, you're scared shitless. He's going to say things you don't want to hear. Best thing to do is to scare him away, and if you can't do that, charge him with something and put him away for as long as possible—until everyone forgets about him. By the time he sees daylight again, you'll be retired from government service and raking in cash as a privateer. The perpetual "revolving door" at the DOJ.

That's the analogy, the parallel world that explains Downing's outrageous behavior. As far as I am concerned, the only possible way it made sense. Nothing else fit the picture.

But I hadn't reached all these conclusions just yet. I hadn't yet had the "pleasure" of meeting Kevin Downing and Karen Kelly. I knew they were talking to my attorneys as if Hector and Moran were a couple of Baltimore drug dealers, but I figured that was just part of their "bad cop" routine, and the "good cops" would come out later. I couldn't assess them until we met face-to-face. Once I look into someone's eyes, I know. And that was about to happen.

In June 2007, Geneva was sliding into the most beautiful time of the year. All those thick gray clouds over the Alps were dissolving, the lake was calm and crystal blue, and the girls in the streets were shedding their heavy coats and strolling around in micro skirts and tight blouses. It was summer outside, but winter in my head, full of thunderclouds and doubts about what the hell I was doing. A mental downpour hammered at my logic.

*What's the matter with you, dumbass? Saint-Tropez's not good enough anymore? Haven't had enough thrills in your life yet? Want to wind up in prison somewhere? Gotta get revenge now instead of just getting laid?*

Well, I guess the answers to those three self-examinations were "I'm still a hammer looking for nails," and "No," "No," "No," and "Yes."

So I packed my bags, along with a briefcase full of files, backups on CDs, and something I called my "NOC" list, after the Non-Official Cover list of secret agents from the *Mission Impossible* films. Those were my aces in the hole, the names of the illicit depositors. Now, I had no intention in hell of turning that list over unless I got some guarantees first, but I had to be ready if the sun shone. And if you think I'd been careful before, now I was super cautious. If somehow the Swiss got a line on what I was doing, they might toss my flat while I was gone, so I swept it clean of any evidence, opened a safe-deposit box at a boutique bank, and locked up full copies of my treasure trove, with duplicates at Poncet's office too.

Once again I told no one where I was going, not my friends or Thais or my maid, and I didn't book a ticket to Washington. The Geneva airport was only fifteen minutes from my flat. I took a cab and bought a ticket to Boston again, to throw anyone in Geneva off the scent, and I paid cash.

————

The US Department of Justice resides in an enormous stone building on Pennsylvania Avenue NW in downtown Washington, DC. The entrance is adorned with four fifty-foot columns topped by majestic Roman scrolls, and the whole thing looks like some ominous temple to omnipotent gods. Paul Hector, Rick Moran, and I trotted up the wide slate stairs in our best suits. The lawyers were hauling respectable, overstuffed briefcases and breaking a sweat, but I was going in "light," with nothing except business cards, a small notebook, and a pen. We passed through the magnetometers, and just inside the department's Great Hall, I spotted this towering art deco statue of a half-nude woman, the "Spirit of Justice," wearing a toga with her arms raised to heaven. She'd been sculpted with one full breast exposed, except it wasn't exposed anymore, because the department had spent eight thousand bucks on fancy drapes to cover up that wayward nipple. I should have known right then and there that this tight-assed temple was no place for a Birkenfeld.

A summer intern law student retrieved us and we walked a long hallway, past officious-looking government attorneys, federal agents, and slick-suited women clicking their heels on the marble. Then it was up an elevator to a higher floor and down another long hallway to the Tax Division, where the intern opened the door to a big conference room and ducked away as fast as he could.

Kevin Downing was in the chairman's spot at the table's bow, braced by Karen Kelly and a guy named Matthew Kutz who turned out to be an IRS criminal investigator, otherwise known as a Treasury Agent. I looked at Downing and it flashed through my brain: *Uh-oh, this dude thinks he's Elliot Ness*—with his short brown hair, ice blue eyes, pug nose, heavy jaw, and snake lips. Karen Kelly was small and bulging from a Kmart brown suit, with tiny dark eyes and a permanent frown beneath a lifeless flat hairdo; she seemed dumb as a box of rocks. Matt Kutz was slim in a boxy, oversized pale blue suit, with a flattop haircut as if he thought he was a fighter. But more friendly faced, probably because he wasn't a DOJ guy.

My attorneys put their cases down and smiled proudly. "Good morning, everyone," said Paul. "We'd like to introduce you to our client, Mr. Bradley Birkenfeld."

I nodded and smiled, but before I could get a word of greeting out, Karen Kelly, almost rising out of her seat in anger, jabbed a finger at me and snapped loudly, "You're no whistle-blower! You're nothing but a tipster!"

I jerked my head back, stunned.

*Excuse me? Did we have some horrible one-night stand I don't remember?*

Rick pulled out a chair for me as I whispered to him, "What the fuck is *this*? This is the kind of meeting you brought me to?"

"Just relax," he muttered. "We're already here. Opening shots is all."

But he was wrong. Downing glared at me as if I'd just shown up at his barbecue carrying a dead skunk. I sat down with my lawyers and took a deep breath.

"All right, let's start with your name again," Downing grunted. "Spell it for us." I spelled it. Then he said, "Your attorneys have been claiming you've got some sort of information we might be interested in, Mr. Birkenfeld."

"Yeah," Karen Kelly sneered. "A once-in-a-lifetime case."

I was already thinking I'd like to dive over the table and choke the stupid bitch, but I ignored her. I reached into my calmest spot and kept it cool.

"You *should* be interested, Mr. Downing," I said, "since it involves one of the largest banks in the world, which has been defrauding American taxpayers for decades."

"And which bank is that again?"

"UBS, AG. The Union Bank of Switzerland."

Something flickered across his face, like a mental gulp.

"And you've been helping them do it," Kelly snapped.

I leaned back in my chair and cocked my head, letting my "I'll eat you for lunch" smile crawl across my lips.

"If you don't want to hear it, just let me know. I'm sure someone else will find it fascinating."

"I'd certainly like to hear it," said Matthew Kutz.

*Well*, I thought, *one brain out of three.*

"Okay, Mr. Birkenfeld," said Downing. "Tell it."

And I did. Over the next two hours, I recounted all my career moves, how I'd started at Credit Suisse, moved to Barclays, and then hit the top of the pyramid at UBS. I told them about how UBS had trained us all on soliciting North American clients, as well as on how to avoid scrutiny by federal agents such as themselves, and I told them about my scores of hunter-gatherer trips. By noontime my mouth was bone dry and my stomach was rumbling, but all they'd offered us were glasses of lukewarm water, as if we were in some sort of interrogation cell. I wondered if the portrait on the wall of current Attorney General Alberto Gonzales had a camera stuck in one eyeball, or maybe the whole room was bugged, because all they did was take some notes.

Finally Downing looked at his watch and started packing up his papers.

"All right, Mr. Birkenfeld," he said. "Send over all this documentary proof you allegedly have, and we'll look it over."

"No offense, Mr. Downing," I said, "but you won't understand it without a translator. That would be me, so I'll deliver it personally and go through it all with you."

His expression curdled, but Matthew Kutz touched his sleeve and nodded. The IRS guy knew what kind of stuff I was talking about. Rick Moran broke in.

"May we discuss immunity for Mr. Birkenfeld, and a subpoena?"

Downing looked at me. "Requesting such things is usually indicative of guilt."

"I don't need protection from you," I said. "I need it from the Swiss. I'm already breaking every Swiss law on the books just by being here."

"Well, you're expecting too much," he said. "And way too early."

Karen Kelly snapped at me again. It seemed to be her only means of communication. "We know the only reason you're here is to get some kind of whistle-blower award."

That really pissed me off. I got up from my chair and my attorneys came to their feet as well. Maybe they thought I was going to stab my Montblanc in her eye.

"Gentlemen, and lady," I said with perfect control. "I started this process a year and a half ago, long before the reward you speak of existed. When I began whistle-blowing, internally at the bank, I was risking everything. The only reward I might have gotten was hard time in a Swiss prison. If such a monetary reward exists here now, it's your doing, not mine."

"All right." Downing waved a dismissive hand. "We'll see you soon."

Out on the street, I tore open my tie. We tried to hail a cab, but it was lunchtime in the capital, so we started hoofing it back over to my lawyers' office.

"Well, that wasn't so bad." Paul was trying to put a rosy blush on a corpse.

"It fucking sucked," I said.

"They're just playing hardball," said Rick. "You'll see. They'll soften up."

We walked for a while in silence, and I was thinking about how wrong these two guys might be. The whole DOJ reception still tasted like curdled milk in my mouth. Their attitudes just didn't make sense.

"What's the status on this whistle-blower award thing?" I asked.

"The IRS is saying it'll be fifteen to thirty percent of any illicit monies recovered as a result of inside information."

We'd actually discussed this brand-new regulation when it first showed up on the radar, back in December 2006. But what I didn't realize was that Hector had then discussed it with Downing, prior to their first meeting. He'd even suggested that the DOJ start their own whistle-blower award program. Forced error! It appeared that Paul was totally ignorant of the anti-whistle-blower dynamic pervading Washington, so all he'd done was to infuriate the same people he was bringing my case to. That's why Karen Kelly was already on a slow burn even before our first encounter took place.

I, however, understood right away that such a program was pretty much a teaser, meant to lure people into talking. Even if UBS were to be prosecuted, any recoveries were a long, long way off. The odds were I'd get thirty percent of zero. But still, I figured the attraction might kick my attorneys into higher gear.

"Tell you what. File for it. If you get it for me, you'll get twelve percent of whatever I get. We'll add that to our agreement."

They liked that idea.

I hate to admit it, but I spent that night in my hotel room brooding. The Four Seasons isn't exactly a Motel 6, so shelling out six Franklins to sit alone in my room, drinking and muttering to myself, seemed exorbitant, but I had to figure this one out. It didn't make sense that these DOJ people were so hostile, when I was ready to deliver a slew of touchdowns to their team. Then I remembered how in Boston those white-collared FBI clowns had reacted to me in much the same way. Maybe Downing and Kelly just didn't like people they regarded as "snitches." Or maybe they thought of me as a threat to their careers; somebody who could pull off a coup they'd been failing at for decades. Clearly, at the very least, Karen Kelly thought I was some sort of carpetbagger, in it just for the money. But Downing: I couldn't figure him out. That one would take me a while longer.

Then I recalled how once, as military cadets at Norwich, we had to ford a river, holding our rifles above our heads. The water got deeper and deeper, and when it surged above our chests and reached our throats, some of the guys started to panic and turned back. I never did. I came out the other side, soaked and breathless but with my honor intact. This thing with the DOJ was looking very similar. "Forge ahead," I said to myself. "It's a test."

But the next meeting in that stuffy conference room wasn't much better. Downing had a puss on like his mommy had tossed out his favorite pajamas, and Karen Kelly looked like she'd slept in that bulging suit without washing her hair. Only Matt Kutz seemed fresh, calm, and nonjudgmental. The Treasury agent was sincerely interested in following the money, rather than swaying with any political winds.

Page by page I showed them sheaves of UBS documents, all solid evidence of the bank's intent, operations, snubbing of American laws, and urgent email to us private bankers demanding greater results. I detailed the processes of opening numbered accounts and how they were maintained, something that surely no US government agent had ever been privy to before. I even sketched layouts of our underground vaults, and exactly what kinds of treasures were secreted down there by North American clients: jewels, cash, bearer bonds, artwork, even gold and silver bars worth many millions of dollars.

Yet in response, Downing's questions sailed off on absurd, irrelevant tangents. He wanted to know how much money I made, how I made it, how often, and intimate details about my personal lifestyle, as if he were comparing his government bureaucrat salary and suburban lifestyle to mine. It was like a frickin' audit. Matthew Kutz, however, took copious notes and asked pertinent questions about trust structures, client fees, and the banking products UBS pushed on its secret account holders. But after four hours, Downing's ignorance of international finance made me think the guy could barely balance his own checkbook. And Karen Kelly seemed dumb as a fence post, repeating her mantra of the day before.

"Let's be honest, Mr. Birkenfeld. You're only here for a payoff."

"That's right," I said. "I'm hoping for the Nobel Peace Prize."

Rick Moran toed me under the table.

"All right," Downing said as he pushed my four-inch pile of documents aside. "Let's talk about some of these client names."

"Let's talk about immunity and a subpoena for Mr. Birkenfeld," said Paul Hector.

"I think we've made our position clear on this," Downing growled. "What we've got here so far is flimsy at best, and—"

I cut him off. "I'll talk about one client."

The room went silent and they all stared at me.

"Abdul Aziz Abbas," I said.

"And who might that be?" Downing asked.

"An Iraqi national, lives in New York City. He's actually a personal client of my boss, Christian Bovay, but I had access to all his records. As a matter of fact, he's such a big dog that Bovay has a separate telephone line in his office, just reserved for Abbas. It's like the red phone from the Kremlin to the White House."

"And that's unusual?"

"Unprecedented," I said. "Nobody but Bovay was allowed to answer that phone. I know because, when I was fairly new at the bank, it was ringing off the hook and Bovay wasn't there. So I walked into his office and answered it. A foreign-accented voice on the other end of the line exploded at me. 'Who is this and why are you answering this phone?!'"

"All right," Downing grunted. "And what sort of holdings did this Abbas have at UBS?"

"Four hundred and twenty million dollars in six numbered accounts. Plus, he's got a $40 million duplex condo on the forty-sixth and forty-seventh floors at the Olympic Tower complex in downtown Manhattan."(Exhibit 15.)

Matthew Kutz whistled. "That's a freaking lot of money."

"That's right, Mr. Kutz. You're starting to get it. And just think, we had *nineteen thousand* such clients in our Swiss branches."

"And how did this alleged undeclared account holder make his money?" Karen Kelly asked. I actually had her attention for the first time in two days.

"He made his money through illegal oil sales with Saddam Hussein's regime, and he's the single largest account holder on the American Desk." Christian Bovay had confirmed all of this to me.

I understood, of course, that the actual names of clients should not be revealed without a subpoena or other legal compulsion to speak about it. However, I had no qualms in voluntarily spilling these particularly filthy beans. After all, this was a post-9/11 world, and this guy Abbas had terrorism written all over him. *Sorry, my Swiss friends, but terrorism trumps Swiss banking secrecy.* In fact, many in the Bush administration thought that the 9/11 attacks were aided by Saddam Hussein. So the prosecutors at the DOJ in Washington, DC, of all people, would want to know this . . . or so I thought.

By this time, I had all of their undivided attention. Their eyes were riveted on me, waiting for what I might say next.

"Oh, there's one other thing you should know."

"What's that?" Downing asked.

"I understand that Abbas is good friends with Rudy Giuliani."

It was the proverbial needle-across-the-record moment. Downing, who is from New York, immediately thrust his open hand at my face and said in a loud tone, "We're not interested in non-Americans!" I tried to interject, but he kept repeating this mantra, almost in a panic. It was like a child plugging his fingers in his ears, shutting his eyes tightly, and humming loudly to avoid unpleasant news.

*Not interested in non-Americans? This bank is run by non-Americans, you dumb jackass,* I thought. Downing was obviously full of shit. This had struck a nerve in him. There was something there. Giuliani was his homeboy, and was way up in the presidential polls. I suddenly saw the three Feds in front of me as dumbass monkeys: *See No Evil, Hear No Evil, Speak No Evil.*

Okay. I moved on to another area of which Downing & Company were completely ignorant.

"Here's a way that you can checkmate the bank on the first move of the game." I told them that six months from then, in early

December 2007, the Art Basel Exhibition would be held in Miami. "UBS is the main sponsor of this event, and they do it for one reason: to have their private bankers on the American Desk fly in from Switzerland and recruit wealthy Americans to open secret Swiss accounts. And those employees will be flying in under UBS America's cover. Make no mistake about it. UBS America is neck-deep in this."

I wasn't even sure that Downing was hearing me. He was still shaken up by the Giuliani thing. But I went on.

"I know the names of each UBS private banker who is flying to Miami, in which hotels they'll stay, their cell phone numbers, and their email addresses. All of them will falsely indicate on their customs declarations that they're traveling for pleasure instead of for business, in violation of US law. They are all instructed to do this by the bank. Each of them will be carrying UBS-issued encrypted laptop computers and BlackBerrys. Those laptops contain the account data on their respective clients, and each one of these bankers has up to two hundred American clients. You get your hands on those laptops, and it's game, set, match."

I slid a large spreadsheet across the table, with all the hard intelligence I'd just enumerated: full names, cell phone numbers, and email addresses of each of these UBS bankers, along with the hotels they'd be staying at.

"Here's your master list," I said. "It's a post-9/11 world. You guys can monitor almost anything going on almost anywhere on earth. This is a piece of cake. All you have to do is take these names and interface with Homeland Security. You'll know exactly when they're flying in, and you can intercept them either at the airport or at their hotels, along with their laptops and BlackBerrys. But you have to move in very quickly and in a highly coordinated manner, because the laptops and BlackBerrys have 'panic buttons' that, when pushed, immediately wipe the devices clean of all data. You can't let these guys have an opportunity to push those buttons. It has to be a quick takedown."

Downing and Kelly had the facial expressions of paper-pushing bureaucrats, that "don't tell me how to do my job" look written all over them. You know the look. It's the same one you see while standing in a painfully slow line at the registry of motor vehicles or the post office.

But I took one more shot at getting them to understand I was handing them the largest winning lottery ticket of their lives.

"With each banker having up to two hundred accounts, you'll easily have the data of over a thousand American UBS account holders in one fell swoop!"

"You watch too much TV," Downing blurted out. "That's Hollywood." He immediately dismissed the entire idea. But TV had nothing to do with it, and I hardly even watch TV. Downing clearly didn't want to utilize methods that he hadn't thought of first. Hell, I might actually get credit for this—instead of him! We can't have that!

Make no mistake about it. This plan would have worked. The US law enforcement authorities would not only have had the account data on over 1,000 American account holders at UBS, but several of their private bankers in custody as well. The bankers could then have been squeezed for more information, corroborating the stuff I'd already given to the DOJ. Slam dunk, right?

Wrong. Suddenly that was it. Meeting over. Downing and Kelly stood up and marched to the door, with Kutz following along like a confused puppy.

"We'll give you one more shot at this," Downing snapped at me and my attorneys. "Come up with some serious information about *American tax-evaders*, and we might consider your needs."

Then they were gone. Shortly after that, we were too.

"What the fuck was that?" I fumed as the three of us managed to stuff ourselves into a cab.

"I think maybe you scared them," Rick said.

Rick nodded. "That thing about Abbas and Giuliani. *That* had to be the one name you gave them? Jesus, Brad."

"Well, if they can't stand the heat," I said. "At least that'll give them a taste of what I've really got here. Maybe now they'll want to deal."

"Fingers crossed," said Rick.

"Listen, gents," I said. "I'm giving them one more shot, and that's it."

But that shot was a dud. The next session took less than an hour. Matthew Kutz wasn't there, and Downing and Kelly behaved as if they'd gone to confession and their priest had warned them to stop dancing with the devil. Hector and Moran tried one more time to get me some sort of subpoena or grant of immunity, but Downing acted as if he were deaf.

"We're going to examine all these documents thoroughly, and then we'll advise you of our position."

"When can we contact you?" Paul asked.

"Don't call us. We'll call you."

"Sounds familiar," Rick muttered.

And then we were out on the street again. I've felt disheartened once or twice in my life, but this was one of my low points. I'd come all this way to hand-deliver a victory to the American taxpayer and a tar-and-feather party to the outrageously corrupt Swiss system, and all I'd gotten was a kick in the ass. Honestly, I felt bitch-slapped.

"This isn't going to work," I said to my lawyers. "Let's take this to someone who's going to listen. Let's take it to the US Senate."

"The Senate?" Rick stopped walking and looked at me. Then he pointed over to Capitol Hill. "You mean those guys?"

"That's right. Get me a subpoena to testify before the US Senate. Do that, and I'll give those senators the whole shebang, client names included—addresses, phone numbers, names of their yachts and girlfriends and racehorses. Those DOJ goons can go fuck themselves."

"Okay, Brad. We'll try it," Paul said. "Where are you going to be?"

"Back home."

"In Geneva?"

"Yeah, at the moment I'm feeling more at home back there."

I took a taxi to my hotel. I felt totally exhausted, as if I'd run a three-day marathon wearing lead boots. And I was pissed as hell. I walked into my hotel room, and for a moment I felt like trashing the place as if I were Keith Richards on coke, which probably seems redundant. I tore off my stupid suit, had a stiff whisky from the minifridge, and was about to go out to a park somewhere and smoke a big fat Havana when my cell phone buzzed.

*What fresh hell is this?* I wondered as I picked it up. But then I smiled. It was my buddy from London, Ladjel Jafarli.

"*La-djel*!" I forced a vocal smile. "How are you, buddy?"

"Very fine, Brad. And you?"

"Livin' the dream."

He laughed. "I don't suppose you happen to be in the States. I'm in Washington attending an executive off-site conference."

"Really?" I thought fast. I'd met Ladjel in Morocco during my stint for Barclays, and he was super discreet; but I still wasn't going to tell anyone what I was doing. "I'm down here too! Been hunting-gathering in Virginia."

"No! Is it by any chance all wrapped up?"

"Like a Christmas present."

"Tell you what, Brad. Let's go to Cancún for some R&R."

"Great idea! I'll book flights for us."

"No need. I've already taken care of that."

It took about a nanosecond for me to accept. I sorely needed a break, a head-clearing, and jetting off to Mexico for a few days sounded to me like a shrink's prescription. I told him where I was staying.

"Excellent!" he said. "Pick you up in two hours."

On the button two hours later, a long black limousine pulled up in front of the hotel and Ladjel jumped out and pumped my hand, his white teeth gleaming in the sunshine. Algerian born, he had wavy black hair and eyes that made girls swoon, and having been raised in Geneva he was fluent in French. A wonderful guy and generous friend, much like Mario Staggl or Sanjay Kumar; a guy I knew I could trust and have great fun with.

However, I didn't dare tell him what I was up to. We drove off to Dulles, all smiles and ready to party. Ladjel knew I was out of UBS and he'd also heard about my lawsuit, but I could tell from our exchanges that he knew nothing about my internal whistle-blowing, and certainly nothing about what I was actually doing in Washington. I said, which was true, that I'd started working for a friend in private equity and planned to make that my new game. He had plenty of ideas and contacts, and we chatted about all the possibilities.

When we got to Dulles the limo drove right past the terminals and around to the private jet park, where a gleaming white Citation X was sitting on the blazing tarmac. I laughed.

"I thought we were going commercial."

"Don't be bourgeois!" Ladjel said. "What's the point of being a high roller if you don't use 'The Bird'?"

So we jetted off to Cancún, just the two of us in that gleaming steel tube with its camel-colored leather seats, two pilots, a very comely flight attendant, and plenty of scotch. Ladjel's firm in London didn't own the airplane, but they had "private jet shares," which meant the sleek beast was at his disposal. While en route, he booked us into the Ritz-Carlton, a five-star resort at the tip of Cancún. I remember that four-day adventure as a swirl of green, pink, and blue. Emerald palm trees bowed over the manicured grounds, swaying in the Atlantic breeze as we drank by the pool. Pink hues were everywhere; the tablecloths, lounge chairs, the stucco bridge leading to the yacht basin, and the sun-pinkened skin of beautiful, well-off women. The bay was crystal blue, and we sailed on it, dove in it, and I felt as if the water was rinsing the creepy slime of Washington from my body and brain. Ladjel and I talked about business, fun, and girls, but still I never mentioned the real purpose of my recent foray in the US capital. We laughed a lot, had fun, and then finally surrendered to life's requirements and got back on the jet, rested, suntanned, and ready to face our next challenges.

Per US regulations, private jets entering American airspace from Mexico have to set down at the first available airport for Customs and Immigration checks. So we landed in El Paso, where I couldn't help remarking to Ladjel on the absurdity of ICE's efficiency at the airport, while just a few miles south of us Mexican "drug mules" were fording the river and easily slipping past the Border Patrol.

"Yes, your country has some very interesting theories on border security," he remarked.

"Washington doesn't give a damn about the border," I said. "They'll take votes from anyone who can pull the lever, even if he just killed the mayor of Juárez."

The jet sat on the tarmac for a while, and then two uniformed ICE agents came aboard. They looked at my US passport, gave it back, and then perused Ladjel's Swiss passport.

"Please step out of the aircraft, Mr. Jafarli," one of them said. "This won't take long."

Ladjel shrugged and got up, while I grinned, toasted him, and kept on sipping until he came back after about fifteen minutes.

"So, did they do a thorough cavity search?"

"No," he said. "I was supremely grateful to not have to bend over. But it was a bit odd. They copied my passport, asked a few harmless questions, and let me go."

"Well, you do look like a terrorist, got a Swiss passport, live in London, and you're a Managing Director at Credit Suisse. A high-class bad guy, but definitely dangerous."

A few hours later we landed at Dulles. I thanked him profusely for the getaway, promised to repay him somehow, sometime soon in London, and after a bear hug we parted ways. He jetted off to England, and I booked the first seat I could get to Geneva. I was feeling renewed and no longer so worried about my misadventures with the DOJ. I figured there were plenty of other agencies and people in Washington, much smarter folks who'd appreciate what I was trying to do. We'd just have to find them and turn that page.

A week went by. Having heard nothing from Hector and Moran, I finally got itchy and called them up, from a pay phone of course.

"Anything from those dickheads at the DOJ?"

"Nothing yet," said Paul.

"So, what's happening with the Senate?"

"We're working on it, Brad."

"Well, work a little faster, Paul. I'm not getting any younger over here."

I hung up, frustrated. They were nice guys, but that's not a quality you necessarily want in a lawyer. It didn't give me that warm and fuzzy feeling having to coach these dudes on what to do, who to go to, how to come up with creative approaches. But they were still the only "non-conflicted" attorneys I'd been able to find, and at least they seemed honest.

A couple of days after that, my cell phone buzzed in my flat. It was Ladjel calling from London, and he sounded uncharacteristically tense.

"Brad, I just got off the phone with someone from Compliance at UBS."

"You're starting to keep bad company," I quipped, not yet getting the tenor of his tone.

"You may not have any friends at that bank anymore," he said. "However, luckily for us, I still do. Listen, someone sent them a letter, allegedly from me. But as God is my witness, it *wasn't* from me. Give me your fax number."

"What's this all about, Ladjel?"

"You'll see shortly, and you won't like it." Then he added, "And Bradley, watch your ass."

I gave him the number and he rang off. A few minutes later my fax machine came to life and spat out a single page. I looked at it, and as I read it I felt the heat flooding my legs and scorching my chest. It was addressed to the Legal department of UBS Headquarters, Geneva, and here it is, verbatim.

July, 2007

UBS AG
c/o Wealth Management and Business Banking
for Legal Department
2, Rue de la Confederation
CH-1204 Geneva

Dear UBS Geneva:

I am informing you of your Wealth Management/Key Clients ex-employee, Bradley Birkenfeld, attempting to cause a malicious legal problem against your bank.

Recently, in spite of your sealed Swiss Court settlement with his employment, he has knowingly attempted to contact US Justice Department authorities to divulge proprietary bank procedures that may be in violation of US laws.

To date, the US Justice Department, Washington,

DC, office is considering issuing subpoenas to certain UBS bank officials as well as the bank itself. And to reward him for such whistle-blower initiatives.

Please check with your lawyers on Mr. Birkenfeld's vindictive and unprofessional actuations, as he resides in our Switzerland.

I assume you shall keep my contacting you in strictest confidence. I am also a Swiss citizen.

Sincerely,
L. Jafarli
London

I read it again, and then again. And then I read it one more fucking time while my ears nearly popped from the steam spitting out of my brain. The language was weird, stilted, as if someone were trying to impersonate a foreign national writing in English. "Unprofessional *actuations*"? Ladjel's English was perfect, much more fluid than this piece of garbage. And Ladjel's name was at the bottom, but it wasn't a signature. It was typed. A signature's like a fingerprint. If you're an impostor pulling a scam, you type it.

I walked to my veranda, flung the French doors open, and stared at the distant Swiss Alps beyond the lake. I didn't even realize that the fax had fluttered from my fingers and curled up on the floor. No one, and I mean not a single soul except my lawyers in Geneva and Washington, knew that I'd been to the Department of Justice. Neither firm knew of my friend Ladjel, and Ladjel didn't have a clue about my activities in Washington. Even if he had, I knew he'd never screw me this way, then show me the evidence and pretend to be warning me off like a concerned friend. Hell, he *was* my friend and had been for years! He was trying to save my skin.

But who was trying to skin me? Then I suddenly remembered that Customs stop in Texas. They'd pulled Ladjel off the plane, alone, just to get his particulars, probably on orders from . . . Kevin Fucking Downing. And if Downing, how did he know where I was going after my trip to DC? Perhaps he'd tapped my phone and put a tail on me;

they could've followed us to Dulles, then simply demanded the flight plan for the Citation X. When we headed back, Customs would've already had their marching orders, and the DOJ their dupe to use: Ladjel, a highly reputable investment banker with a Swiss passport.

My blood boiled. Someone inside the US government, either Downing and his fucking cohorts or someone else, was trying to get me thrown into a Swiss prison cell.

Or, worse, they were going to get me killed.

# CHAPTER 9

## TIGHTROPE

*"There is only one way to avoid criticism: Do nothing,*
*say nothing, and be nothing."*
—*ARISTOTLE, GREEK PHILOSOPHER*

WHEN YOUR OWN GOVERNMENT betrays you, it's a mule
kick in the guts.

I grew up believing in the infrangible bedrock of our American
system of justice. That's what I was taught as a kid: That no matter what might happen, my rights as an American citizen would be
assured by the Constitution and the Bill of Rights, the greatest documents authored on earth since the Ten Commandments and the
Magna Carta. And if I were to be accused of breaking the laws of the
land, my fate wouldn't be decided by one petty law enforcement officer—perhaps bitter, corrupt, and with an axe to grind—but instead
by "Twelve Angry Men," a jury of my peers, all good and true.

Yes, there were days in American history of which none of us
patriots were proud, yet they'd been corrected whenever they
occurred. And of course there'd also been rogues in government,
even of recent memory. However, I'd never imagined that something
like what I'd just experienced could ever happen to me. American
prosecutors and government agents couldn't turn rogue anymore.
There were checks and balances, steely-eyed watchers scrutinizing
the guardians. This wasn't Berlin of the 1930s, and the Department

of Justice wasn't the Gestapo. That's what I firmly believed. But now I felt like some Mafia foot soldier who'd decided, for the collective good, to rat on the Godfather and reveal every blood-spattered tale of the omertà, and had wound up spilling to an FBI agent named Michael Corleone.

The Jafarli letter shattered my world. I was no longer sure who I could trust. It wasn't something as prosaic as discovering a cheating spouse. It was like being thunderstruck by the revelation that your entire family had banded together, taken out a $5 million insurance policy on your life, and hired a hit man to put a bullet in the back of your skull.

I'd hate to admit this to Ladjel, but I went over every word of every conversation we'd had since his first call to me at the Four Seasons in Washington, and then all through our Mexico getaway and up to our last handshake and hugs at Dulles Airport. At least, that is, every word I could recall, because some portions of our time were inebriated. But nothing stood out; no strange slip-ups by Ladjel, no awkward probes, no overly curious queries on his part about my dealings with UBS, my planned career choices for the future, or satisfaction or lack thereof with the lawsuit results. I vetted him in my head and he came up clean. But it was ugly having to do it and I felt ashamed—and angry that those fuckers at the DOJ had made me do it.

It was them, all right. The suspect list was a simple, five-fingered exercise. My brother Doug knew what I was doing, because I'd finally told him about it while passing through Boston on this last trip. But it sure as hell wasn't Doug, unless he was somehow still pissed off over some adolescent squabble we'd had as kids. One finger down. And it wasn't Ladjel; two fingers down. And certainly not my two attorneys, unless they'd been taught in law school to take their clients' money and then get them knocked off. That was four fingers down, and the last one was Downing and the DOJ. That famous Marlon Brando line from *On the Waterfront* screamed in my head. "It was you, Charlie. It was *you*."

But why the hell would Downing do it? The Department of Justice and Kevin Downing had set me up; they'd tailed me and

Ladjel to Mexico, had Ladjel pulled off the plane to a run a back-
ground check on him, then stolen his identity and used him in some
dark scheme to expose me and make me back off. But why? It didn't
make sense, unless what they really wanted was to shut me up. And
as much as I already couldn't stomach Kevin Downing, somebody
else had to be pulling his strings. *Who's your fucking puppet master,
Pinocchio?*

Somebody up there hated me, as much or even more than
Downing, but I knew I wasn't going to find out who. It didn't matter all that much. The DOJ was all-powerful. I was up against a
dragon. I'd have to be extra careful now with my phone calls, email,
faxes, and what I said to whom. I still had people who I thought
were great friends working inside UBS, but could I trust them?
The only people I felt I could completely count on were Doug and
my best buddy from the State Street days, Rick James, but they
weren't in Geneva. As long as I stayed in Switzerland I'd be a lone
wolf, keeping the hunters at bay.

For a minute I thought about packing up, folding my tent, and
taking off, just so the Swiss couldn't put the shackles on me. But that
thought was short-lived. I was now a marked man in both Europe
and the States, so rather than run, I figured the best tactic would be
a counterattack. I'd take that phony Ladjel Jafarli letter and shove
it right up the DOJ's ass. I suddenly decided that this time I wasn't
going to sneak around and rotate pay phones. If anyone was listening, which at that point I was sure they were, I wanted them to hear
my defiance. I called Hector and Moran in Washington.

"Listen up, gentlemen," I said. "I'm going to send you a fax right
from my home office."

"Okay, Brad." Rick sounded curious. "But is that secure?"

"Doesn't matter. I've already been blown, and not in a good way."

I sent the fax off, and five minutes later they were both on the
phone and breathless.

"I can't *believe* this," said Paul. "Is this some kind of a prank?"

"Only if I'm Batman and Kevin Downing's the Joker."

"Are you absolutely sure, Brad," said Rick, "that this couldn't
have been your friend Ladjel turning you in to UBS?"

"Are you absolutely sure, Rick," I said, "that your wife isn't banging the pool boy?"

"Pretty damn sure," he said.

"Same thing. Ladjel and I have been friends for ten years. He's successful, wealthy, true blue, and has no reason to fuck me or kiss UBS's ass. No motive. Besides, Ladjel never knew a thing about this, so it couldn't have been him. This letter was a forgery."

"Fair enough," Rick said. "What do you want us to do?"

"I want you to take that letter, fax it right over to Kevin Downing, and say, 'What the fuck is this shit?' He's going to deny knowing anything about it, but at least he'll know we're on to him. And right after that, I want you to call the IRS and SEC and, most importantly, the Senate. I don't care if you have to sell your firstborn, but get me that subpoena to testify. Are we clear?"

"All right," Paul sighed. "Fasten your seat belt."

"We're already in a nosedive here," I said. "Hurry up."

I hung up, and I admit I slammed the phone down pretty hard. I wanted them to get the message that I wasn't thrilled with their choices so far and they'd better start playing hardball. *Nice guys finish last.* But things were moving too fast; no time to switch horses. I'd just have to keep whipping their flanks.

Hector and Moran did as instructed, and Downing reacted as predicted. They faxed him the Jafarli letter, along with one of their own, demanding a full explanation. When he didn't respond, they called him up, and he actually chortled like a schoolboy who'd been caught sneaking peeks up girls' skirts at recess.

"I have no idea who sent this," Downing said. "But it's clear that your client has numerous enemies, which doesn't surprise me. He should take precautions."

Slimy bastard.

Right after that, Haig Simonian published his scandalous article in the *Financial Times*. I sat out on my veranda, drinking espresso and grinning from ear to ear. According to Haig, some anonymous Swiss banker who called himself only "Tarantula" had contacted him and ripped apart Swiss banking, exposing years of its secrecy and corruption. Haig wrote that there was no way for him to confirm the morbid details, but his considerable experience in financial matters led him to believe that Tarantula was legit. By the next morning, all the other papers had picked it up and it was already causing some serious tremors in every bank from Zurich to Lugano.

Meanwhile, my legal starlings did start burning up the phone lines, trying to get me immunity from the IRS and the SEC and a "friendly subpoena" from the Senate Permanent Subcommittee on Investigations. I figured with all that in play and with the DOJ's pathetic ploy exposed, Downing and his cohorts would be less inclined to pull any more antics. But my faith in the palliative effects of logical thinking didn't last long.

A couple of days later, I got a call from James Wood, who was still grinding away at UBS, but had moved over to the South Africa desk as I'd warned him to do.

"Bradley, listen to this one, mate."

"I'm listening, James."

"One of our friends in the Legal Department had one too many brandies last night. He blurted out that the US Department of Justice just sent something called a 'target letter' to UBS Legal, I think perhaps to Peter Kurer himself. Apparently the letter's a warning to UBS, stating the bank's now under formal criminal investigation by the American authorities!"

"Well, that's interesting," I said in as offhand a manner as I could, since I'd bolted upright in my chair.

"Bloody hell, Brad!" James exclaimed. "You were right!"

"It's been known to happen on occasion," I said. "Just watch your ass, James."

"And you, yours," James said.

"Don't worry." I forced a laugh. "It's my favorite piece of real estate."

But *fuck*. I was furious! Talk about showing your hand! It was almost like the DOJ was saying to the Swiss, "We're going to have to look in your drawers. Better hide the porn!" Whatever their agenda was, I knew it had nothing to do with seeking justice for the American taxpayer.

That was enough. I was done dealing with those DOJ clowns. I called up Hector and Moran, told them the latest, and said, "*Fuck* the DOJ. I'm not dealing with those assholes. I'm booking airline tickets, and you guys better have somewhere for me to go."

---

It was August 31, 2007, when Hector and Moran first made contact with the US Senate. I'd coached them on what to say and whom to approach, but I knew it wouldn't be an easy row to hoe. Senator Carl Levin, the powerful chairman of the Senate Permanent Subcommittee on Investigations, was a lifelong Democrat and no friend of the Bush administration, which included the Department of Justice. I figured he'd find my offer to testify interesting, inasmuch as no one before me had ever proposed breaking the Swiss banks and telling exactly how they'd been defrauding American taxpayers for decades. But you couldn't just drag a finger down the Capitol Hill phone directory and give Carl a call. My attorneys got some staffer on the line and said, "We've got an American client, who's also a Swiss banker, and he'd like to blow the whistle on all the nefarious Swiss banking practices." The response was a bit cool, something akin to "That's nice. And I've got a bridge in Brooklyn that's going up for sale real cheap." Not so easy. It was going to take more than a few phone calls and a letter. But I stayed cool and told them to wait a couple of weeks, let it all sink in, and hit them up again.

In mid-September I told my lawyers to "end-run" the DOJ and reach back out to the IRS, including two special agents assigned to the IRS Senate detail, John Reeves and John McDougal. I wanted the IRS to know that I was still willing to cooperate, but since the DOJ was about as friendly as a junkyard dog, we were going much higher. I had a two-tiered tactic in mind. The IRS had to be kept in the loop about the fact that I was going full steam ahead as a whistle-blower; plus I knew they were dying to hear the whole story, which I'd only tell if I had a subpoena to protect me from the Swiss. The IRS couldn't grant it, but the Senate could.

Right after that, I had Hector and Moran push the Senate's doorbell again. This time something had changed, probably due to

Haig Simonian's article, which had been picked up by all the major financial papers and web sites. Once again my lawyers offered my detailed testimony, in person and at the committee's convenience. But they also emphasized the caveat: "Our client *must* have a subpoena, otherwise he won't be able to testify without risking his freedom. We'd appreciate such generous consideration in exchange for such groundbreaking revelations." Basically they were saying, "Turn us down, and you'll all have some 'splainin' to do."

On October 9, Hector and Moran called me up in Geneva, and I could tell they were practically fist-bumping each other.

"We got it, Brad! The Select Committee just issued you a subpoena!"

"Great. Fax me a copy," I said, though I was thinking, *'Bout fucking time. If you'd gone this route in the first place, I wouldn't have that mad dog Downing yapping at my heels.* But all I added was "I'll start packing my bags."

Still, I was excited and at last optimistic. Somebody was finally going to listen to what I had to say, and it wouldn't be a couple of bitter bureaucrats in some dead-end job. This was it, the Big Show, and this time I was going to take along every single piece of hard-hitting evidence I had. I also realized that my testimony before Levin's committee could avalanche into further consequences over which I'd have no control, so I had no idea how long I'd be in the States. I paid my housekeeper three months in advance and told her to keep the plants alive.

Then I headed for the airport, admittedly a bit edgy, since it was all too possible that the Swiss National Police might be waiting at the gate with a warrant. But hell, I'd always been something of a high roller, so I tossed the dice again.

---

Washington, DC, in October is a whole lot better than the nation's capital in June. It was cool and breezy and the leaves were turning, although in counterpoint to the weather, things for me were heating up. I set up the "bunker" at Doug's place in Weymouth, just outside

Boston, and I should have bought shares in Delta Airlines with the number of times I jetted back and forth. Doug, as I've mentioned before, is a meticulous and talented trial attorney, and as I ran down the details of everything I'd been doing, he started a dossier of evidence that later on would save my skin. He completely supported my whistle-blowing, but just like me, he was dismayed and pissed off at the way the Department of Justice was treating me like Lucky Luciano. Doug regarded his duties as an attorney much like a physician adheres to the Hippocratic oath. He was stunned to discover that the DOJ viewed their vows as "flexible," and eventually he'd grow to be even more furious than I was.

Over the course of the next month, I worked with Hector and Moran to set the stage for my upcoming Senate testimony, as well as ensuring that my whistle-blowing status was rock solid with the IRS. On October 12 we had a sit-down in my attorneys' office with a couple of IRS Legal and Compliance agents. I gave them more documents and testimony to garnish a clear picture of the massive scandal, and I told them I was about to tell everything to Carl Levin's committee, and after that they'd get that whole shebang too. They were polite, solicitous, and very grateful. After all, Congress funds the IRS. The DOJ, on the other hand, always secretive and scandalous, was as useless as a screen door on a submarine.

Throughout the rest of October we started shipping over preliminary evidentiary documents to the Senate. I wanted the committee to do some reading, even though I knew they wouldn't understand the material without my "translation." But if I just walked in there with a two-foot pile of papers, their heads would probably explode. At the same time, I had Hector and Moran keep on tugging at the DOJ, asking Downing for immunity and piecemealing him with more tidbits of evidence. I knew the fucker would keep on snubbing us, which he did; but it kept him off the scent of what I was really about to do: a Hail Mary pass right over his career. Then I had Rick and Paul contact the Securities and Exchange Commission, giving them a heads-up, too, on what was about to go down. With all these reach-outs, no one would be able to say later on that Birkenfeld was loath to cooperate.

On November 6, a huge story broke on CBS News and was soon

picked up by all the financials, including the *Wall Street Journal*. Down in Sao Paulo, Brazil, a UBS private banker based out of Zurich was suddenly arrested, along with nineteen Brazilians accused of scheming to help Brazilian companies evade taxes by laundering money through UBS and Credit Suisse, my old alma maters. The Brazilian police had raided forty-four different sites in a sweep dubbed "Operation Switzerland," seizing $4 million in Brazilian and US cash, and estimating those companies were black-market-laundering $4.1 million per month and hiding it all in Swiss banks!

Quick as Flash Gordon, I made copies of those breaking-news articles and had my lawyers express them off with cover letters to the Senate, IRS, SEC, and DOJ. The letters basically said, "Told ya, boys!" But the underlying message was "Even the freakin' Brazilians are smarter than you boneheads." This Brazilian sting operation on UBS and Credit Suisse was extremely similar to the tactics I'd suggested the DOJ employ in the United States (I guess the Brazilians watch too much TV as well!). Five days later I was walking up the steps of the Capitol building.

On November 13, Senator Carl Levin was busy. Translation: He wasn't going to personally sit through my testimony, but would instead have it summarized by his staff. For the most part, big-time senators only preside over public hearings, which are often televised on C-SPAN. Otherwise they'd get nothing else done. Whether or not they ever really get anything done is a matter of opinion.

My testimony was to be held in a large boardroom across the way from Levin's office. As I walked down those hallowed halls with Paul, both of us wearing respectable suits and ties and hauling the mother lode of Swiss secrets, I felt like I'd finally arrived at the Emerald City to see the Great Oz. A full two years had passed since I'd first discovered the Three-Page Memo and had sworn to implode that evil Swiss castle, and now I was hurtling toward the end zone. But I couldn't help wondering if they were going to treat me like a slimy rat, the way the DOJ had. I was about to find out. We were greeted by a couple of young interns and politely escorted inside.

The boardroom was large, about twenty by thirty feet, with a long conference table as big as a Boston Whaler and portraits of scowling senators lining the baize green walls. At one end of the table sat a female stenographer, polished nails already poised above her machine's keys. Across the table sat Robert "Bob" L. Roach, Senator Levin's counsel and chief investigator—about forty-five, with a big square jaw, Roman nose, steel-rimmed glasses, and bristly brown hair going gray at the temples. On one side of Roach sat two "majority," or Democrat, staffers, and on the other side two "minority" Republican staffers. The chairs on our side of the table were empty, but before we could sit down Roach stood up and right away the stenographer starting pecking.

"Mr. Birkenfeld," he intoned, "please raise your right hand."

I did so, while he asked, "Do you swear to tell the whole truth, nothing but the truth . . . ?"

I wanted to say, "You bet your ass I will," but I just said, "I do." I felt elated. It was all finally going to be on the record. And even better than that, Kevin Downing wasn't going to hear any of it unless he begged for a transcript copy. *Dumbass.*

Bob Roach was polite and gracious, although fairly humorless, never cracking a smile. He thanked me for my appearance and there were nods all around the table. Copies of everything my attorneys had provided were set out in neat stacks before his committee staffers, and Paul and I had volumes more to distribute. That took awhile, and then I gave them an overview of who I was, my role in Swiss banking over the past ten years, and how I'd come to the decision to blow the whistle on a cult-like club from which no other "agent" had ever come in from the cold. They were all very attentive, as if I were spinning a tale of mystery and intrigue, which I was, except that every word of it was true.

Before them lay reams of documents: many in English, some in French or German, including UBS memoranda, PowerPoint presentations, internal accounting missives, and confidential spreadsheets (Document 1). These were smart folks, but they didn't know much about the internal workings of secret Swiss banking, because no one before had ever revealed such details. This was their first day at school and I had to not only educate them on the basics, but then walk them through the connective tissue.

That first session with the Senate took nine hours, with a half-hour break for lunch. After the first hour, their brows were deeply creased and their eyes bugging out. These guys were government tax-issue experts who knew they'd been scammed for years, yet really had no idea how. But they looked at me as if they were the presidents of a blood bank that had been drained of its precious fluids over the course of decades, and here I was telling them the true tale of Dracula.

Some folks have claimed that Bradley Birkenfeld really didn't know all that much, and that even without my whistle-blowing, secret Swiss banking would have collapsed on its own. Well, Bob Roach and the Senate would disagree. They were attentive as hell, and I suggest you be too, because this is the crux of my story, the sharp blast of my whistle.

I'm going to tell you now what I told them. Read it carefully so you don't think I was just some rumormonger with a few breathless tales to tell. It was everything I'd learned, all the mud I'd slogged through for years. I gave it to them piece by piece, and they sat there stunned as if I were skinning a hippopotamus right there on their pristine, shiny mahogany table. I am footnoted multiple times throughout the US Senate reports of July 17 and 25, 2008. I am also recognized as the one person who provided the Senate Committee countless internal UBS documents and strategies.

First, I told them what UBS was doing, how they were doing it, and how long they'd concealed it. Then, I detailed the physical locations and operations of all the UBS private banking offices involved, in Geneva, Lugano, and Zurich. After that, I gave them a sheet as long as your arm with all the UBS private bankers involved—full names, phone numbers, email addresses, their UBS internal codes, and all the cities they'd worked in. Putting a nice bow on those bombshells, I then gave them the names of all the UBS senior executives involved in the US offshore business, supported by an internal UBS organization chart. I also connected the dots with the UBS offices and personnel in the United States, who were helping to facilitate and perpetuate this massive tax fraud against the US government.

"I'd like to suggest," I said. "No, actually, I insist that the DOJ,

IRS, and SEC match those entire phone lists with Homeland Security." I was offering up the same suggestions to them that I'd offered to the DOJ.

"Why is that, Mr. Birkenfeld?" Bob Roach asked.

"Because all UBS private bankers have had their passports scanned during previous visits to the States. You're going to find some very interesting matches pop up."

The staffers glanced at one another and scribbled notes. The stenographer kept hammering away.

"But let's talk about assets for a bit," I said as I shuffled some papers. "The total number of US accounts opened and maintained by UBS in Switzerland is nineteen thousand."

You could have heard a fly sneeze in that boardroom.

"And," I went on, "the total assets in those US accounts, acquired and invested by UBS in Switzerland, is *$20 billion*."

Eyes blinked. One of the staffers wearing glasses took them off and wiped them, almost comically, as if that might help him hear me better.

"This does not even include offshore trusts and companies with bank accounts external to UBS, as well as the endless hidden treasures in thousands of safe-deposit boxes. Oh, and please note that the value of a Swiss franc, or CHF, is slightly higher than the dollar, so you might want to bump that figure up accordingly. Further, the total revenue on US secret accounts generated by UBS in Switzerland averages $200 million per year. That would be $2 *billion* in untaxed revenue over the last decade alone. I'm afraid I can't give you the precise figures for prior decades, but you can safely assume that this has been going on since World War II."

Did I have their attention yet? Let's just say none of them looked at their watches—not once.

I had to "translate" the UBS internal accounting breakdown of assets and revenue by sector, class, and month. Then I hit them with a detailed list of the cities, hotels, length of stays, and frequency that UBS private bankers traveled to the United States, plus the number of existing and prospective client meetings that took place during those trips. You might be wondering how I had all this information compiled so perfectly. Well, just remember that I had two years to do it, fueled by lots of pissed-offedness. Resourceful and relentless.

That took about three hours, and then we broke for lunch. Paul and I had sandwiches in the Senate commissary, where the committee staffers stayed away from me as if they were sequestered jurors and I was the state's star witness, which was pretty much the situation. We came back in and Bob Roach reminded me that I was still under oath.

"I'm fully aware, sir," I said, and then I swung back into the evidence. "Let's talk about how UBS categorizes its US clients, and how they treat them according to their net worth. Key Clients are those with $25 million or more; High Net Worth Clients, $10 to $25 million. Core Clients are those holding $2 to $10 million, and Mass Affluent Clients have the smallest UBS accounts, of $2 to $3 million. They're all conveniently placed in Portfolio Management mandates with a standard investment strategy of funds. Ironically, a majority of those funds are UBS products, created by the investment bank. Each of these clients is serviced according to his or her value, and the cost of such service is proportional. You might want to note that with 19,000 such accounts at the bank, *every one* of them falls into one of these categories."

The amounts were staggering. I didn't blame the staffers for loosening their ties. I carried on.

"Shall we discuss how UBS openly and shamelessly trained all of us private bankers to avoid scrutiny while here in the States?"

Nods all around. I selected my next sheaf of evidence, the UBS in-house training materials (Document 3).

"Here you can clearly see how the bank trained us on various techniques, such as when and how to indicate business or pleasure on US Customs forms. Please note in Paragraph 2 that our managers suggest frequently rotating hotel rooms to conceal our identities. You will see further down that our clients must be referred to using only code names, and that our business cards had to be reprinted with the title 'Wealth Manager' and 'UBS' removed. On the next page you'll see the ironclad rule about us never carrying client portfolios on our persons, but instead having them FedExed over to the States to our hotels or local UBS offices. In the spy trade, those are called 'dead drops.' Below that you'll find the specific techniques for encrypting client information on our PDAs, or 'palm' devices, as well as the bank's purchase and distribution to us of IBM-encrypted laptops."

I stopped for a moment and looked up. "By the way, I refused to carry any such encrypted devices."

"And why was that, Mr. Birkenfeld?" Roach asked.

"I was a Swiss resident, working in full compliance with Swiss law, and I wasn't going to behave like a criminal."

"But you understood the clandestine nature of these techniques, and their purpose."

"I understood fully," I said. "No one was twisting my arm. My negative feelings about these issues bloomed later."

That struck another chord and Roach nodded respectfully. I wasn't one of those witnesses pretending "the devil made me do it."

"I'd like to mention at this point," I said, "that prior to this committee's invitation to testify, and issuance of a subpoena so I could freely do so, I have made numerous attempts to bring this information to the Department of Justice."

I let that one sink in for a long beat too. They had to know what a bunch of bureaucratic dumbasses were working over at Justice.

"Unfortunately, the DOJ refused to grant me immunity or issue me a subpoena, which made it impossible for me to reveal to them everything I've brought to you. As a matter of fact, I even offered to have myself electronically wired, work out of a special office at the Justice Department, and travel back and forth to Switzerland, meeting with Swiss bankers and clients in order to gather more information."

"That was a courageous offer, Mr. Birkenfeld," said Roach. "I assume you chose the better part of valor and changed your mind."

"No, sir. Kevin Downing at the DOJ rejected my offer out of hand. You'd have to ask him why."

"We'll do just that," said one of the Republican staff members.

"Perhaps someone else will undertake that mission in the future," I said. "To that end, you should know that UBS has two main off-site centers for annual conferences of all the UBS bankers from Zurich,

Geneva, and Lugano. These meetings cover a range of topics from investment products, account pricing, marketing, client referrals, VIP events, and often have motivational speakers, which sort of amuses me because the vast sums of money involved are motivation enough. The two sites are the UBS Wolfsberg Castle complex outside Zurich and the Montreux Palace Hotel outside Geneva. When the meetings are in session, the sites are off-limits to anyone but UBS private bankers and executives. You'd have to have someone on the inside, like me."

I smiled and shrugged apologetically. Clearly they weren't going to get another American who'd worked in Swiss banking, at least not in this decade or the next. Then I distributed five copies of a colored tri-fold brochure. I'd held that one back for effect.

"This is the UBS 'Fund Facts' brochure," I said. "The bank printed thousands of them quarterly, in German, French, English, and Italian, and those of us on the foreign investor desks carried them with us, handing them out to prospective clients. You'll note that the brochures clearly market the sales of investment products, as well as the bank's offer to advise these clients on an ongoing basis. I'm sure I don't have to tell you that we UBS private bankers were not licensed to sell or advise US clients on investments. As a matter of fact, after our clients perused these materials, we openly instructed them to discuss these investments with us only if they were traveling outside the Continental United States. In other words, 'find a clean pay phone.'"

At that point, the session was deep into the late afternoon. But I can tell you that no one looked like they wanted to leave. It was like they were snuggled in their beds with a nightlight on, unable to put down the latest John Grisham novel. I shuffled some more papers and smiled with some irony.

"Oh, this one's the UBS in-house, very nicely printed, Counter-Surveillance Case Study booklet. We were trained on this, extensively, by the bank's Security and Compliance personnel, which you might find ironic."

Their eyes bugged out again, as they read about how we were to act like the German spies who'd been smuggled into the United States from submarines back in the 1940s.

"And now, please turn to the next document, this Three-Page

Memo. This was a document called 'Cross-Border Banking Policies,' ostensibly issued in November 2004. You might be surprised, just as I was, to discover it contains extensive verbiage expressly forbidding us bankers to do exactly what the bank had been urging and training us to do for years on end."

I gave them a minute to read through that backstabbing piece of shit that had set me on fire and brought me to this very place. Some of the staffers shook their heads and muttered to each other. I heard one of them whisper, "Do you *believe* this?"

"The next document," I said, "is an updated ten-page version of the same set of policies, which once again contradicts the actual activities of UBS. This one was issued recently, in June 2007. I'm afraid I can't tell you how I acquired it, but let's just say I have many friends across various departments at UBS."

After each of my distributions, there were slews of questions, with Roach often deferring to staff members who needed some help. "What does this figure mean, Mr. Birkenfeld?" "Could you please further define the term *Net New Money*?" "How did you choose which venues to attend in order to meet new clients?" Honestly, I reveled in coaching them all through the materials, because they were genuinely fascinated and grateful, unlike that dumbass Downing. The hours flew by and at long last Bob Roach looked at his watch. It was already past five p.m.

"Mr. Birkenfeld, you've given us so much valuable material that I think we're going to have to do some serious studying and homework." He looked around and got nods from his staff members. "We'll have to continue this at our next session. Is there anything else you'd like to provide as we wrap this up today?"

"Maybe just this," I said as I took out multiple copies of something I'd held back. I stood up, passed them around, and sat down again. "Those are all the names of my clients at UBS, including all the North Americans. You'll also find the details of their numbered accounts, asset holdings, offshore companies, and trusts I helped them establish to conceal their identities, and the progression of investments, with untaxed income in bold. Following my clients is an extensive list of clients serviced by my immediate boss, Christian Bovay, by his superior in Zurich, Martin Liechti, as well as those of Raoul Weil, a higher-ranking managing director of the entire operation worldwide. These are just a portion of the forty-five hundred accounts serviced in Geneva and of the nineteen thousand in total."

Igor Olenicoff was at the top of that list, along with Abdul Aziz Abbas, and scores of other Americans or US residents who'd been evading taxes. I wasn't happy about having to turn over some of those clients, like Olenicoff, but it wasn't as if I could pick and choose. If I held anything back, I knew I'd be toast.

Eventually the committee would come to know all these clients intimately, as would the IRS. Most of those people would throw up their hands, admit their guilt, sign on to an amnesty program, pay their fines and back taxes, and thereby remain safe from any public revelations.

"Holy shit," someone whispered after reading the name of a Hollywood celebrity.

"A small fish," I said. "Only $20 million. Igor Olenicoff, my largest client, had $200 million in his portfolio."

I let them keep on reading while I gathered up my papers and packed them away. When Paul and I left for the day, nearly unnoticed, they were still sitting there reading. As I closed the door behind me, I heard one of them gasp.

"No! Not *her*. You've *got* to be kidding me!"

———

One week later there was a second session with the Senate. But this time something had shifted in Carl Levin's boardroom. I could sense an undercurrent of rage in the committee staffers, not directed at myself, but at the very idea that the United States had been so abused, for so long, by an ostensible European ally. Granted, I had brought them volumes of evidence about the dealings of only one Swiss banking institution, yet one couldn't ignore the conclusion that the Swiss government's legal constructs had fomented and, by logical progression, encouraged UBS's criminal behavior across international lines, as if they were a global cartel. The other 130 private banks just in

Geneva were complicit in the same devious business as UBS, but at different levels.

Once again I delivered more bad news. I added fire to their ire by informing them that while UBS was certainly the biggest offender of all the Swiss banks, they were certainly not alone. Just as I'd done with the DOJ, I spilled many beans on Credit Suisse, where I'd first been immersed in the whole Swiss shell game.

But the Senate Committee, unlike the Department of Justice, refrained from shooting the messenger. The staffers had clearly done their homework, boning up on the voluminous materials I'd given them during our first session, and there were many more questions and requests for clarifications. It seemed to me that they were powdering their cannons for a broadside soon to be unleashed, and I hoped it was going to be aimed at all the government's thus far incompetent law enforcement bodies. At times the staffers, as they asked more questions, seemed almost embarrassed.

*How could we not have known about all this? How could it be that the Internal Revenue Service, the Securities and Exchange Commission, and the Department of Justice have allowed this to go on under our very noses for decades? We have to rely on a single American citizen with a conscience to slay this dragon?*

Bob Roach swore me in again, and I began by first commenting on and reviewing a letter that, the day before, my lawyers had sent to the Committee, the DOJ, and the SEC. That letter was the result of inside information I'd just received from one of my mates still inside UBS, in which he told me that the bank had just issued instructions about altering the nature of its offshore business with US customers.

"Gentlemen, it appears that UBS is starting to circle the wagons. Before you begin thinking that this might be the result of leaks from these closed-door sessions, I believe I can explain why."

"Please do, Mr. Birkenfeld," said Roach.

"About two months ago, while I was still in Geneva, the Department of Justice sent UBS a target letter. That letter essentially warned the bank that it was under investigation. Personally, I would regard that as a gross tactical error, but we are now witnessing the results.

UBS has been warned, thereby making your efforts to discover their current practices all the more difficult. They are instituting travel bans and document destruction."

Someone slapped the table and hissed, "Christ." I simply raised an eyebrow and shrugged.

Over the rest of that day's session, which was as long as the first, we all got deep in the weeds. I had to review lots of the documents and information I'd already provided, because these things were admittedly difficult to understand unless you'd worked in Swiss banking. But I also made sure to take some time to summarize all the steps I'd taken, first as an internal whistle-blower at UBS, and then the high risks I'd taken to bring the information to the US government. I wanted them to understand what I'd had to do, that even after leaving UBS I'd acquired up-to-date intelligence from inside the bank, used multiple pay phones and fax machines from rotating hotels to pass it on to my lawyers and then to the DOJ. I provided proof that I'd often traveled to European cities outside Geneva, for no other reason than to FedEx evidence from a secure location, and flown back and forth on my own dime. I wanted all my efforts on the Congressional record.

After that, I politely explained why previous attempts by US authorities to rein in the Swiss behavior were useless.

"The Qualified Intermediary Agreement, or QI," I said, "was designed to force US investors, and the Swiss banks that court them, to formally state the nature and holdings of offshore accounts. It was an attempt to convert all 'undeclared' secret numbered accounts to 'declared' accounts. I'm sorry to inform you that UBS has developed tactics to circumvent that agreement and uses them frequently. My guess is that most other Swiss banks are doing the exact same thing."

The folks in the room looked pretty sheepish. Clearly nothing they'd tried before was working.

"How do you suggest we counter these tactics?" one of the staff members asked.

"I'd suggest the US government get serious," I said. "A full-on assault against Swiss secret banking practices. I'd suggest legislation, and with it, prosecution. Some pressure on the Department of Justice to actually do something might help."

They all looked at each other, and I could tell that's what they already had in mind.

"I have no desire to harm my colleagues," I said, "those at my level who've been bound by Swiss law. However, those above them, the managing directors, board executives, bank chairmen, the designers and, if you'll excuse the expression, the financial pimps. I can help you catch them at their game."

"Will you?" Roach asked.

"I will."

And that's pretty much how that second long session wrapped up. They thanked me, I thanked them, and I left with my lawyer, after assuring them that further information would be forthcoming.

I'm guessing it was within the next twenty-four hours that Carl Levin was briefed by Bob Roach. Levin and the senators on his Committee went nuts, calling immediately for open hearings on Switzerland's flouting of American laws. I'm also guessing that Levin made a call to the Department of Justice and screamed his head off. Why is that my guess? Because two days after my last session, Kevin Downing called my attorneys. He ranted and raved, apoplectic that I'd gone to the Senate, testified, and taken his precious investigation public.

The politicians had gotten out front on this, causing an enormous embarrassment for the DOJ; they could no longer suppress my evidence or the brewing scandal. However, no open accusations of corruption or obstruction of justice flew between Senate Democrats and Republicans, because both sides knew full well that they all had dirty fish in the fire. But they had no choice now except to excavate the Swiss numbered accounts and hold their breath, with no way of knowing which rats would scurry out. It must have been rough on those poor politicians. I wonder how many of them called their Swiss bankers in a panic. Though my testimony was secret, I knew that a storm was raging on Capitol Hill.

As for me, I just sat back with a smile and watched it all happen. I'd just pulled the pin on a hand grenade and tossed it into the room, and I was waiting to see who was left standing.

For the first time in history, Swiss banking secrecy looked about to collapse like a house of cards.

# PART III

# CHAPTER 10

## HUNTED

*"You must be the change you wish to see in the world."*
—*MAHATMA GANDHI, INDIAN LEADER*

IT WAS JANUARY 2008 and I was back in Geneva. A free man again, at least for the moment.

Cold winds blustered across the lake and the Swiss Alps were slathered in snow, but breathing in that frigid air was like getting a hit of pure oxygen. It was good to be far, far away from the slimy tentacles of the ungrateful Department of Justice. I had spilled my guts to the US Senate, given them everything I had, and I intended to keep on giving to the Committee as well as to the IRS and the SEC. The responses from those government bodies had been thankful, even warm, but I had no illusions about my precarious position. Carl Levin and his staff viewed me as a courageous whistle-blower, while Kevin Downing still saw me as a scorpion in his bedroom slipper.

The Department of Justice had let me go home to Geneva, but I was certain that Downing was out to get me, some way, somehow. He was furious that I'd pissed in his Cheerios and turned to other branches of the US government. With what I'd revealed to the Senate, I knew that Downing would now have no choice but to start seeking indictments, and I was pretty damn sure that one of them would have my name on it. Carl Levin's committee might see me as a gift from the gods, but the irony was that the Senate could protect me from the Swiss, but *not* from that vengeful prick Downing, who could still have me indicted as a coconspirator in tax fraud. If he could pull that off, I knew he would. No doubt about it.

Still, with the pops of the New Year champagne corks, I was at last released from the stress of bouncing from one federal agency to another, able to take a break from trying to prove my verity and worth.

I wasn't going to sit in my beautiful flat in Geneva and brood. Life goes on, and there were deals to make, parties to attend, and maybe a few women to woo. I threw myself back into some private equity deals with my close friend Dave, a guy with an eye for great start-ups and matching investors. I winged over to Mumbai and met with the Indian Minister of Oil and Gas, where we signed a deal for the purchase of American coal, the "clean" type.

Then I flew over to Beijing and Shanghai, meeting with senior Chinese officials and pitching my coal deal, as well as some prime real estate opportunities in Europe. Naturally I had some fun in between, and you already know what kind. But all in all, I felt like I was in a state of limbo, waiting for the axe to fall.

In between brokering international deals, I kept on feeding more information to various American government agencies. Kevin Downing had blown me off when I offered to serve as an ongoing informant, but the Senate, IRS, and SEC were still hungry for anything I could provide. So I turned myself into an undercover agent, hobnobbing with all my friends still working at UBS and coaxing the secrets out of them. They had no idea what I was doing with their fun new facts; it must have seemed like old-boy-network office gossip, over dinner and plenty of alcohol. James Woods and I had dinner one night at Restaurant Les Armures up in the Old Town. It's a pretty little place that spills out onto the cobblestones of Rue du Soleil Levant (Street of the Levantine Sun).

"So, how's it going over there in the black magic kingdom, James?" I asked him as we enjoyed our French cuisine.

"It's a bloody horror show, Brad! You should see the panic. All sorts of travel bans, new security protocols, and if anyone even mentions a trip to the States, Bovay has a shit fit! I am so glad I listened to you and switched to South Africa."

"I'm glad you did too, James." I smiled.

"It's almost as if someone is feeding the Americans UBS's money-hunting tactics, in real time! Every move the bank makes is instantly thwarted."

He said that innocently, and I replied in kind.

"Interesting theory, James. But no one would do that, unless he or she wanted to wind up locked away in a dungeon in Zurich."

"I know. But you should see Martin Liechti's latest directive. Don't bloody go anywhere unless I approve it!"

I laughed. "I'd love to see that memo, just for shits and giggles."

"I'll send you a copy. But don't tell a soul."

"Cross my heart. More wine?"

In about mid-January, the *Financial Times* broke another big story about UBS. Haig Simonian authored the piece and in it he quoted bank officials who'd announced with a flourish that UBS would be ending all secret relationships with US clients, in effect closing down their numbered accounts. I knew my former Swiss bosses too well, which meant that I knew the whole thing was a red herring, an attempt to cool the heat. But it didn't cool mine, because I also knew that if that idiot Kevin Downing and his DOJ bumblers hadn't warned UBS with their "target letter," we could have rolled up the entire operation, just as the Brazilians had done. It was as if I'd fingered a mansion in the suburbs for a crack den, whorehouse, and weapons cache, and the cops had said, "Really? Let's go knock on the door and ask."

But at the very least I could rub their noses in it, so I dictated a cover letter to my lawyers and had them send it, along with copies of the *Financial Times* article, to the SEC, IRS, Senate, and DOJ. I know that probably seems like I was fanning the flames of my own fire while being burned at the stake, but it was part of my next tactical phase. And besides, by now you understand that I don't retreat under fire.

Meanwhile, I gathered more and more info on what they were actually doing over at UBS. And what they were doing was circling the wagons, destroying incriminating evidence that pointed to illicit relationships with American clients, rerouting their hunter-gatherers to target countries that didn't seem to care much about tax fraud, and moving assets to other jurisdictions with new offshore structures. They were telling everyone to stay away from the States. They should have done the same thing with France, because eventually their shenanigans there would cost them a shocking 1.1 billion euros in frozen funds in escrow, with a high risk of up to 6 billion in fines! Well, you can't fix stupid, or arrogant. By this time, I had my secret communications methods down pat: moving from pay phones to Internet cafes, taking short "vacations" outside Geneva, and FedExing packages to Hector and Moran. It was all fresh intel.

In February Hector and Moran brought both the SEC and the Senate up to date on my activities. Those were telephone calls, but shortly thereafter in March I had them start funneling active intelligence and documentation to both bodies. Later that month I fired off another broadside, more information showing that the UBS big dogs were basically trying to figure out how to outsmart the US Department of Justice, which shouldn't have been a problem given the DOJ's miniscule minds. My instincts told me that sooner or later the DOJ was going to go after me, so I'd better keep doing my "charitable works" as a way to counter their claims. I felt like I was doing well: smart moves, preemptive strikes, all of which I'd use to parry the stiletto that Kevin Downing wanted to plunge into my spine.

Then came the indictments. And they were sealed.

A sealed indictment means you don't tell the guy you're going to bust that he's about to be taken down. I'm pretty sure that if Downing and his bosses could have gotten away with it, they would have snuck out to pay phones themselves and called lots of Swiss cell numbers— the ones I'd given to the Senate. But thanks to my efforts, the Senate had a hard list of all the Swiss perps, the UBS managers making it all happen, and so did the IRS and the SEC. They'd turned them all over to the DOJ and said, "Go get these international tax fraud criminals!" Well, I'm pretty sure that Downing busted a gut when he saw the source of the intel—me—but he had no choice at this point. And if he fucked up the indictments, lots of fat fingers would be pointing his way. My guess is that his bosses, Kevin O'Connor, and above him the Attorney General, probably said, "Do what you have to do. We'll handle anything 'sensitive' later." That might be supposition, but in the end that's how it worked out, so I'll stick with my assessment.

At the top of the hit list was Igor Olenicoff. Downing could have had his name when I first walked into the DOJ, but he'd refused to give me a subpoena, so he only discovered Olenicoff as a result of my Senate testimony. He was probably drooling at the prospect of dropping the hammer on Igor, because he was linked directly to me. But then Downing discovered what the rest of the world already knew: Olenicoff was already being prosecuted by the IRS and the US Attorney's office in Orange County, California! Downing couldn't go after him because he'd already been snagged. I'm sure that one pissed him off and made him even more determined to nail me to a cross.

But Igor was no fool (Forbes 400 list). He had already hired a former DOJ prosecutor from the exact same office that was prosecuting him to mount his defense (remember that revolving door?), and to avoid the public embarrassment of being indicted, quickly pled guilty to a *single* felony count of filing a false tax return for 2002! He admitted to tax evasion and failing to inform the IRS about his offshore accounts in the Bahamas, Liechtenstein, the UK, and Switzerland—with apologies, of course. The government decided he could make it all good by paying a fine of $52,018,460.36 and repatriating all of his money to the States. Igor smiled and took out his checkbook. For a guy worth more than $2 billion, it was chump change. Ironically, it was later uncovered through discovery in a civil lawsuit against Igor Olenicoff that he and his son (Andrei) had opened their Barclays Bank account in the Bahamas with Yugoslavian passports. Yet neither one was born in Yugoslavia, they did not reside in Yugoslavia, nor did either of them work in Yugoslavia. The Olenicoff scams continued . . .

In case you're thinking that Olenicoff was just a fun-loving, basically upstanding, sometimes forgetful billionaire with a few quirks (you know, a regular Joe), note this. He was "selective" about honoring his commitments. Proudly displayed in front of numerous offices of his "Olen Properties" were beautiful, expensive sculptures—all unlicensed copies. Over the years he'd recruited two world-class sculptors, Don Wakefield and John Raimondi, to submit detailed proposals of original works, with mockups, photographs, dimensions, and prices. Wakefield and Raimondi never heard from Igor again, because he had the sculptures knocked off by a Chinese artist (the Chinese have made copyright infringement and patent theft into national pastimes). Both enraged artists sued Olenicoff, federal juries found him guilty as charged, and he was ordered to pay Wakefield $450,000 in damages, and Raimondi $640,000. Again, that was parking-meter money to Igor, yet it might have cost him less to just pay for the original works and not need his lawyers. But, used to getting his way, Igor chose to appeal the verdicts rather than pay the artists.

In the end, Olenicoff got away with all of it. At his sentencing hearing in that spring of 2008, Igor blamed his plight on everyone else: his lawyers, accountants, UBS, and me—for giving him such bad advice! Prosecutors nodded solemnly and argued *against* his serving any prison sentence, even though the sentencing guidelines called for three years in stir. They did agree that he'd have to suffer some indignity, since he'd been using offshore accounts to avoid paying taxes since 1992, but he had no prior convictions and his crimes had "hurt no one financially." They lobbied hard for a slap on the wrist. Why? Because Igor has low friends in high places.

US District Court Judge Cormac Carney sentenced Igor to two years' probation and 120 hours of community service. His former DOJ prosecutor-attorney called it "the deal of the century." It was, and as a result Igor was free to go after me. But we'll get to that later.

Meanwhile, although the rest of the indictments were sealed, somehow all of my former UBS bosses—Christian Bovay, Michel Guignard, Martin Liechti, and Raoul Weil—suddenly received word from Swiss authorities that they were all "wanted men" by the US government. Did someone in the US Department of Justice have a tight relationship with someone in the Swiss Ministry of Justice? Can't say for sure, but Hillary Clinton, the soon-to-be new Secretary of State, certainly did (that wouldn't come out until she decided she wanted to be the leader of the Free World). The Swiss, however, were not about to break their own legal "codes of ethics" and ship big-money bankers off to jail in Washington. All those guys had to do was stay home in Switzerland, or at least just travel anywhere *except* the United States, and keep on bringing in that illicit cash. Simple, right?

One might think so, unless you're an arrogant, swaggering, puffed-up dude like Martin Liechti. Martin thought he was invincible, untouchable. Unlike many of my white-socked Swiss managers, Martin acted like an international gadfly, jetting around the world in his thousand-dollar suits, gelled brown hair, and permanent tan. He'd been warned to watch his ass, but he wasn't about to let the Americans dictate the terms of his business trips. So in mid-April Martin boarded a flight for the Bahamas, probably to snag some more fat cats and make sure that tan kept its glow. His flight itinerary routed through Miami, where he'd have to switch planes, but he probably figured he'd be able to just walk from one terminal to the other. Wrong. First he had to clear Customs, and that's where his name popped up at Passport Control. A couple of icy ICE men took his elbow and his suitcase and invited him for a little chat.

Strangely, although Martin's face was on a DOJ "wanted" list, he wasn't swept off to court or arraigned by any judge. Federal agents from the Department of Justice informed him that he was being detained as a "material witness" in a burgeoning international tax fraud case. By merely detaining Liechti on a material witness warrant instead of an arrest warrant, Downing and his cohorts at DOJ had total control of his fate. For the time being, there would be no court appearance, no nasty federal judge making decisions, as long as he played ball. They escorted him off to a five-star hotel in Miami, locked him up in a fashionable suite, and posted round-the-clock gunmen to make sure he didn't go for a swim and keep on swimming. Aside from that inconvenience, he was told to just cool his heels and enjoy the weather. And that's where he stayed for four months, until "invited" to testify before Carl Levin's soon-to-be-televised open hearings.

My cell phone buzzed in my flat in Geneva. It was Jacques Leuba, and I could hear the sounds of lunchtime somewhere. He'd left the office.

"Bradley, have you heard the latest? It's *incroyable!*"

"What's unbelievable, *mon ami?*"

"Martin Liechti. He's just been arrested in Miami! The bank's denying it, but he's been overdue from his trip for a week. Christian's been trying to call him, but he doesn't answer his cell phone, and his secretary's starting to stutter."

"Maybe she's got early Alzheimer's."

"Don't be glib, she's not even thirty. A reporter from the *Financial Times* has been calling over here, trying to confirm the story, but we've all been told to shut up."

I knew that had to be Haig, who'd been slightly skeptical of my bombshell at the beginning but was now all over it and publishing every new UBS scandal.

"Well, Jacques," I said. "I guess you reap what you sow."

He laughed. "I can tell that you're heartbroken, Bradley."

"Hey, I feel sorry for the guy. He could wind up in prison, and American prisons aren't exactly the Ritz. Some big dude named Bubba might make Martin his wife."

"You're brutal. Want to have lunch?"

"Not today, Jacques, but soon."

"All right. I'll let you know if I hear any more gossip."

"Thanks, buddy."

We hung up and I exhaled a long sigh. Martin Liechti, busted. Downing was starting to actually do something, taking down Swiss bankers and clients, knocking them off like pawns. Part of me was happy about it. After all, that's what I wanted, for all those arrogant, ungrateful Swiss assholes to pay. But the other part of me reacted like a mole inside a terror network. I'd been feeding the authorities hard intelligence, but when the commandos finally showed up, they'd be killing everyone in sight, including me. Some of the stuff I'd delivered was as persuasive as a smoking gun, such as Martin Liechti's memo to all Americas Desk bankers, blatantly telling them to up their game in the States. It was bombshell stuff, and had no doubt served as ammunition for his detainment. And still, over the course of a long year, Hector and Moran had been trying to get me immunity from prosecution, pleading that I'd only played a minor role in the vast Swiss scheme; they'd failed. Only the DOJ could grant me immunity, and Downing kept slamming the door in their faces. With

Liechti's detainment it was now all too clear that I wasn't going to get a pass.

I called my attorneys up and told them about Liechti. You'd think that these guys, Hector and Moran, representing a whistle-blower in the tax fraud case of the century, would have already known about Martin Liechti's demise. They didn't.

"Oh, now that's interesting news," said Rick.

"Ya think?" I scoffed.

"Well, what are you going to do now?" Paul asked.

I sighed and shook my head. They should have been telling me what they planned to do! I just told them I'd be thinking it over and would let them know.

If you've done any skiing, you know what it's like when you take a hard fall on a black diamond slope, lose a ski, and just keep on tumbling, sliding, wondering when something's going to break your fall. That's how I felt at the time, but my instinct was to just jam a ski pole in the ice and stand up, straight and tall. I had only two choices. I could stay in Geneva forever, lie low, keep doing my business deals, give up on the whole whistle-blower thing, and never go back to America. Or I could keep my head up, flaunt my righteous cause, go back into the fray, and face the hard music—no matter what discordant tune Downing decided to play.

Liechti's capture was the signal for me. My bosses were hunted men and I knew my days were numbered as well. Kevin Downing wasn't going to grant me immunity from anything, ever. He wanted me in chains more than he wanted the truth. And I wasn't going to spend the rest of my life in Europe, always looking over my shoulder, unable to see my family and friends in the States. I wasn't built that way. It was time for a showdown.

The idea of getting some sort of award at the end of my efforts wasn't even on my radar at the time, because nothing like that had ever played out to the benefit of any other informant like me. It was simply a question: Was I going to stick to my guns? My old military training kicked in; nothing matters but the mission.

Then I looked around my flat, all the beautiful accoutrements, the comforts, and I thought about my Swiss chalet in Zermatt, my cars, my best buddies in Geneva and lovely lady friends, and everything else I could still enjoy if I'd just let the whole thing go. I knew if I went back to the States I might never see any of my life here again. As a matter of fact, the only thing I might be seeing for a long, long time would be iron bars and weak sunlight streaming through a concrete slit window. I asked myself over and over: "Is it worth it?"

The answer came back from somewhere. *Birkenfelds don't act like fugitives. Birkenfelds don't hide. Birkenfelds don't run.* I called Hector and Moran back.

"Okay guys, listen up. I want you to arrange another meeting, with both the SEC and the Senate."

"They just called us," Rick said. "They've requested follow-up meetings with you. What do you want us to say to them?"

I rolled my eyes. "Well, tell them hell yes!"

"You're going to come back here?" Paul sounded incredulous. "Especially with one of your bosses just getting busted?"

"I'm not a criminal, and I'm not going to act like one. I don't give a fuck what that moron Downing says, thinks, or does."

"All right, Brad," said Rick. "We'll get on the horn to the SEC and the Committee."

"Honk it loud," I said. "But don't blow it."

It was the first week of May 2008. I took a deep breath and started packing, but it felt different than preparing for any previous trip. This time I really had no idea when I'd be coming back, if ever. Spring was in full bloom in Geneva; it would be even warmer in the States. A couple of suits? Sure, those would do for now. Polo shirts, slacks, and jeans? Okay. Then I looked around some more in my closet for my favorite parka and chuckled out loud, remembering a line from an old Mafia movie where the hit man, with a big bulge under his jacket, shows up at his victim's house. "We're takin' a little walk. You ain't gonna need your coat." I finished up the clothing options quickly, but was much more careful about packing up all my latest UBS evidence and documentation. Then I picked up a forgotten envelope from the table in front of my green leather couch, an invitation to my upcoming high school reunion in the States. I opened it up, thinking about all the years of adventures I'd had since those innocent schoolboy times and wishing things could be that simple again. Then I booked a seat on a late-night flight, one way to Boston, and called my brother Doug in Weymouth.

"I'm coming into Boston tomorrow."

"What the hell for?" Doug demanded. He'd been carefully tracking all the intrigues going on with my case, and he knew Martin Liechti had just been nabbed.

"High school reunion."

"Are you out of your mind?!"

I laughed. "No, I'm coming in for more meetings with the Senate and the SEC, and to finish this thing with Downing once and for all. The reunion's just a side trip."

Looking around my apartment just before heading out the door, I glanced down at my coffee table in front of the fireplace. A Monopoly board game was on it. I walked over there, opened the box, pulled out the cards from the game, and found it—the *Get Out of Jail Free* card, with the image of some silly-ass-looking mustachioed dude wearing a top hat. I placed the card in my wallet and walked out.

Just before boarding the plane, I found an airport pay phone and called Haig Simonian. It was too late to find him over at the *Financial Times*, but by now I had his cell number and he knew my voice. I didn't have to announce myself as "Tarantula." I could tell I'd woken him up.

"Evening, Haig. Sorry about the late hour. I'm about to board a flight for the States. Just wanted you to know what's going on, in case I disappear."

He sighed and wished me good luck. I think he was worried about losing his "Deep Throat," the kind of source that comes around only once in a newsman's career.

It was a long flight, maybe the longest of my relatively young, carefree life. But at least I was in Business Class with plenty of room for my long legs. I had a couple of stiff drinks to little effect and pushed my food away. I knew I wasn't going to sleep much, so I scrolled through the menu of feature-length movies. I smiled and chose *The Fugitive* with Harrison Ford.

If you're Boston-born and raised, flying into Logan always feels good. At dawn the bay glistens blue and silver and you can see the furled sails of that beautiful four-master, the USS *Constitution*, better known as "Old Ironsides." The Hancock Tower, cocooned in huge windows and gleaming, jabs majestically up from the skyline, like the Twin Towers once did in New York. I looked down at all that as we circled for a landing, thinking about how this was the place I'd begun my banking career, and the place where I'd probably end it.

I got off the plane, hefted my carry-on, and started heading for Passport Control. There weren't a lot of other passengers around. A sleepy airline employee at the gate counter didn't even look at me, until he saw what I saw. Ambush.

I watched as four uniformed ICE agents came striding over from a darkened hallway. I could feel the stares from the few other passengers around me, but I knew by then what was happening and I just nodded and smiled at the government's hit men.

"Would you come with us, please?" one of them said. It wasn't a request.

We left the ramp area, one ICE guy leading and the others following. We passed into a separate room, with long rows of empty seats and a lady in a crisp white uniform shirt, sitting at a big desk like a Supreme Court judge, sipping coffee and eyeing me like I might be a kiddie-porn peddler. We kept on going, into something like an interrogation room, where they took my bag, laid it on a long table, and told me to sit down. I did.

One of them put his foot up on a chair, like he'd watched too many episodes of Law and Order. His fingers tapped the butt of his sidearm.

"There's a warrant for your arrest, Mr. Birkenfeld. Department of Justice."

"Really?" I said. "I wonder what that's all about."

They looked at each other and sneered. Another one leaned over me.

"Are you carrying more than $10,000 in cash on your person?"

"No," I said. "Credit cards are much lighter."

He didn't like that much, so this time he growled it.

"I'll ask you again. Are you carrying more than $10,000 in cash on your person?"

I cocked my head and gave him my Birkenfeld grin. "Tell me something," I said. "Is English your first language?"

They hauled me out of my chair, spun me around, and slapped the cuffs on me. Then they threw me into a holding cell.

I missed the high school reunion.

# CHAPTER 11

# THE TWILIGHT ZONE

*"I am shocked—shocked—to find that
gambling is going on in here!"*
—*CAPTAIN RENAULT, CASABLANCA*

I'VE NEVER LIKED FLORIDA all that much.

Not that I have anything against Disney World or Mickey Mouse, and Daytona's a fine motor speedway, even though it's not Formula One. Miami can be fun if you like the beaches, bikinis, and Latin nightlife, which I generally do, but it's not Saint-Tropez or Cancún. So, other than some light entertainment, I've always thought of the state as sort of flat, barren, and humid, a place to escape from New England winters when your bones are aching and you're craving a lounge chair and drinks with pastel umbrellas. If you're still relatively young, a visit to Florida can be like a bleak peek at your future: lots of sweet old folks with blue hair, moving slowly. God's waiting room.

But apparently Florida's a great place to arraign an international tax fraud conspirator, even if his place of US residence is in Boston. And apparently Kevin Downing loved it, because he dragged me all the way to Fort Lauderdale to be harangued by a Southern District of Florida judge. Downing could have chosen Boston, or even New York or Washington, DC, but those venues would have been too convenient for me.

When word reached me from Hector and Moran that I'd have to fly down to Florida, on my own dime, just to be formally bitch-slapped, I figured Downing just wanted to make me sweat, which certainly happens the minute you step off a plane in Fort Lauderdale in June. This was a classic case of forum shopping.

Maybe most of this is bitter speculation on my part. But the fact is that Kevin Downing decided that Ground Zero for my case proceedings would be as far away from my residence as he could manage, while still remaining on the Eastern Seaboard. That also meant that with every appearance—and there would be many—personnel from Washington would have to be there too. Perhaps the Department of Justice has a secret mileage program, so when they travel all over the place to prosecute tax criminals, using your tax dollars to do so, they rack up free airline trips, hotel stays, and vacations. At any rate, they spend your money like drunken sailors while claiming they're doing everything they can to save it.

A month had passed since I'd landed in Boston, knowing full well that with Martin Liechti's detainment I probably wouldn't make it to curbside. The Customs and Border Protection guys had kept me at the airport for an hour, then stuffed me like a street perp in the back of a patrol car, driven me over to Winthrop, and locked me up for the night in an old New England jail. It wasn't too bad. I had my own cell and a good book, *Five Years to Freedom*, an incredible true tale by former US Army Special Forces officer James N. Rowe about his imprisonment in a North Vietnamese bamboo cage for five years. It put things in perspective.

In the morning the sheriffs drove me from the local jail in Winthrop over to the federal courthouse in Boston to face my first judge, a "Judge Judy"-type woman with little patience for government bullshit. Boston judges don't go much for drama; they've seen too much real crime in Southie. Downing wasn't there, but he had two of his US attorneys on hand, neither of whom ever disclosed to the judge the fact that I'd come to the States to give further testimony. Downing had also pressured Moran, my attorney that day, not to reveal to the judge that I had come forward to volunteer the information on Swiss banks a year earlier. Downing essentially forbade Moran from revealing the truth of why I had returned from Switzerland: to continue my Senate and SEC meetings to singlehandedly expose the largest tax fraud in the history of the United States. Nope. He was just coming in for a high school reunion. So the DOJ force-fed a blatant lie to a federal judge and presented me as a dangerous international criminal who'd fly the coop the first chance I got.

But the judge wasn't buying it.

"Government," she said to Downing's flunky. "From what I can see here, Mr. Birkenfeld has no prior arrests."

"Your Honor," the DOJ prosecutor sputtered, "he's a major player in a federal tax fraud case. We'd like him held until his arraignment."

"Taxes." The judge hissed the word as if she'd been audited once or twice herself. "You've already got his passport, so he's not going anywhere. And you don't even have an arraignment date set."

"Well, Your Honor . . ."

"You want me to jail him indefinitely?"

"We're looking at only about a month."

"Nonsense!" The judge jabbed a finger at me. "Mr. Birkenfeld, you're released on your own recognizance. Show up again whenever and wherever you're told."

"Yes, ma'am," I said.

"But, Your Honor," the DOJ goon tried one more time.

"Next case!"

And that was that. I recovered my luggage, which I knew had been thoroughly searched. But there was nothing in there to find, other than a few of my favorite cigars and Swiss chocolates. I assumed that Downing's flunkies had also made copies of every piece of paper and all the computer discs in my briefcase, although that didn't matter since I was going to turn over everything anyway. My brother Doug drove me back to his condo in Weymouth.

Doug was already furious with the DOJ, but now my arrest had him mumbling curses and stomping around the condo. He'd been speculating, as I had, that sooner or later Downing would throw the book at me; but the DOJ's flagrant abuse of power compounded by their blatant humiliation tactics made his blood boil. Yet I wasn't humiliated; I was just getting started. I told Doug that I'd planned to meet again with the SEC and the Senate, but now my plans had changed. Downing was pressuring Hector and Moran to deliver me back to the DOJ for a "full debriefing." Maybe he thought the shock of my arrest would have me curled up in a corner, crying. I called my lawyers and told them to set it up. It was time for a face-off.

A few days later I flew down to Washington and strode back into that fine, venerable old building, the one with the expensive drapes covering up exposed sculpture nipples. Rick Moran tagged along, but his head was hung low like a kid whose father keeps telling him, "Don't do it that way," and he'd done it that way anyway. Downing held court in his pristine conference room, with Karen Kelly sitting there like his yappy little Chihuahua, along with an Assistant US Attorney named Jeff Neiman. This guy looked like he'd barely graduated from law school, had gelled black hair and a fresh golf tan, and worked out of the US Attorney's Office, Southern District of Florida. He stood barely over five feet tall and had a disturbingly distracting lisp. His pants were about two inches short, exposing a pair of mismatched socks. It made me think of that character in the classic movie *My Cousin Vinny*, the trial lawyer with the terrible stutter. I didn't figure out what Neiman was doing there until later.

Downing was clearly pissed that I'd appeared before a New England judge who didn't go his way. He'd wanted me locked up so he could sweat me for as long as he pleased, Iranian-style. And here I was, walking around like a free man. He practically pounded the table.

"All right, Birkenfeld. Now we want the names! *All* the names."

"I gave them all to the Senate, and the IRS as well," I said with a shrug. "If you'd given me a subpoena when we asked for it, you could have had them last year."

Jeff Neiman's eyes flickered at Downing. He was probably thinking: *Why didn't you just give him a subpoena?* But he didn't say a word, so right away I knew who was higher up on the totem pole. Downing.

"Well, wise guy," Downing snapped. "We want them *now*."

But it was simply a childish game and I knew it. The DOJ already had all my evidence because the Senate had shared it with every relevant agency. This was about Downing trying to intimidate me by having me arrested and indicted, as if that was the straw that would finally break my back. None of his behavior made sense for a logical, mature criminal justice professional. I was already a whistle-blower, a walk-in, a volunteer, in effect having confessed to my full participation in the illegal activities I'd brought to light. So what more could he possibly come up with? He simply wanted the drama, a show for his acolytes. So I played along, took out a copy of the long, detailed list of Swiss bankers and clients that I'd given to Bob Roach and the Senate Select Committee, and slid it across the table.

"There you go," I said. "The rest of the government already has this, so I guess you can too."

He snatched it away, puffed up, and flicked the papers with a finger as if he'd just broken John Gotti. Meanwhile, I took out my wallet and pulled out my yellow *Get Out of Jail Free* card, the one I'd taken from my flat in Geneva (Exhibit 16). I slid it across the table. Downing, Kelly, and Neiman bent forward and stared at the card.

"So?" I said. "Will this work now?"

All three of them sat there, stunned. If they thought they were going to break me, I'd just shattered their fantasies.

"And by the way," I said, "I have prearranged meetings with the SEC and the Senate, and I intend to honor those commitments."

I thought Downing was going to have a stroke. He banged his chair back, stood up, and yelled, shooting a finger at my face.

"You will *not* meet with, or talk to, anyone from the Senate or the SEC! Is that clear, Birkenfeld?"

My lawyers later advised Carl Levin (senator) and Robert Khuzami (SEC) in writing that with those words, Kevin Downing might have committed not just one, but *two* federal felonies, pointing them to 18 U.S. Code § 1505 which makes it a federal crime to impede, intimidate, or obstruct any witness before a Congressional committee or investigative agency, such as the SEC. Just as Judge Kaplan had said about Downing and the DOJ team in the notorious KPMG case, the very same people who were duty bound to protect the constitutional rights of the American people were instead violating them. Downing was shaping up to be a recidivist.

I just cocked my head at him and smiled. And then I looked over at Jeff Neiman. The baby DA just sat there, immobile and expression-less as a library lion. He'd just witnessed a DOJ prosecutor trying to intimidate a government witness from cooperating with sister federal agencies. In my view, Downing's actions were clearly over the line, but Neiman didn't utter a word. My lawyers subsequently reported this outrage to the DOJ. As far as I know, however, Downing was never dis-ciplined for it. Apparently the KPMG case had taught Kevin Downing nothing about browbeating witnesses, and the rest of his crew were too cowed to open their mouths.

I gathered up my papers and started to leave.

"We'll see you at your arraignment," Downing snapped. "Don't even think about not showing up."

"We'll be there," said Rick. I think those were the first words my lawyer uttered that day, and the last. Words of surrender. We parted ways outside. I had nothing kind to say to him.

On June 19, 2008, I stepped off the plane in Fort Lauderdale and got hit with another blast of heat, appearing before Federal Magis-trate Barry S. Seltzer, Southern District of Florida. Beside me in the steamy courtroom stood Rick Moran, and across the aisle were scowl-ing Downing and his coat-holder, Jeff Neiman. As Seltzer strode out from his chambers to the bench, I knew I'd made the correct deci-sion about entering my plea: *Guilty as charged.* He was white, medium height, middle-aged, and swaggered in his black robes like he was a Supreme Court kingpin. In fact, magistrates are at the bottom of the federal court food chain, like baby judges, and I sensed a Napoleon complex. I'd also read some of Seltzer's "reviews." Apparently he didn't like bankers, as he falsely tried to compare me to Marc Rich[2] in his courtroom—no shortage of civil servant jackasses here. So pleading *not* guilty would have been like red-flagging a bull.

You might be wondering why I entered my confessional plea,

---

2   Marc Rich was a renowned oil trader, indicted for tax evasion and profiteering during the US–Iran oil embargo. He fled to Switzerland to avoid prosecution. Rich's former wife, Denise, funneled millions of dollars to the Clinton Presidential Library and to earlier political campaigns. On the last day of his presidency, Bill Clinton called then–Deputy Attorney General Eric Holder to ask for the DOJ's blessing for Rich's pardon. And the deal was done.

instead of trying to argue my innocence. Well, I wasn't remotely innocent in the eyes of the law, or my own. I'd already submitted tons of evidence attesting to my participation in the whole Swiss scheme, so I knew that fighting the indictment was just going to stoke Downing's and Seltzer's hatred. If I forced this thing to go to trial, Downing would summon his minions and whip their flanks until they convinced a jury that I was another Charles Manson. I wasn't about to give him that license.

I was already focusing down the road on the next stage in the process, my sentencing hearing. It would be at that point that my lawyers could mount a solid case for leniency. After all, Igor Olenicoff had already returned to his real estate empire in California and was joyfully making back the millions he'd had to pay out in fines. He was free as a bird, so why shouldn't I be? The government wouldn't really let Igor ride off into the sunset while locking me up in a federal penitentiary, would they? Soon enough, I reasoned, all of my Swiss bosses would be rounded up and would start talking like scared teenagers busted for pushing weed. When the government finally realized how important my testimony would be at the trials of the Swiss, and that I was not just a whistle-blower but was facilitating the return of hundreds of millions to the American taxpayer, they'd throw in the towel and withdraw the charges. Right?

Kevin Downing sneered throughout the plea hearing, pretty much claiming that I'd committed every imaginable sin short of armed robbery and child abuse. Since I'd already preemptively agreed to a guilty plea, the government had prepared its case document: *United States of America vs. Bradley Birkenfeld*. The "Statement of Facts" at the top of the first page said that all parties agreed that "had this case proceeded to trial, the United States would have proven the following facts beyond a reasonable doubt, and that the following facts are true and correct and are sufficient to support a plea of guilty."

In other words: "This is what the defendant told us he did, but we're going to make it look like we uncovered it all by ourselves."

What followed were six single-spaced pages, including every detail of all my nefarious activities, the Olenicoff gambit, and all the dirty doings of UBS, which was referred to only as "the bank."

But everything on that charge sheet was all the information, verbatim, that I'd laid out in detailed testimony to the Senate, IRS, SEC, and ultimately to the DOJ. Are you getting this? I'd walked in and handed them the keys to the evil kingdom, and now they wanted me hanged for coming up with the keys!

Most of it was focused on Olenicoff. He'd already been convicted, and since I was his confessed facilitator—slam dunk for the DOJ. *We've already bagged the big dog, and now we've got his pimp.* The last line said "The tax loss associated with the conspiracy involving the evasion of income taxes of the approximate $200 million Igor Olenicoff concealed offshore is $7,261,387 million, exclusive of penalties and interest." The clear implication was that I was responsible for that taxpayer loss. But believe me, if I'd been able to take out a checkbook and write them a check on the spot, Downing would have torn it up. He didn't want the truth or compensation; he wanted me punished.

Magistrate Seltzer asked a few perfunctory questions, seemingly just to hear himself talk.

"So, Mr. Birkenfeld. You have a residence in Switzerland. Where?"

"In Zermatt, Your Honor."

"I've been there," he said, as if trying to impress us all with his worldliness. "The town with no cars."

Rick Moran made an attempt to interject something positive.

"Your Honor, Mr. Birkenfeld came in on his own volition."

Seltzer looked at him. "Yes, of course. And I'd like to see his bank account records."

"Well," Moran said, "I'm afraid the Swiss refuse to release those records."

"Ahh," Seltzer sneered. "Just like Marc Rich."

*Now there's an objective comparison,* I thought. *Why not Manuel Noriega or Saddam Hussein?*

Seltzer then instructed us to formalize the plea. On the last page were spaces for all our signatures: Downing's, Neiman's, Moran's, and mine. We passed it around and signed off. Downing scrawled his name with a flourish. I penned mine like the victim of a bad divorce.

Seltzer hardly looked at me as he pushed my papers aside and prepared for his next big case. The courtroom echoed with the sounds of his clerk slamming a date and time stamp on the government's victory. Then Seltzer laced his chubby fingers together and stared me down.

"Guilty plea entered," he growled. "Mr. Birkenfeld, I'm setting your bail at $100,000. Pay it in Boston and appear at Probation. You'll be wearing an ankle monitor. Date of sentencing to be determined." He banged his gavel.

I left and headed back north.

I sat there on the flight to Boston thinking about bail, brooding over the indignity of it. The money wasn't a huge issue, but I'd decided to use a bail bondsman. I knew I wasn't going to be skipping bail or trying to hide somewhere, and I hate losing interest on my own savings. The ankle monitor was going to bug me more, the feeling of being inexorably linked, night and day, to Kevin Downing, as if he'd be sneering over my shoulder. He already had my passport, so where did he think I was going to flee to? Hole in the Wall, Wyoming, like Butch Cassidy?

*He'll probably have it packed with C-4,* I thought, *so if he thinks I'm going to bolt he can use a remote detonator and blow my leg off.*

All through the flight I kept on trying to figure out Downing's psychotic obsession with me, but as we neared Boston I stopped gazing out the window and looked around the cabin. There were a number of well-dressed women on the plane, with fresh tans and full shopping bags.

That suddenly made me think about all the wives of the thousands of Americans holding secret Swiss accounts, and how most of them probably had no idea what their husbands had been doing during all those "business trips" to Zurich and Geneva. I wondered how many of those women had discovered their husbands' philanderings, full-time girlfriends, gambling habits, and stripper addictions, and had filed for divorces and agreed to settlements, having no idea they were ignorant of the many hidden millions that should have been theirs. I was pretty sure that, along with American taxpayers, hundreds of such women had also been screwed by the Swiss, and not in a good way. I was thinking that their divorce lawyers should revisit their settlements, because most of them were surely fraudulent.

———————

As the heat of July settled its steamy skin over Washington, Senator Carl Levin's Permanent Subcommittee on Investigations was in high gear, preparing for their first open hearings on Tax Haven Banks and US Tax Compliance. For many years, in the back halls of Congress, its members had been grumbling about the abuse of American tax regulations by foreign banks, but they hadn't been able to prove it. They were powerful men and women, yet much like a heavy artillery battery with nothing but empty cannons, they'd been impotent. Then I'd showed up with crates of ammunition, and now they were loading up, slamming the breaches, ready to yank the firing cords.

If there's one thing that members of Congress love more than their overblown salaries, endless vacations, free healthcare, and bloated staffs, it's press coverage. As the Committee prepared for its onstage-live debut, they were getting plenty of it. In May, Haig Simonian had published an article in the *Financial Times* about UBS executives imposing an official travel ban and telling their staffs to avoid the United States, because Capitol Hill was finally righteously pissed. Right after that, *The New York Times* had started to dig, with a major piece about wealthy Americans falling under scrutiny as the Department of Justice, IRS, and Senate Select Committee pointed their fingers at UBS.

With my guilty plea down in Florida, Haig then splashed my story all over the financial pages. Just ten days later, the DOJ filed a "John Doe" summons with a federal court, demanding that UBS reveal the names of 19,000 anonymous Americans holding undeclared accounts. Every single material fact contained in that summons had been voluntarily supplied by me to the DOJ, SEC, Senate, and IRS—19,000 names, more than 52,000 accounts, and $20 billion in assets. The DOJ had simply cut, pasted, and taken all the credit. It should have been called the "Bradley Birkenfeld" summons!

UBS, of course, refused the demand, claiming its hands were tied due to Swiss banking secrecy laws. That snubbing really enraged our American lawmakers. Simonian warned in another *Financial Times* article that the Swiss would soon be facing a withering American broadside, and right after that the cannons boomed. The US government petitioned a federal court to force UBS to release all the names, and the judge said "Hell yes" and issued his order. *The New York Times* was now running stories nearly every day. The fire was burning under my ex-bosses' asses, who realized if they didn't somehow comply from their hideout in Switzerland, hundreds of UBS Americas branches might be waking up to federal agents armed with warrants and padlocks.

During that time between my plea down in Florida and the hearings coming up in mid-July, I was in Boston, following the firestorm with a degree of glee. Doug would head off to work at his practice and I'd ensconce myself in "the bunker," a bedroom piled with carefully ordered legal files, stacks of the latest newspapers and magazines, a computer, and my constantly buzzing cell phone. Mostly I talked to my lawyers, even though my faith in them had waned. Plenty of reporters were trying to reach me, but I wisely lay low on that. I knew myself too well, that I'd likely say what was on my mind, especially regarding the DOJ. That wouldn't help me much at my sentencing hearing, a date for which hadn't been set. I like wearing shorts in the summer, so that black ankle monitor hung from my foot like an oversized G-Shock watch. Try taking a shower with one of those on your leg. It was a constant reminder that we're all slaves to the government, but most of us don't have to wear our shackles in public.

On July 3, Paul Hector called me up with some news.

"Brad, Bob Roach just reached out to us. He'd like you to come back down to Washington and help with the Committee's investigation."

"Always happy to help," I said. "Got a date?"

"July 9th."

"I'll be there."

It was a very good sign, or so I thought at the time. The Senate, unlike the DOJ, wasn't pretending that I had no further value. They clearly saw me as the linchpin of their case, the guy who could help them nail the Swiss. Every evening when Doug came home we'd review the day's developments, and he agreed that this bore good tidings.

But it didn't play out the way I was hoping. I met with Roach and one of his investigators. They needed more help in excavating Martin Liechti's role as a UBS kingpin; I was pleased to do the digging and it went well. I headed back home to wait for my invitation to Carl Levin's hearings, but then Hector and Moran called and hit me with the bad news.

"You're not going to appear at the hearings, Brad. They don't want you to testify."

"Why the fuck not?"

"We're not sure, but they said 'no.' We think it's Downing blocking you from testifying."

"Those DOJ cowards are afraid of what I might say."

"Probably so." Hector and Moran sounded all beaten up. "We're sorry."

So Downing must have blocked my appearance at the Senate's open hearings, no doubt claiming it would compromise the DOJ's case. He was right; it would have, because if I'd appeared there would have been a public outcry against putting me in jail. The whole world would have known, in real time, exactly who had exposed all the Swiss Goldfingers, and also that I was about to be tarred and feathered for it. On the other hand, the Committee members were probably relieved. They had no way to control me or tailor my testimony. What if I'd held something back from them before? What if I suddenly turned to Senator John Kerry and said, "By the way, Senator, your bosom buddy so-and-so has an account in Geneva!" It was better for them to let me sit home and watch it all on TV.

Which I did. On July 17, I settled myself on Doug's sofa, sat back, popped open a beer, and flicked on C-SPAN. The big show I'd scripted myself was about to make its "Broadway" debut. Senator Carl Levin, a Michigan Democrat, assumed his seat as Chairman of the Permanent Subcommittee on Investigations. As usual, he was dressed in a plain dark suit and red tie, with his gray hair in a sloppy comb-over and those half-lens reading glasses perched on the tip of his nose. Frankly, I liked the guy—for a senator, that is. He's one of those old-fashioned lawmakers who's always worked in Washington as if he believes he's a servant to the people. To his left sat Norm Coleman, a Republican from Minnesota, much younger than Levin, clean-cut and baby-faced. The two opposing senators worked the stage like a smooth comedy duo without any laughs. Apparently I'd catalyzed a rare bipartisan, cooperative effort.

Levin opened up with a long, carefully prepared statement, which he read from his podium while also checking out his audience over the blades of those glasses, like Ebenezer Scrooge.

"Good morning, everybody. About fifty tax havens operate in the world today. Their twin hallmarks are secrecy and tax avoidance. Some tax havens are little-known places like Andorra and Vanuatu that few Americans have heard of. Others, like Switzerland and Liechtenstein, are notorious for operating behind a ring of secrecy. *Billions* and billions of dollars' worth of US assets find their way into these secrecy tax havens, aided by banks, trust companies, accountants, lawyers, and others. Each year the US Treasury loses up to $100 billion in tax revenues from offshore tax abuses. Tax havens are engaged in economic warfare against the United States and against honest, hardworking American taxpayers."

Levin then went on to say that during the course of the proceedings, the Committee would be exposing the dirty deeds of two banks, Liechtenstein's LGT and Switzerland's UBS AG. However, he stated that while UBS officials had agreed to give testimony, LGT had refused to cooperate. Apparently LGT also had a whistle-blower, who'd secretly shipped off 12,000 pages of evidence to the US government in February 2008, four months *after* I'd first given mine to the Committee. But that whistle-blower couldn't be present, because he was now on Liechtenstein's most-wanted criminal list, had gone into the US Witness Protection Program, and had a $10 million price on his head! Levin said he'd be making a brief appearance, but only via a recorded interview with Bob Roach, concealed in shadow. His life was in danger.

"Dumbasses," I spat at the TV. "You could have had me right there in the flesh!"

"We have also managed," Levin said, "to pierce some of the layers of Swiss secrecy that for too long have made Switzerland the place to bank for people with something to hide."

"*You* pierced it? I flayed it open, and you guys just held out your cups!"

"In late 2007," Levin continued, "the Subcommittee took the deposition of Bradley Birkenfeld, who worked for more than twelve years as a private banker in Switzerland, including four years at the Geneva office of UBS . . ."

*Here we go. My time to finally shine.*

"In 2008, Mr. Birkenfeld was charged and pled guilty to conspiring with a US citizen, Igor Olenicoff, to defraud the IRS of $7.2 million in taxes owed on $200 million of assets hidden in secret accounts in Switzerland and Liechtenstein . . ."

I nearly threw my beer at the screen. "That's how you debut your star informant? What the fuck? How about 'Mr. Birkenfeld bravely came forward of his own volition, taking extreme risks, and gave us the reams of evidence without which we'd never be having these proceedings'?" I was grinding my teeth as Levin went on.

"In connection with this prosecution, the United States also detained, as a material witness, a senior UBS private banking official from Switzerland, Martin Liechti, then traveling on business in Florida. These enforcement actions appear to represent the first time that the United States has criminally prosecuted a Swiss banker for helping a US taxpayer evade US taxes. And Mr. Liechti is here today. I want to express my appreciation to the Justice Department and to the US Attorney for the Southern District of Florida for making him available."

Well, that made me feel a little bit better. Martin was going to be in the hot seat and I'd get to watch him squirm. Hearing him confess might almost make up for my public flogging.

Levin carried on with a long litany of all the wild and crazy schemes used by Swiss bankers to defraud the American government. It was clear to me that Bob Roach and his team had simply summarized all of my evidence into a courtroom-style drama that their boss could read out like a brilliant prosecutor. Then he wrapped up his opening statement with the news of another groundbreaking legislative bill that would subsequently solve all these problems, the "Stop Tax Haven Abuse Act." It was cosponsored by Levin, Coleman, and Senator Barack Obama.

But Obama, who was allegedly very concerned about all those poor Americans being taken advantage of by sneering Swiss criminals, hadn't shown up at the hearings. In fact, Senator Obama hadn't attended a single meeting of the Committee, of which he was a member! He was on the stump all over the country, racing down the home stretch to become America's first black president. Appearing on the Committee's dais might also have proved a bit sticky, since one of Obama's major supporters, and favorite golf partner, was Robert Wolf, *Chairman of UBS Americas*. In fact, the fifth-largest bundled money contributors to Obama's presidential campaign were UBS Americas employees. At the time, no one knew very much about Barack Obama, except that he was young, hip, eloquent, and the Generation X Democrats' greatest hope. When Senator Coleman took the mike and laid into Swiss tax abuse, he clearly didn't know much about Obama's buddies either.

"To be clear," Coleman said, "our focus is on UBS's operations out of Switzerland. UBS has a large number of personnel based here in the United States, and they, like us, must be surely appalled at what the Subcommittee has uncovered."

*Appalled? They were aiding and abetting it, numb-nuts!*

"But there is a fundamental question that must be asked of UBS," Coleman posed. "And that is, when you are sending Swiss bankers, twenty UBS bankers taking over three hundred trips since 2003, somebody in America has to know what is going on . . . this kind of activity in this country cannot simply have occurred without folks here intentionally turning a blind eye. . . . I would sure like to find out what the folks in America knew about these transactions."

"If you do try to really find out," I scoffed, "you'll lose that cushy job of yours. Look around that chamber. Half the politicians around you will be calling their accountants and attorneys at lunch today, screaming 'get me amnesty'!"

Finally, it was time to talk to the witnesses, the first of whom made me sick to my stomach: Kevin O'Connor, Associate Attorney General, Department of Justice, a big guy with a bulldog face and close-cropped black hair. He was Kevin Downing's boss, and no doubt the guy who'd been giving Downing his marching orders. Next to him sat Douglas Shulman, Commissioner of the IRS, a slim dude with a trembling demeanor who looked exactly like what he was, an accountant. Both of them were hunched forward and wound tight, as if unsure whether they might get a beating from Levin, who thanked them for coming, asked them to stand and raise their right hands, and swore them in.

Shulman presented his statement, which included all the magnificent techniques the IRS would be using to pursue American tax-evaders, including the Qualified Intermediary Agreement (which UBS had circumvented time and again), and the John Doe Summons (which so far UBS had thumbed its nose at). Then he mentioned folks like me and my ears pricked up.

"The final and very important tool that I will mention this morning is informants," said Shulman. "Informants have been valuable sources of information for IRS civil and criminal investigations into offshore tax evasion. With the new whistle-blower standards that reward informants, we are hopeful that we will get additional input on potential violations."

He was talking about me, and inviting anyone else like me who might be out there to come forward and, if their information was valuable, perhaps be handsomely rewarded by the IRS. The irony was that he was sitting next to one of the biggest haters of informants in Washington. Elbow to elbow, one wanted to give a whistle-blower a crown, and the other wanted to take his head off.

*Washington, DC.*

When Kevin O'Connor got his turn, I actually laughed out loud. I'd never seen him in person or heard him speak before, and for a guy who looked like Sean Hannity's beefy big brother, he had a voice like a squeaky old lady. O'Connor told the chairman how wonderful his Committee was, and then listed all the fabulous investigative work being done by the DOJ's Tax Division in conjunction with the IRS. Levin's staffers put up a big chart listing all of UBS's techniques for bringing in Net New Money and making sure no one found out who it belonged to. When he asked O'Connor if he'd ever seen these things before, O'Connor answered, "Yes, because Bradley Birkenfeld told us about them."

*Thanks, Dick Tracy. So why do you want me in prison?*

Senator Coleman then uttered something dumbfounding. "We've got to put a stop to this!" It was as if, until that morning, he'd never heard a word about secret Swiss numbered accounts and had suddenly discovered that American citizens were actually using them!

Then all eyes turned to watch as Senator John Kerry walked into the chamber and took a seat on the dais. Kerry wasn't a member of the Committee, so he thanked Levin for allowing him to "sit in," and then he fawned for a while over their very important investigation into secret Swiss banking. I shook my head and hissed out loud, "Jesus Christ, if they only knew."

Just four years before, I'd sat in John Kerry's office, having a one-on-one with the senator just after he lost the 2004 presidential election to George Bush. He wanted to thank me for the massive fund-raising I'd done for his campaign. That's right; I'd attended two of his fund-raisers, in his Nantucket and Georgetown homes, and then I'd rustled up half a million dollars for him in Switzerland and contributed money myself. The guy who'd brought me into the senator's inner circle was Jack Manning (Exhibit 11), Kerry's best friend and CEO of Boston Capital, a mega real estate firm and fifth-largest owner of apartments in the United States (147,000 apartments in forty-eight states). Manning, whose net worth is $1.8 billion (Forbes 400 list), is a huge Democrat fund-raiser and had been a regular guest at the Clinton White House. As a matter of fact, Manning had once made fund-raising history by hosting Bill Clinton and Al Gore at a $25,000-per-person event at his Boston mansion in 1998, together, on the *same* evening. At the time they were the sitting president and vice president, a huge "no fucking way" for the Secret Service. But Manning had pulled it off.

Now, four years later, I was nearly pissing myself as I watched Kerry opine in his sober tones about the damages done to the American taxpayer.

Kerry went on, in his self-aggrandizing way, to recall his time on the Senate Banking Committee, during which he'd led investigations into the notorious Bahamas bank BCCI, which was hiding money for Panamanian dictator Manuel Noriega and an up-and-coming jihadi named Osama bin Laden. "We also passed some amendments in the Banking Committee that came to be known as the Kerry Amendments, which required transparency in reporting . . ."

Ah, yes, the "Kerry Amendments." He was there to talk about himself, and probably to make sure things didn't get out of hand. Unbelievably, he then politely asked O'Connor and Shulman why the DOJ and the IRS hadn't been doing a better job of catching these international banking thieves! Really?

Eventually Kerry ran out of gas. He'd swooped in, grabbed the limelight, acted like Batman saving the day, and then he was gone. Senator Levin then had his staff present the recorded interview with the LGT whistle-blower, now living in a witness protection program under an assumed name. The guy was in silhouette on a huge TV monitor, but he clearly had a completely bald head, Dumbo ears, was wearing glasses, and spoke with a very distinctive Liechtenstein Swiss-German accent. I smacked my forehead. "Jesus! If any of this guy's new neighbors are watching this, they'll know right away exactly who he is!" I was glad I hadn't tried for any anonymous informant deal. I wouldn't trust the Justice Department to protect my cat, if I had one.

Levin then trotted out a pair of indicted Americans who'd held secret accounts with LGT. Both men refused to answer any questions, claiming their Fifth Amendment constitutional rights. The Committee already knew they weren't going to cooperate, so why drag them out in public? It was all for show. "See what badasses we are?"

Finally Senator Levin called Martin Liechti up to the witness table, along with his attorney. I felt this strange wave of relief flooding up through my chest. Here, at last, they were going to publicly rip one of my arrogant UBS managers into little tiny pieces, make him pay for running this international craps game and cleaning the table of US taxpayer money. Liechti looked a little pale in his plain gray suit, even though he'd been sitting around a five-star pool at the

Ritz-Carlton Hotel in Miami. He stood up to be sworn in, sat down again, and . . .

Pled the Fifth!

"Mr. Chairman, on advice of my counsel, I assert my rights under the Fifth Amendment to the US Constitution, and I respectfully decline to answer your questions."

What the fuck? Liechti wasn't going to cooperate? He wasn't going to talk? The DOJ had been detaining him for four months in a luxury suite, supposedly so they could squeeze the secrets out of him and deliver him like a birthday present to this noble body of lawmakers. And, just to make certain that he'd sing like a bird for Levin, as we learned years later, Liechti and the DOJ entered into a secret nonprosecution agreement (NPA) two weeks prior to the Congressional hearing (Document 4). The NPA required Liechti to cooperate and answer all questions put to him by the government as a condition to avoid prosecution. Simple, right?

Well, guess what? *Levin and the Committee didn't know about that secret DOJ deal.* Liechti sat there and arrogantly pled the Fifth, and Levin shrugged and dismissed him as an uncooperative witness!

Kevin O'Connor didn't utter a single word of protest. Kevin Downing, who was sitting behind his boss, didn't even flinch. They both knew they'd gotten Liechti's sworn promise to talk, but when he refused, no one from the DOJ batted an eyelash!

I was stunned, and the rest of it was just a blur. UBS delivered a single witness, the bank's brand new Chief Financial Officer, Mark Branson, who fell all over himself promising that the bank hadn't realized what terrible deeds it was doing, and that going forward nothing like it would ever happen again, and that of course UBS would fully cooperate with the US Congress and the Justice Department (my ass). *Fully cooperate? Really? Your top dog just refused to cooperate and pled the Fifth in an open Senate hearing, you lying weasel!* Branson had obviously been chosen by the bank to appear because he'd spent his career in Japan, and could innocently claim that he hadn't been part of these practices in Switzerland. He was also a Brit, so he didn't have that evil Swiss-German accent. He was squeaky clean.

"I am here to make it absolutely clear that UBS regrets any

compliance failures that may have occurred." Yeah, it is called complying with the law!

*May have occurred?* Branson then admitted to every piece of damning evidence I'd provided, but claimed that UBS management hadn't known about any of it, and was genuinely "appalled"! When asked to explain an Exhibit, which happened to be the UBS instruction manual on countersurveillance techniques I'd provided, he claimed (under oath) that the training was only concerned with maintaining the anonymity of account holders, in compliance with Swiss law. Senator Coleman asked him, "Since UBS has more than 30,000 UBS Americas employees, who in the United States branches was aware of the bank's illegal practices here?"

"I have no knowledge that anyone in the United States was aware."

*Christ!* Right away I had flashbacks to my parties in Long Island and Fisher Island with Richard Ziegelasch, Executive Director at UBS International, based in New York City. Martin Liechti had sent me directly to Ziegelasch to drum up more rich American clients to deposit their assets in Switzerland, because he hobnobbed with the the richest of the rich. Ziegelasch was the one who'd arranged my private introduction to some of them. *No one in the United States knew?*

I realized that nothing was going to happen here, at least not in any public forum. Branson was there to serve as UBS's fall guy and the Senate's whipping boy. It was all a political dog-and-pony show. "Vote for us! See how hard we're working for you?"

Levin ended the hearings, promising that US lawmakers were going to get to the bottom of all this, and smacked his gavel.

A week later Levin's Committee held another grueling C-SPAN session. I watched it, but it was more of the same. UBS promised to negotiate in good faith regarding turning over the names of its 19,000 American account holders. The senators said, "Thank you very much."

I said, "You naive idiots. You're going to have to take a chainsaw to UBS's balls before they'll even squeak out one name."

I still couldn't fathom why they'd let Liechti off the hook. I thought that maybe because he'd pled the Fifth in public O'Connor and Downing simply hadn't wanted to stand up in those hallowed Congressional chambers and scream, "We object! Make him talk or let's put him in jail!"

Yeah, that had to be it. They still had him in custody down in Miami. Now they were going to throw the book at him, just like they'd thrown it at me. At least if I had to go to prison, he would too. Maybe we'd be cell mates, and then I could laugh in his face every day while we both made license plates.

In August Congress took their yearly month-long recess so they could all go off to play golf and sail. It's a tradition that harkens back to long before Edison invented the lightbulb, when Washington was just too hot to get any of the people's work done. Never mind that we've had air-conditioning now since the mid–twentieth century.

When Congress isn't in session, it's the perfect time to stab them in the back. They're not around to gather up their minions and fight the good fight. So August was the perfect time for Kevin Downing to arrange for Martin Liechti to be quietly released, two weeks after the hearing. Liechti was told to keep his mouth shut and then put on a plane back to Switzerland. Nobody knew. It didn't even make the papers.

But *I* knew, because I still had good friends in Switzerland. I called my lawyers and told them to call that idiot Downing and demand to know why he'd just let the mastermind of Swiss corruption go home.

Rick Moran got Downing on the phone.

"You just let Martin Liechti go free? He's the key to this investigation. He's also the key to Brad's case! Why, for God's sake?"

Downing just laughed and hung up.

# CHAPTER 12

## BLOWUP

*"Money plays the largest part in determining
the course of history."*
—KARL MARX, GERMAN ECONOMIST

ON THE HEELS OF that summer, the storm clouds began to gather.

Across the world's financial markets, autumn 2008 was hurricane season. I could almost hear a rumble like rolling thunder. It was the sound of a tsunami, sucking the breath from the stock markets, crushing the real estate bubble into bursting, and heading straight for the towers of Swiss secret banking.

Most of the American media was focused on a different drama, a clash of titans. Presidential hopefuls Barack Obama and John McCain were battling it out in a bloody arena, with Joe Biden and Sarah Palin hunched in the ring corners, icing their fighters' black-and-blue eyes and shoving them back out for yet another round. That was the fodder for the masses, the stuff that brought in millions in television advertising money between rounds of breathless debates. So the public didn't really notice the earthquake punching cracks in the underground vaults in Zurich and Geneva. But those of us who'd spent our professional careers in international banking certainly did. And one ex–Swiss banker in particular, a convicted scapegoat who'd set off the first explosion, paid little mind to anything else.

Carl Levin and his fellow senators on the Permanent Subcommittee on Investigations were on the march. They were joined by powerful bipartisan friends, Claire McCaskill, Tom Coburn, and others, who all realized that the loss of millions in taxpayer revenues was something with which their constituents could identify, since so many of them were losing their homes. Just behind the Senate, the IRS smelled blood in the water, and they were hungrier than ever for convictions and fines. At the back of the pack, the Department of Justice had no choice but to follow along, while yapping as loud as they possibly could so that someone might think they were leading.

In November, Raoul Weil, my former überboss and head of UBS Global Wealth Management, was indicted by a grand jury in Florida for aiding and abetting American tax abusers. Weil just shrugged it off, confident that the Swiss government would never respond to American demands for his extradition. After all, if Switzerland started turning over its biggest bankers, there'd be no one left to run the casino. But I knew Raoul, and I knew he was an arrogant son of a bitch, and that sooner or later he'd find himself ensnared somewhere like Martin Liechti had. Maybe this time the DOJ would have no choice but to put him on trial.

Mark Branson, the UBS Chief Financial Officer who'd testified under oath before Levin's committee and had sworn to cooperate with the "John Doe" summons, had gone back to Switzerland and apparently forgotten his promise. Doug Shulman, the Commissioner of the IRS, was still fairly new in his position, an appointment that generally runs for five years, and he intended to keep his position. He didn't look like a hard-ass, but looks can be deceiving. In short order the IRS opened full-throttle in its lawsuit against UBS in a Florida District Court, demanding the release of the 19,000 names of American secret account holders, and this time they won. As we all know too well, the IRS has frightening powers. When it sues a major financial institution that then fails to cooperate, that institution often finds itself mortally wounded—privileges revoked, accounts frozen, fines levied each day in the millions of dollars—and thus unable to operate. At UBS headquarters in Zurich, Geneva, and Lugano, my former bosses were pissing down their legs.

During that time I was back in Boston, planning my next moves with Doug. I took a long hard look at the progression of events since I'd first come forward to American authorities, and the scorecard on my side came up short. I'd taken my case to the Department of Justice, and now I was wearing an ankle monitor, virtually under house arrest, and awaiting a verdict which, given my strokes of luck so far, would likely include a prison term. The Senate had taken my evidence, then used it to build the biggest case against Swiss bank secrecy in history. But then they'd treated me like a pariah, kept me in the back room like some pregnant teenage daughter of a *Father Knows Best* family in the 1950s.

You might think this next part is strange, especially given my ugly experience with State Street Bank, but I no longer trusted anyone in Washington and felt much safer in Boston. It felt to me like the old colonial days, when the seat of power in Washington was still infested with powder-wigged Brits and Boston was the center of rebels and tea parties. I was no longer going to commute to the capital, running back and forth with my hat in my hand, trusting men with questionable talents who'd spent their professional careers in that culture. I fired Paul Hector and Rick Moran. It was something I should have done long before.

Then I did some extensive research and came up with a venerable Boston firm, Todd & Weld, LLP, and hired one of their most experienced attorneys, David Meier, to pick up my case. Meier had served for twelve years as the Chief of Homicide in the Suffolk County District Attorney's Office and had a reputation for defending the wrongfully accused. In 2007 he'd been recognized as "Lawyer of the Year" by *Massachusetts Lawyers Weekly*. He seemed battle-hardened, knowledgeable, enthusiastic, and had no federal government connections. A Boston guy unsullied by Washington. David Meier contacted the DOJ and informed them that going forward, he'd be handling my case. Kevin Downing responded courteously with something like "Who the hell are *you?*"

Downing didn't like the fact that I'd fired Hector and Moran, who he had been able to control. Seems I had a lot of nerve hiring some attorney in Boston who he couldn't just summon over to the Department of Justice for a browbeating whenever he pleased. Meier ignored Downing's seethe and pressed for a confirmation date for my sentencing down in Florida.

"I want it delayed," Downing snapped. "I've petitioned the Court for a continuance, and I suggest you assent to that. Otherwise you can forget about me submitting any motions for leniency."

That wasn't the first time Downing stalled my sentencing hearing. He'd already done it with Hector and Moran, and he'd do it again, *three* more times over the course of a year, for no other reason than to keep me sitting on razor blades. Think this country has ironclad laws designed to protect the rights of American citizens? It does, but only *you* have to abide by them, while the lawmakers abuse the hell out of them.

However, while Downing was getting great satisfaction from letting me twist in the wind, he didn't realize that he was actually doing me a *huge* favor. I had nothing to do but to work on my case, so I turned my attention to finding out more about the IRS whistle-blower award program. UBS hadn't yet been forced by the government to pay any penalties or fines, but I felt in my bones it was coming. A number of well-intentioned nonprofit support groups had reached out to me, such as POGO, the Project on Government Oversight, and GAP, the Government Accountability Project. But while they railed against my indictment and had thousands of people signing petitions in my favor, they had no "teeth" when it came to turning my situation around, or maybe getting me paid for my efforts on the back end.

That's when I discovered the National Whistleblower Center in Washington. It was a small organization yet staffed by talented, knowledgeable folks who firmly believed in protecting informants like myself. The NWC's Executive Director was Stephen M. Kohn, also a law partner at Kohn, Kohn & Colapinto, cited as the best whistle-blower firm inside the Beltway. Kohn had represented Linda Tripp, the Department of Defense employee who'd outed Bill Clinton and Monica Lewinsky. Tripp had suffered withering retaliations, sued the government, and won a $595,000 award plus full reinstatement to her previous position, with retroactive benefits. Kohn was obviously my guy.

Steve flew up to Boston and we met at the Langham Hotel. I liked him right away; he was diminutive, intense, with curly gray hair, wire-rimmed glasses, and a steel-trap intellect. He already had years of experience representing whistle-blowers, testifying in Congress, and writing several comprehensive books on the subject, but he understood that I was talking about something unprecedented. Then another talented lawyer who Steve had recommended join our team, Dean Zerbe, flew up and we met at the Hilton Hotel at the airport. Dean was a real savvy tax lawyer and was the author of the whistle-blowing law in the Senate Finance Committee. If you want to ask about the Constitution, ask Thomas Jefferson. If you want to know about the IRS whistle-blowing law, ask Dean Zerbe. Dean was stunned when I showed up with all the evidence of my whistle-blowing history, filed, tabbed, and supported by reams of UBS documents.

"This is incredible! I can't believe all this stuff!" Dean gasped. "We won't even have to go through the usual hours of client interviews. How'd you do all this, Brad?"

I pulled up my pant leg and showed him my black ankle monitor. "Well, I've had a lot of time on my hands."

A few days later, Steve and Dean made the trip together and we met once more, at the Boston Harbor Hotel. I signed a retainer agreement.

"It's going to be a battle," said Steve. "But you're well armed, Brad."

"And dangerous." I smiled.

Steve Kohn and Dean Zerbe fired their first shot at the Senate, filing for a transcript copy of my depositions. They needed that transcript in order to demonstrate to the IRS just how much I'd given the government. But Bob Roach refused the request, citing Committee rules. Really? My own words were being withheld, from me? It would take six more months of wrangling before Steve and Dean were finally allowed to review the transcript, in a secure room on

Capitol Hill. It confirmed everything I'd told them, but they weren't allowed to make copies.

Still, I was starting to feel optimistic. Not so much about my sentencing, which had been delayed yet again by Downing, but about someday getting some sort of financial retribution for everything I'd had to endure. Every newspaper and blog that covered my case railed against the injustices done and slammed the government for trying to persecute their own best informant. None of it had any impact, but I knew it would help Steve and Dean's case. As the New Year's bells rang once again and I hobbled into 2009, I felt a little less shackled, ready for some hope and change.

Yet those platitudes I dreamed about were mine, rather than that of America's new president. Certainly, just like most Americans who'd learned their history and lived through stormy times of racial oppression, I sincerely wished Barack Obama the best of everything, and hoped he'd raise our country up to a new plateau of harmony and fine ideals. But at the same time, like most Americans who'd been burned before by the campaign promises of politicians, my attitude was wait and see. I was sort of like a cop who's seen too much blood and has lost his faith in humanity. As an international banker I'd seen too much corruption and abuse of wealth to have much faith left in my leaders. I'd given campaign contributions to politicians of every stripe; not because I believed the bullshit they were selling, but because they'd then introduce me to their wealthy friends. It had worked every time, and I'd come to view politics as the "cake" that's fed to the masses, while behind our backs the deals are already done. So while I liked the new president's promises—superb universal healthcare, racial harmony, no more fighting other people's endless wars—I figured he'd renege on half of it and screw the rest up. He did.

Then there was that other small item, Obama's choice for a new Attorney General. Bush's Attorney General, Alberto Gonzales, had been replaced by Michael Mukasey after Gonzales was accused of "politicizing" the DOJ and using it to punish George Bush's enemies. Now Mukasey was out; Eric Holder was in, and he'd turn out to be the biggest "politicizer" the Department had ever had. The new AG was also the guy who'd recommended the pardon of Marc Rich, the billionaire oil king who'd screwed the United States out of tons of tax revenue (ironically Rich's attorney, Bob Tomajan, had $25 million in a Swiss secret numbered account at UBS in Zurich). And just prior to his new gig, Holder had been an extremely well-paid lawyer for UBS. So Kevin Downing had a new boss who wasn't likely to love me. Not much hope for a change there.

Boston can be a bitch in the winter, but I like it; always have. After all, I was raised in that area and had spent my winters on hockey rinks and ski slopes, so the bitter winds slicing through the city's concrete canyons and the piles of dirty snow don't move me much. Doug didn't have a fireplace in his condo, but I was warmed by the news of firecrackers going off all over the finance world, especially since I'd lit the fuse.

That grand jury down in Florida that had indicted Raoul Weil had been tapping their feet since November, waiting for the Swiss to show some good faith and turn him over. I knew that wasn't going to happen, and eventually they figured it out too. On January 14, 2009, the presiding pissed-off judge declared Weil a "fugitive from American justice." Problem was, Weil hadn't set foot in the States during his recent tenure with UBS, and he wasn't likely to show up now for a vacation at Graceland. However, when the United States says it's seeking an international banker for high crimes and misdemeanors, INTERPOL, the International Criminal Police Organization, takes notice. Weil was eventually arrested in Italy and tried in a federal court in Florida in the fall of 2015. Despite Martin Liechti's testimony that Weil knew that thousands of accounts didn't comply with US tax law, and UBS' own admissions, Weil was acquitted of all charges. The DOJ never called me to testify! Then, in June 2016, French prosecutors announced that they are seeking to try UBS and Weil for tax evasion.

Maybe that was a big red flag for UBS, because just four days later the bank threw up its hands under withering fire from the US Congress. UBS entered into a deferred prosecution agreement with the DOJ, admitted to "certain conduct," and agreed to pay the US government $780 million in fines. How they came up with that figure, and why the Florida judge agreed to it so quickly, no one will ever really know; but I knew it was only a symbolic wrist-slap. The DPA clearly stated that for the eight-year period from 2000 to 2007, UBS had made $200 million per year from its North American secret accounts, a total of $1.6 billon! And just remember that UBS had approximately $20 *billion* in American account holder cash and securities. Even if that huge amount had all been locked up in a mom-and-pop savings account in Rhode Island, the interest would have been a lot more than what they agreed to pay. Ironically, it would turn out later that the fine was based only on the amounts that I had been able to prove they'd scammed! Still, at least it was something. The US government accepted the terms and got ready to cash a check and take the credit. UBS thought they were off the hook.

Then, bam! The very next day the IRS slammed UBS with yet another motion to enforce the "John Doe" summons and make them turn over the 19,000 names. Maybe UBS had thought their $780 million payout would make it all go away. Wrong. Eric Holder might be the new president's stooge, but Doug Shulman at the IRS had been appointed by George Bush. Seems he was taking his job seriously, and he had full public and Congressional support.

About a week after that, Marcel Rohner, the Chief Executive Officer of UBS, handed in his resignation. UBS announced that Rohner was "retiring," at the tender age of forty-four, but it was obvious he'd been forced to walk the plank. It was February 26, the day of my own forty-fourth birthday, and I couldn't have gotten a better gift! Doug and I opened a bottle of champagne. It went down nicely with my birthday cake and a box of Swiss chocolates.

On March 2, Eric Holder received a distinguished visitor in his Washington headquarters. Eveline Widmer-Schlumpf, Switzerland's Minister of Justice and Police, had jetted over to Washington with her hair on fire. The US Senate Permanent Subcommittee on Investigations, having finally cracked the spine of UBS, had turned its sights on over a dozen other Swiss banks. First on the list was Credit Suisse, where I'd begun my career in private banking; the Senate wanted unconditional surrender. Widmer-Schlumpf, Holder's counterpart in Switzerland, said she only sought "fair and equal treatment" of all the Swiss banks currently under assault. She was begging for mercy. The Department of Justice declined to discuss their boss's response, but apparently Holder told her that more Swiss heads would have to roll. She went home with her tail between her legs.

Two days later the chairman of the board of UBS handed in his resignation. It was Peter Kurer, the man who'd battled me over my bonus, dismissed my UBS whistle-blower complaints, and shit-canned the entire internal investigation. After that he'd risen to the top of the heap, and now he was out on the street. Swiss banking was quickly becoming a target-rich environment.

On that very same day, Senator Carl Levin opened a second round of televised Permanent Subcommittee hearings. Beside him on that long curving dais were Senators Claire McCaskill of Missouri and Tom Coburn of Oklahoma. The government's witnesses were IRS Commissioner Doug Shulman and John A. DiCicco, the Acting Assistant Attorney General of the Tax Department at the US Department of Justice. DiCicco looked just like the hapless civil servant he was: clueless about the facts, adorned in an oversized cheap suit, and he spoke in a mundane, monotonous voice. DOJ's finest.

Nowhere to be seen was Kevin O'Connor, who'd been Kevin Downing's boss. Turns out he had left his job as Associate Attorney General of the United States, the number-three position in the DOJ, to go work as a partner with Rudolph (Rudy) Giuliani—former mayor of New York—at the New York offices of Bracewell & Giuliani, a firm with $325 million in revenues. Of course, the Abdul Aziz Abbas connection jumped to the forefront of my mind. I had informed Downing and the DOJ two years earlier that Abbas was a friend of Giuliani's.

This time Levin was so pissed off you could almost see the steam hissing out of his ears. UBS had been cornered by the IRS, grudgingly admitted its wrongdoings, signed a Deferred Prosecution Agreement, and promised to pay $780 million in fines. However, even though the IRS had then pursued UBS to force them to reveal the names of 19,000 American account holders, and the bank had promised to do that, they were now retreating under cover of "Swiss banking laws."

But what really enraged Levin was that Mark Branson, during

the summer session, had offered up that figure of 19,000 names as a firm and final number. As Levin and his staff had already discovered from my testimony, the real number was more like *52,000* American accounts! Worse than that, since August, six months earlier, when UBS had promised to cooperate by revealing a "substantial number" of its US account holders, the bank had turned over a mere *twelve* names!

It was a shit show. I watched with my feet propped up and a bowl of popcorn on my lap. The gloves were off, and Levin, McCaskill, and Coburn ripped into Branson for now behaving exactly like what he really was: an arrogant stooge and apologist for UBS. Levin actually said, "The only conviction so far in this matter is that of Bradley Birkenfeld, the informant!"

Branson ignored that and deflected ninety percent of the senators' questions about UBS's crimes against America, claiming, "I have no knowledge of that, since I've only been in this position for a year." How convenient for UBS to send an until-then Japan-based employee to answer to Congress for Swiss activities he was not familiar with. Then he stated that the bank would pay the agreed-upon fines, but it wasn't going to turn over even one more name unless compelled to do so by the Swiss government. "The payment of fines is a legal matter that has been resolved in court," Branson sneered. "In regard to the account holder names, that is a matter of negotiations between statesmen." UBS was praying its government, embracing Swiss privacy laws, would save its hide from disclosing an embarrassing list of client names.

I thought Levin was going to take his gavel, spin it across the room, and embed it in Branson's head. After four hours of ugly exchanges, Levin finally adjourned with barely polite formalities, but the message was clear: "We're going to burn your Swiss asses. Now get the hell out of my chambers!"

I hadn't enjoyed a courtroom drama that much since *A Few Good Men*.

As with every great courtroom drama, the most fascinating aspects were those going on behind the scenes: the heated arguments between battling attorneys, the blood-pounding pressures on defendants and victims, and the sub rosa deals. The Swiss secret banking crime and corruption scandal was a blazing firestorm across the world's financial markets, but it was merely the surface. Way down below, powerful people were cooking the books.

On March 6, newly minted US Secretary of State Hillary Rodham Clinton arrived in Zurich for secret talks with her counterpart, Swiss Foreign Minister Micheline Calmy-Rey. Ms. Calmy-Rey was no doubt agitated, as Switzerland's two largest banks, UBS and Credit Suisse, were under assault by American authorities. UBS, with more than 80,000 employees worldwide and hundreds of billions in assets, was hemorrhaging value like a freshly slaughtered steer. The bank's stock had just hit an all-time rock bottom of $7.45 per share, free-falling ninety percent, and it was staring at a charge-off of $53 billion. Calmy-Rey begged her power-sister Clinton for a break. If UBS had to cough up 19,000 American account holders, the rest of its clients would jump ship and drag Switzerland's largest bank to destruction.

Apparently Secretary Clinton had a few creative ideas. Her new boss, President Barack Obama, had made a campaign promise to at last close down the terrorist prison christened by George Bush at Guantánamo Bay, Cuba. Clinton, ever the political expedient, probably didn't express how much she despised Obama (she and her husband had made a devil's deal; Bill would support Obama's candidacy, and Obama would make Hillary Secretary of State, and from that power perch she'd make her hard drive for the presidency, whenever Obama finally got sick of the job). Secretary Clinton suggested perhaps Micheline would consider accepting some low-level terrorists from Guantánamo and resettling them quietly in Switzerland. Just a couple of Chinese Uighur Muslim fellows captured in Afghanistan— basically harmless. Oh, and Obama was also interested in opening up a secret dialogue with the Ayatollahs of Iran. Since the United States had no embassy in Tehran, US interests were represented there by none other than the Swiss. Perhaps the Swiss could put some pressure on Tehran to release an imprisoned American citizen, and in turn Obama would start work right away on denuding those silly sanctions imposed by the Bushies over Iran's nuclear ambitions.

After all, everyone deserved a fair shot at energy independence. The Israelis would freak, but Obama, being the admiring son of a rabid anti-colonialist, didn't much care for them anyway, and he had all those left-leaning American Jews in his pocket. Clinton suggested to Calmy-Rey that those small gestures weren't too much to ask in return for a little leniency on this whole UBS scandal (at the direct expense of the American taxpayers).

Micheline Calmy-Rey promised to think about it, and Hillary Clinton flew off to her next international television appearance. Lo and behold, shortly thereafter, a pair of Chinese Uighurs found themselves blinking in the Swiss springtime sun. A couple of months later, an American hostage in Iran, Roxana Saberi, found herself doing the same in New York. Miraculously, the IRS and Department of Justice gave UBS a stay of execution, while Calmy-Rey informed UBS that they'd better come up with some American account holder names—*lots* of names—because Hillary Clinton had just saved their asses.

I wonder if Clinton was concerned that some of her billionaire friends might get burned, if and when UBS surrendered.

None of us American taxpayers had a hint of what was going on at the time. Ms. Clinton's under-the-table deals with the Swiss wouldn't come out until another whistle-blower, Bradley Manning, dumped thousands of classified US government emails and cables all over the Internet. Included among those were just a few State Department after-action reports about Clinton's quid pro quo with UBS and the Swiss. Whatever further discussions on the subject she had with Calmy-Rey were gone forever, because she'd sent them from her own private email server at home, and then had them destroyed. *Nothing to see here, folks. Move along.*

Even more jaw-dropping revelations would come out later about UBS's expression of gratitude for Hillary's intervention. Up until 2008, UBS had only made small donations to the Clinton Foundation, which brags that its mission is to "convene businesses, governments, NGOs, and individuals to improve global health and wellness, increase opportunity for girls and women, reduce childhood obesity, create economic opportunity and growth, and help communities address the effects of climate change." From my observations, the Foundation, while contributing a small portion of its buckets of donated funds to worthwhile causes, is really a Clinton mini-state, which overpays hundreds of employees to lock in their loyalty and boldly purchases political influence where no man has gone before. At any rate, prior to Clinton's deal with Calmy-Rey, UBS had only seen fit to contribute $60,000 to the Foundation, an amount that wouldn't even cover the bank's annual parking tickets. Afterward the Clinton Foundation's cash registers rang up *$600,000* in UBS gifts. The bank also decided to partner with the Foundation on some inner-city development programs, issuing a $32 million loan at very reasonable rates. Oh, and suddenly UBS also thought that Bill Clinton would make a very fine paid speaker about global affairs, so they paid him *$1.52 million* for a series of fireside chats with the bank's Wealth Management Chief Executive, Bob McCann. It was Bill Clinton's biggest payday since leaving the office of the presidency.

But that's not necessarily tit-for-tat, a quid pro quo, is it? I mean, let's say you're a local small-town legislator and your local bank's having some zoning issues with the town council. You step in and fix the problems, and just by coincidence, the bank turns around and donates thousands to your favorite charity, then partners with that charity to finance its projects, and then pays your politician husband the value of a mansion just to have him sit down for coffee with the bank president. That couldn't be considered bribery, could it? I mean, no one would even raise an eyebrow in your district, right?

You'd be in fucking *jail*.

Anyway, none of Hillary's Mafia-style antics would come out until long after 2009. In the meantime, since no one knew she was massaging the shoulders of Micheline Calmy-Rey, UBS was still in a nosedive. Outraged Swiss citizens, banking customers, and UBS shareholders started calling for heads to roll. Marcel Rohner and Peter Kurer had already fallen on their swords, and on March 17, two more top managers, Michel Guignard and Daniel Perron, were publicly fired. On April 1, UBS closed down its "Art Banking Department" (no more Rodin exhibits or Art Basel extravaganzas, boys). Right after that, if you'd happened to be looking up at the windows of Doug's condo, you might have spotted me dancing a jig. Christian Bovay had just been dumped on the street like a drunken sailor. Fired. Gone. *You're welcome, Valerie!* Just think, if Christian hadn't blown me off about that Three-Page Memo, you probably wouldn't be reading this story. The Swiss should have marched him out to a firing squad, without a blindfold.

On April 2, the G20 Summit on Financial Markets and the World Economy was held in London, bringing together heads of state, finance ministers, and central bank governors from twenty of the world's largest economies. For the first time in history, Switzerland was placed on the summit's "gray list," which meant the country's economic status was now shaky at best. In effect, it was a public slap in the face for being naughty boys.

On April 15, UBS held its annual shareholders' meeting in Zurich. I wish I could have been there along with a couple of clowns, but my friends who attended told me it was nearly a free-for-all, with shareholders screaming at UBS managers and tearing up their annual reports, which weren't worth the high-grade paper stock they'd been printed on. Five days later, trying to reinject some value into its tumbling share prices, the bank sold off its entire Brazilian offshore private banking operations. The sale brought in $2.5 billion, but it still wasn't enough. The bank had just posted a "larger-than-anticipated" loss of $1.7 billion for the first quarter. In other words, "We're fucked."

Well, not so much, because George Bush's Treasury Secretary Hank Paulson, Fed Chairman Ben Bernanke, and New York Fed President Tim Geithner were already playing fast and loose with hundreds of billions in TARP bailout money. Interestingly, Geithner's peccadilloes regarding his own personal finance didn't faze Obama when it came time to appoint Paulson's successor at the Treasury. "Turbo-Tim" failed to pay $35,000 in Medicare and payroll taxes during his employment at the International Monetary Fund from 2001 through 2004, a lapse that was accidentally discovered during an IRS audit. Tim blamed the "error" on his tax software: "Turbo-Tax did it." The new Democrat-controlled Congress nevertheless ignored Geithner's "eye-twitch" and confirmed his appointment.

One of the biggest benefactors of Paulson, Bernanke, and

Geithner's $700 billion shell game was AIG, the mega insurance firm designated "too big to fail." One hundred eighty billion dollars was funneled to AIG, and AIG turned around and slipped $100 billion of that to *twenty* of its foreign bank business partners.

Want to guess who got a huge chunk of your hard-earned and squeezed-from-your-savings-account taxpayer money? That's right: UBS. AIG slipped UBS a cool $5 billion from the bailout received. And nobody knew about it. It didn't come out until Geithner was forced to divulge exactly how he'd spent the people's money. But that's why UBS wasn't too worried about having to write a check for $780 million to the IRS. In public, they cried and whined and had tantrums about it. In private, they were laughing their asses off. Another "deal of the century," and the American taxpayer gets screwed (again).

As the old saying for UBS goes, "You and Us."

Meanwhile, as I was watching this circus from the bunker in Boston, my new defense attorney, David Meier, kept petitioning the Florida court to at last set a sentencing date for my case. Downing delayed it again and again without even a blush. A facile and expert bullshitter, he kept claiming that more evidence regarding my case was still forthcoming, which was incredulous since I happened to be the only witness he had who knew anything about it. So I just kept working on my whistle-blower award tactics with Steve Kohn and Dean Zerbe, while David Meier went around soliciting compliments from government officials about how, without my testimony, they would *never* have been able to nail the Swiss.

But Hillary Clinton had already made damn sure that the Swiss wouldn't really suffer. Micheline Calmy-Rey had promised to pressure UBS into turning over a big chunk of those 19,000 names. In turn, UBS at last came up with a list.

On April 30, 2009, in a district court in Florida, UBS finally responded to the "John Doe" summons and turned over the names of 4,500 American secret account holders. That's 4,500 out of 19,000 American account holders; you do the math. The list was cherry-picked; no one of any significance was on it. They were all trust-fund babies, doctors, small-business owners, and self-made millionaires. No politicians, power players, campaign fund-raisers, defense contractors, or lobbyists. Sacrificial lambs. It was a whitewash, and a super-slick deal for UBS as well as the account holders. Their names would remain anonymous, as long as they came in through the IRS voluntary disclosure program, repatriated their cash and securities, and agreed to pay penalties and fines to the IRS. The recovered assets would accrue to $12 billion and counting; American money returning to American banks.

In all modesty, *I* brought that money back in. *You're welcome, America. Happy to help.*

But UBS had already paid its $780 million penalty. They couldn't be tried all over again and have their punishment recalculated. Double jeopardy, you know. Hillary Clinton and Micheline Calmy-Rey's secret arrangement had produced nice results for all parties involved, and now it was all tied up with a pretty bow. UBS must have had a party in Zurich. "You Only Pay Once."

Kevin Downing kept me hanging, but I didn't mind all that much. I was still a free man, and in some ways I felt like the last man standing after an Old West gunfight. I'd watched with satisfaction as my former UBS bosses fell from their perches, one after another, and the bank was forced to give up its dirtiest business forever. In terms of penalties, they hadn't paid nearly enough for my liking. But in terms of stock value they'd taken a beating, and their arrogant chins now drooped to their chests. Over $200 billion had been withdrawn from the bank by account holders. The stock options held by the senior executives were tied to the bank's stock price, so they were now worthless (I'd cashed my stock in a long time ago, when it was still riding high). As for their reputation as the bank of choice for secret numbered accounts, they were finished, over, well done; stick a fork in it. No American on earth was ever again going to ask UBS for a comfy elevator ride down to their magnificent vaults. And I knew that more bad news was coming. The bank had been scamming plenty of other countries with the same tax fraud schemes, and those countries had now witnessed America getting its payouts. France and Germany were already waking up, just cranking up their investigations. UBS was just in the eye of the storm, getting a little breather. But the back half of the hurricane loomed on the horizon. Things were going to get a lot, lot worse.

In May, Downing at last contacted my attorney, David Meier, with some begrudging news. It seemed he'd run out of fairytales and hapless excuses and couldn't figure out a new way to torment me further. The Southern District of Florida had set a firm date for my sentencing hearing, August 21, 2009, and refused to entertain any further delays. Downing had never let the law impinge on his behavior before, but he was fresh out of ammo. It meant another three months of waiting for us, but we'd been preparing for the fateful date for nearly a year.

"It's about fucking time," I said to Meier. "Batter up."

The day before my court appearance, I packed a small bag and got on a plane to Fort Lauderdale. I knew I wouldn't be there long.

My fate had already been sealed by a rigged system.

# CHAPTER 13

## SCAPEGOAT

*"It is to be regretted that the rich and powerful too often bend the acts of government to their own selfish purposes."*

—ANDREW JACKSON,
AMERICAN PRESIDENT

IT WAS A PERFECT day for a hanging.

Fort Lauderdale in August felt like the closest spot on earth to the sun. The rows of hotels along the beachfront glistened so brightly they were painful to look at, and the roads shimmered like desert mirages. Not a palm frond moved, the air tasted thick like steam mixed with sea brine, and the white-sand beaches were nearly empty because you couldn't plant a foot without wincing. But all of that didn't matter to me much, because all I really saw was the down-turned mouth of Judge William Zloch.

As Zloch strode out from his chambers to the bench, I knew I'd made the correct decision about entering my plea before Magistrate Seltzer: *Guilty as charged.* Zloch was tall and rock-jawed, with lizard green eyes and a shock of thick blond hair. I'd done some research before showing up in his jurisdiction, and I knew he'd been a quarterback for Notre Dame and a Navy lieutenant in the waning days of Vietnam. He also had a reputation as a surly egomaniac; even his closest associates called him intense and overbearing. Lisa Arrowood, a senior partner in David Meier's firm, had referred to Zloch as a "real asshole." He had a penchant for verbally decapitating defendants and lawyers.

Two camps faced Zloch in the kingdom of his courtroom. On the left stood mine, including me, my attorney, David Meier, and one of his local associates. On the right stood "Government," as Zloch would address them: Kevin Downing, Jeffrey Neiman, and a third prosecutor, Michael Ben-Ary. I wasn't sure what Ben-Ary was doing there, except that maybe Downing wanted to keep the odds even, or have someone handy to fetch him lemonade.

There were no witnesses. You don't need witnesses for a lynching. The courtroom gallery was packed with members of the media, but the only friendly observer was my brother Doug, who'd come along to support me. I could feel the intensity of his energy behind me, but no matter what happened, I knew he wouldn't be able to say a word.

The proceedings opened without any raised right hands or oaths to God to tell the whole truth and nothing but that. Kevin Downing and his deputies would be doing most of the talking, and it's a given that government prosecutors will never, ever lie.

There'd been a series of motions between Downing and the Court, as well as David Meier and the Court, prior to us showing up for game day. Downing had submitted a lengthy sentencing memorandum, in which he'd lobbied for a fat chunk of jail time. He claimed in the memo that after my guilty plea he'd allegedly discovered many more crimes I'd committed, particularly with my coconspirator, Mario Staggl (I hadn't been able to keep Mario out of it, because he'd already been named in Olenicoff's confession). It was easy to turn Mario into a supervillain like Dr. Evil, because he wasn't there to defend himself, and never would be. When Zloch asked Downing how he'd made these discoveries, Downing said with a straight face, "Mr. Birkenfeld told us about them."

Zloch didn't even blink at that. I assume by now you've noticed that whenever someone in this story asked how the government managed to crack the code of secret Swiss banking, the answer has always been "Bradley Birkenfeld."

David Meier had submitted our own sentencing memorandum, along with a slew of supporting letters from my "fans." These weren't just cranks, or whiz-kid bloggers who read the *Financial Times*, but powerful people in government who knew what the hell they were talking about. The first one was from Senator Carl Levin (Document 5).

> "Mr. Birkenfeld initiated contact with the Subcommittee and subsequently provided testimonial and documentary information related to his employment as a private banker at UBS in Switzerland. . . . Throughout the Subcommittee investigation, which lasted over 14 months, Mr. Birkenfeld voluntarily made himself available for additional staff interviews and provided additional documents to the Subcommittee. . . . The information provided by Mr. Birkenfeld has been accurate, and enabled the Subcommittee to initiate its investigation into the practices of UBS."

In other words, "We couldn't have done this without him, so give him a fucking break."

Yet another letter had been sent directly to Judge Zloch from Robert Khuzami, Director of the Division of Enforcement of the Securities and Exchange Commission.

> "I am writing to provide the Court with information about Bradley Birkenfeld that the Court may wish to consider in connection with the sentencing of Mr. Birkenfeld."

Khuzami went on for two pages, detailing my repeated voluntary whistle-blowing cooperation and multiple meetings with the SEC, and how all of that had resulted in a successful civil suit against UBS, plus preventing the bank from further violating federal securities laws, and bringing in $200 million to the SEC in penalties.

"For these reasons, we would characterize Mr.
Birkenfeld's cooperation as significant to the Commission's investigation. I *hope* that the information in
this letter is helpful in determining the appropriate
sentence for Mr. Birkenfeld."

In other words, "I *hope* you're not going to be so stupid as to
punish a real American tax hero."

Well, hope springs eternal, but it was clear to me that none of
that had mussed a hair on Zloch's head. Steve Kohn, writing from
the headquarters of the National Whistleblower Center in Washington, DC, had sent a voluminous report to the Senate detailing
the DOJ's incompetence and corruption in handling my case and the
nefarious practices and, yes, lies that had been used to tar and feather
a stand-up whistle-blower. Kohn had urged the Senate to intervene
on my behalf, and Carl Levin had done just that. None of it helped.
I figured Judge Zloch was a Republican.

So the wrangling began. But it wasn't about whether or not the
defendant, me, who'd bounced from one government agency to
another over and over, risking his life and career to help the US government crack the case of unabashed Swiss crimes, should actually be
shown some consideration and get no more punishment than Igor
Olenicoff had. It was all about the *length* of jail time I was going to
serve. Honestly, when the first figures Judge Zloch uttered were "70
to 87 months," I felt a little weak in the knees. *Seven years?*

Downing, just to look good and merciful, had prepared a motion
for a downward departure (less time) from the maximum years I
could get, according to sentencing guidelines prescribed for these
kinds of cases. I knew that was all for show—if it were up to him, he'd
put me away for life. Zloch ignored the motion. He didn't need any
pissant lawyers telling him what to do, but still he was pretty savvy.
Judges are political animals, and he knew that whatever he decided
was going to be plastered all over the newspapers.

"Well," Zloch said to his prosecutors, "the advisory guideline
range at this point is 70 to 87 months. However, the maximum pen-
alty that can be imposed is 60 months because that is the statutory

maximum . . . The Court is never allowed to go *higher* than the statutory maximum, under no circumstances. So, the guideline range
could be 200 months to 250 months, and since the statutory maximum is 60 months, the Court cannot go higher than 60 months."

Downing wasn't happy with that, but he was stuck between a
rock and a hard place. I knew he had wet dreams about me hobbling
out of prison twenty years down the road with a long white beard
like Rip Van Winkle. However, since I was the only guy on earth who
could still help the government with the UBS case, he'd be needing
my cooperation even after the sentencing. In order to get it, he'd
have to file for a 5K1 motion, under which a court can ignore the
sentencing guidelines and statutes. If he didn't file for it, I could tell
him to fuck off and never talk to him or anyone else in the government again.

I actually found myself slightly relieved. Things are pretty bad
when you get a happy jolt from hearing you might only do *five* years
in prison.

Zloch instructed Downing to make his case. As Downing proceeded, I witnessed his rare talent of being able to talk out of two
sides of his mouth. He performed like a ventriloquist holding a
dummy that contradicted everything he said.

"Your Honor, after Mr. Birkenfeld was arrested and an under-
seal indictment was unsealed," Downing said, "Mr. Birkenfeld immediately began to cooperate with the United States government and
provide detailed information about his personal involvement with
what is now known as a massive tax fraud scheme that was committed by UBS's executives, bankers, and others against the United
States government."

Right off the bat Downing was twisting the truth, trying to make
it look like the shock of my arrest had made me talk. But he knew that
I'd already been babbling about the whole thing for a year before his
goons cuffed me in Boston, so the other side of his mouth started to
chatter.

"Prior to his arrest," Downing went on, "and in particular in the
summer of 2007, Mr. Birkenfeld came to the Department of Justice
and started to lay out the parameters of this fraud scheme, gave some

information about the individuals at UBS that were involved, and talked in rather detailed fashion about the parameters of the scheme and how it was conducted."

*Okay,* I thought, *maybe he's actually going to ease off on me, probably because he knows Judge Zloch can ask for his records of my interviews.*

"Mr. Birkenfeld at that time also provided documents to the United States government. So in June of 2007 the US government was in a position to approach UBS, to request that they begin to provide information about its fraud scheme, and that in fact did occur."

*Hey, maybe he's decided he likes me? Maybe he realizes how good I've made him look?* Nope; not so fast. The "dummy" took over.

"Unfortunately," Downing continued as if the whole thing was just so sad to him, "when Mr. Birkenfeld came in, in the summer of 2007, he did not disclose to the United States government his own personal involvement with that fraud scheme."

*What? I didn't tell you I was one of the UBS managing directors making it all happen? I told you I was just the fucking janitor, right? I just happened to witness all this shit while I was cleaning the bathrooms!*

"Nor did he in particular give any details with respect to what is now publicly known to be one of his clients, Mr. Olenicoff, who is one of the largest clients at UBS that was involved with this tax fraud scheme."

*Because you wouldn't give me immunity or a subpoena! That's why I spilled it all to the Senate instead of you!* I felt the blood rushing up to my face and I wanted to scream out in Court, "Goddamn liar!" David Meier must have sensed it because he gripped my arm to keep me steady and silent. Judge Zloch interrupted.

"Just for a reference point," he said to Downing, "what did Mr. Olenicoff end up paying by way of back taxes, interest, and penalties?"

"I think in total it was approximately $53 million, Your Honor."

It was a lot of fucking money, and I saw Zloch raise an eyebrow, almost as if wondering himself why this prosecutor wanted his lottery ticket locked in a slammer. Downing must have realized he was appearing vindictive, not to mention ungrateful.

"I will say," Downing conceded, "that without Mr. Birkenfeld walking into the door of the Department of Justice in the summer of

2007, I doubt as of today that this massive fraud scheme would have been discovered by the United States government."

*You slimy bastard. So you should be dropping the charges, right?*

"Moreover, by allowing us to begin our investigation back in June of 2007, that investigation now has resulted in not only changing the way in which we obtain foreign evidence from banks in Switzerland, it has caused the Swiss government to come and enter into new tax treaties with the United States government through which the United States government will now obtain tax information in civil tax cases, which never happened before, and more readily obtain them in criminal cases."

At that point my head was swimming. Downing's testimony was totally schizophrenic. Love me, hate me, trash me, tout me. But then came the kicker.

"And, if I might, Your Honor," Downing now said in this phony, almost mournful tone, "but for Mr. Birkenfeld failing to disclose his involvement with the fraud and the US clients that he aided and assisted in tax evasion, I believe we well would have *non-prosecuted* Mr. Birkenfeld."

*What? You could have had every name on the first day we met. All you had to do was issue a subpoena or a grant of immunity. But you fucking hate whistle-blowers and that's why you prosecuted me!*

"But given the fact that he refused to provide that information and led us down a course where we had to start to investigate Mr. Birkenfeld and his activities, that is why we are here today, that is why he was indicted, and that's why he pled."

*Bullshit! I pled because I'd already told you about everything I'd done and I wasn't going to pretend that I hadn't. It's called integrity. Look it up. But not in the DOJ handbook. You won't find it there.*

Zloch then asked Downing how many tax-evaders had been snared due to my testimony, and Downing had no choice but to admit I'd delivered my entire portfolio.

"Now, you said something that has great significance," Zloch said to Downing, "and I just want to make sure that I am clear on your statement. And that is that but for Mr. Birkenfeld, this scheme would still be ongoing?"

Since Carl Levin had already stated exactly that in his letter, Downing couldn't refute it. It must have tasted like Liquid-Plumr® drain cleaner as he cleared his throat and confessed.

"I have no reason to believe that we would have any other means to have disclosed what was going on, but for an insider in that scheme providing detailed information, which Mr. Birkenfeld did."

Both Downing and his "dummy" were babbling simultaneously now. "He did provide it! No, he didn't!" I was shaking my head, thinking that what he really needed was a court-appointed therapist. But then he stuck the knife in my ribs because he just couldn't help himself.

"I *do* know when Mr. Birkenfeld came in the door, he seemed to be motivated by the new whistle-blower statute that applies to tax cases."

*Piece of lying shit!* What Downing failed to share with the judge is that I had retained my attorneys to contact the DOJ regarding UBS and other Swiss banks in mid-2006, long before the IRS whistle-blower statute became law. He had to paint me as some sort of greedy scumbag to make sure Judge Zloch didn't suddenly turn around and toss the case out of court.

"But again," Zloch pressed him, "but for Mr. Birkenfeld this scheme would not have been discovered by the United States government?"

Downing nodded. "I believe that, Your Honor, yes."

Well, at least it was now all stated and recorded, in perpetuity, in the official legal proceedings of a federal district court. "None of this could have happened without Birkenfeld." But that fact still wouldn't have any impact on my sentencing if my lawyer couldn't pull a rabbit out of his hat. Now it was David Meier's turn.

"Your Honor, on behalf of Mr. Birkenfeld, I appreciate Mr. Downing's candor and forthrightness with the Court with respect to the general role or the characterization of Mr. Birkenfeld through all the responses to the Court's question."

*In other words, Your Honor, when you forced Downing to tell the truth about Brad's central role in this international tax case, he got cornered and had to.*

"As I have set forth on behalf of Mr. Birkenfeld in his sentencing memorandum and the attached exhibits," Meier continued, "and the Government in its 5K1 motion details, I respectfully suggest that based on these facts and circumstances the Court ought to grant the motion and depart downward."

*In other words, since everyone knows what's going on here, let's get off this nonsense about a seven-year sentence and talk turkey.*

Zloch agreed with Meier's plea. "The Court finds that Mr. Birkenfeld has rendered substantial assistance to the United States government. The Government concedes that point. Accordingly, the Court will consider a departure below the advisory guideline range."

That sounded pretty good. But then he added, "Having granted the government's motion, the Court reserves the right to impose any sentence authorized by law."

*Uh-oh . . .*

Zloch called me up to the podium. I'd seen enough real trials on TV to know that this was the part where anything could happen. I was cool on the outside; no sweaty palms. But inside my head the thoughts were careening around like pinballs.

"Good morning, Your Honor," I said.

Zloch didn't return the greeting.

"Bradley Birkenfeld, you now being again before this court, and you previously having pled guilty to the offense charged in the one-count indictment of the United States of America vs. Bradley Birkenfeld, and the Court having previously adjudged you guilty . . . Do you or does anyone on your behalf now have any legal reason to show why the sentence of the law should not be pronounced upon you?"

Well, I could think of a thousand reasons not to impose any sentence on me at all. But I'd already pled guilty, and unless my brother Doug suddenly jumped up and yelled that I wasn't really Bradley Birkenfeld at all, but some nutty impostor, there were no "legal" reasons not to impose a sentence.

"No, Your Honor," I said.

Zloch nodded. "No legal reason having been shown as to why sentence should not now be imposed, the Court will receive whatever information or evidence may be offered in extenuation or mitigation of punishment."

Meier got up again. This was his shot. I wanted to cross my fingers but I didn't dare move a muscle.

"Respectfully," Meier said, "I am asking the Court in recognition of these unique and extraordinary circumstances to depart downward some eighty percent, so that Mr. Birkenfeld's advisory guideline range falls with Zone B of the sentencing guidelines, and to thereafter, in the Court's discretion, to fashion what I suggest most respectfully is a fair and reasonable sentence, which would require Mr. Birkenfeld to be on probation for a period of five years and to serve an appropriate period as a condition of that in home detention, perhaps six months or nine months."

*That's what I'm talking about! No jail time, five years' probation, and just locked up in Doug's condo, living on Chinese takeout.*

"I suggest to the Court," Meier continued, "that this is indeed an extraordinary case. Two days ago, the Commissioner of the Internal Revenue Service announced that there has been an historic agreement with the Swiss government by which the IRS would be able to gain access to thousands of UBS accounts of American taxpayers. In that announcement the Commissioner stated that the world of international taxes has changed drastically."

*That's it, David, now tell them why.*

"I submit most respectfully to the Court that the individual who in essence sounded the alarm, who in essence provided the road map to the IRS, to the Department of Justice, to the Securities and Exchange Commission, to Senator Levin's Subcommittee to enable the United States Government to drastically change the world of international taxes, stands before the Court to be sentenced today."

Meier carried on, once again laying out for the Court everything I'd done for the US government. He recounted for Judge Zloch how I'd risked my career and life to come forward, had scores of meetings with and presented my evidence to multiple government agencies, and how even right after being arrested I'd kept it up as if I hadn't been screwed. He told Zloch that the only reason the DOJ hadn't gotten everything they wanted from me was because they'd refused to protect me. But he said it all in very polite terms. He was no Johnnie Cochran, the Shakespearean lawyer who'd gotten O. J.

Simpson off. And unfortunately, I was no celebrity murderer. I was just a scapegoated banker and none of this was being televised.

Meier ended his progression of facts with his plea, once again, that I be given nothing more than probation and home confinement. Then the Judge asked me to state my case.

"Mr. Birkenfeld, what would you like to say, sir?"

I took a deep breath and gave it my best shot.

"Thank you, Your Honor, for giving me the opportunity to speak this morning. I would like to express my regret for my actions as it brings me here today."

I figured if you admit you're guilty, you'd better say you're sorry if you're looking for a break.

"UBS recruited me and trained me, as well as my colleagues, and pressured and incentivized us financially to do this business without advising us of the consequences. When I put my concerns in writing to the UBS Legal and Compliance departments in Switzerland, they refused to address any of my concerns. Soon after this, I realized there was a cover-up of the corporation, and I was determined to contact the US authorities to expose this scandal, which I did. I want to thank you, Your Honor, for taking these circumstances into consideration and I'm happy to answer any questions you have."

"I have no questions, Mr. Birkenfeld," said Zloch.

*Really?* I was stunned. *You've got me right in front of you, and you don't have a single question? You don't want to hear from me why I gave everything to everyone, except the DOJ?*

"Is there anything else you would like to bring to the Court's attention?" Zloch asked.

He clearly wasn't going to ask me anything that might lead to revealing the DOJ's gross incompetence. All I could do was stand up for myself.

"Yes, Your Honor, there is something else I would like to add. That is when I sensed that this was wrong, this conduct. I wanted to make sure that I came forward fully to cooperate with the US authorities and the US agencies. The problem I had was that I was under Swiss law as a resident of Switzerland, and if I divulged any names without a subpoena, I would go to jail in Switzerland where I lived at the time and had been for the previous fifteen years. So that was my problem in that regard. But I wanted to try and start this process and give as much information as I could without breaking that bank secrecy and finding myself in jeopardy in Switzerland, where I lived."

*There. Get it? Now ask Kevin Downing why they hell he wouldn't grant me immunity or a subpoena!*

But all Zloch said was "All right. Thank you." He wasn't going to pin Downing to the wall and watch him twitch like a butterfly. He turned to Downing.

"All right, what say the United States?"

Downing puffed up, just the way I'd seen him whenever we were face-to-face at the DOJ. Now he was going to get his pound of flesh.

"Well, briefly, Your Honor. I think you get a sense of the dilemma that Mr. Birkenfeld intentionally put himself in."

Then he went on to list all the reasons why I should be thrown in prison.

"Number One: Birkenfeld knew what he was doing when he went to Switzerland to work in Swiss banking." *Of course I did. I didn't go there to become a ski instructor.* "Number Two: When Birkenfeld decided to be a whistle-blower, he had transferred all the funds of Mr. Olenicoff from UBS to other banks so that he and Mr. Staggl could continue aiding and assisting Mr. Olenicoff committing tax evasion." *I didn't choose to move Igor's money out of UBS. He did!* "Number Three: The whistle-blower letter appears to me to be a setup to find a way to get compensation from UBS after he decided to take his scheme with Mr. Olenicoff elsewhere." *What the fuck? That's bullshit and pure speculation. Isn't my attorney going to yell, "I object!"?*

"Finally, when he came to the United States government he came in to be a whistle-blower. He wanted to earn money by disclosing the wrongdoing of others. He refused to disclose his own wrongdoing." *That's a lie! Did you forget I walked into a DOJ conference room in Washington, DC, and told you exactly what I was doing as a private banker at UBS in Geneva, Switzerland?* "That is why the government charged Mr. Birkenfeld. That's why he was indicted. That's why we are seeking jail time." *Bullshit. You want me in jail so you can show that you actually did something and got one lousy conviction, even if it's the wrong conviction!*

"As to his bank secrecy claim? We made it clear to Mr. Birkenfeld and his lawyers that we would seek a court order that would give him the necessary legal compulsion that would show the Swiss government that he was compelled." *Jesus Christ! You could have gotten a court order in one flat hour! You denied me a subpoena every time we met!* "But finally, I must say to you, Mr. Olenicoff would be in jail had Mr. Birkenfeld come in, in 2007, and disclosed that information. We did not have the evidence that Mr. Birkenfeld provided after Mr. Olenicoff pled." *So, I have to go to prison because you incompetent fools weren't even aware of Olenicoff until I turned him in?* "That is why we are here today, and that is why the US government seeks jail time for Mr. Birkenfeld. That's all, Your Honor."

I was seething. I turned and looked at David Meier, but he didn't say a word, and he obviously wasn't going to. I mentally smacked myself on the forehead. *You're real good at picking lawyers, Brad. You're a fine fucking judge of that profession.* I barely heard Downing's final wrap-up.

"Your Honor, might I add one more point?"

"Sure." Zloch nodded.

"I wanted to end on also a positive note. We do intend on continuing to utilize Mr. Birkenfeld in conducting investigations and bringing cases against other UBS clients and other clients of Mr. Birkenfeld, and we do anticipate that we may be back to this Court."

"For a motion for a reduction of sentence?"

"That is correct, Your Honor."

I had to admit, Downing had a lot of fucking nerve. He was blatantly saying he wanted to squeeze every last drop out of me, and in return he might come back to court someday and get me some mercy. To me that was blatant extortion, but apparently to Judge Zloch it sounded oh-so-generous.

"All right, Mr. Birkenfeld," said Zloch. "Step up to the podium, please."

*Here we go . . .*

"The Court, being fully informed of the facts and circumstances surrounding the crime, and no legal reason having been shown as to why sentence should not now be imposed . . . It is the judgment of the Court and the sentence of the law that Bradley Birkenfeld is hereby committed to the custody of the United States Bureau of Prisons to be imprisoned for a term of forty months as to the one-count indictment."

*Three years and four months . . . Holy shit.*

"It is further ordered that Mr. Birkenfeld shall pay to the United States a total fine of $30,000."

*Thirty thousand bucks? I've already spent twice that amount just dragging my ass back and forth for the US government. I should be getting a rebate!*

"Upon release from imprisonment, Mr. Birkenfeld shall be placed on supervised release for a term of three years."

*Three years in the slammer, and three more on probation? Jesus.*

"It is further ordered that Mr. Birkenfeld shall pay immediately to the United States a special assessment of $100."

*What's that for? Lunch?*

"Does the Defense have any objection to the manner or procedure in which sentence has been imposed, or that this hearing has been conducted, Mr. Meier?"

"No, Your Honor," Meier said.

"Mr. Birkenfeld?"

I hesitated for a moment. But then I said, "No, Your Honor."

I had objections exploding out of my ears, but I knew I was on very thin ice with a handpicked judge who was a real ornery prick. Zloch could still increase my jail time with the stroke of a pen.

He turned to Downing. "Any from the Government?"

"No, Your Honor," said Downing. He was barely concealing his victory grin.

"Mr. Birkenfeld, you are to surrender yourself at the federal facility designated by the Bureau of Prisons no later than noon on January 8, 2010. Is there anything else from the Defense?"

"No, Your Honor," said Meier.

"From the Government?"

"No, Your Honor," said Downing.

"All right, counsel, thank you very much. The Court appreciates your efforts."

Zloch raised his gavel and smacked his wooden podium. It sounded like a gunshot. Then he actually smiled.

"Everyone have a great weekend. The Court is in recess."

*A great weekend.* I couldn't believe he'd actually said that. I felt like Alice in fucking Wonderland. I don't remember much of what happened after that, except that we had a bunch of papers to sign and I forked over a hundred bucks in cash, which I guess was supposed to cover the copy-machine expenses. Downing said something to Meier about making me available for further cooperation until my date of incarceration. The two of them stayed in the courtroom and chatted. When opposing lawyers discuss your fate, it's never about anything good and I didn't want to hear it.

In a side room in the courthouse that day, Downing made a rather blunt comment to David Meier about my prior lawyers whom I had fired a year earlier, Hector and Moran. "This is what happens when you've got lawyers who don't know what they're doing." Thanks for that great referral, Bob Bennett!

I walked out with Doug into the steaming heat of noon. He was so furious he wasn't able to talk. We slipped into the car, ripped off our ties, cranked the air conditioner, and headed for our hotel. I turned and looked at his square-set jaw and his eyes blazing out at nothing ahead.

"Well, look on the bright side, Brother," I sighed. "At least I'll be able to get this fucking ankle jewelry off."

# CHAPTER 14

## CAMP CUPCAKE

*"Colonel Hogan, if you ever escape . . . be a good
fellow and take me with you."*

—SERGEANT SCHULTZ,
HOGAN'S HEROES

SCHUYLKILL FEDERAL CORRECTIONAL FACILITY—2012
Lopez made his break for freedom one sunny Sunday morning.

It wasn't exactly *The Great Escape*, but it sure as hell was dramatic. He came barreling down the barracks aisle, doing a flat-out five-minute mile in his prison work boots, and he slammed through the fire door at the end of the block and sprinted for the woods. Right after that came a fat guard we called Waddles, pounding along and wheezing lung steam, his keys and baton slapping his belt. There was no way Waddles was going to catch Lopez. That kid was fast.

From my perch on my bunk I raised an eyebrow, then turned back to my copy of *Prison Legal News*, finding my place again in an article about appeals for sentence reductions. One of my buddies in "Camp One" had a hearing coming up and had to prepare a good argument for getting some time dropped from his "bid." For a white-collar criminal, Normy was fairly illiterate and needed my help. I enjoyed doing that for lots of the guys, and by now I had scores of "clients" in the block. I'd research their cases, write their briefs, track down pro bono attorneys, and find cracks in the government's stupid reasons for keeping them locked up. For me, it was a satisfying way to buck the system. For them, I was an in-house Clarence Darrow, the closest thing to a public defender they had.

A prisoner named Anwar strolled by my cubicle. He was a sweet, elderly black dude from Philly who'd gotten twenty years for possessing half a snack-bag of crack. We enjoyed singing Motown together after lights-out. I'd start from my bunk with "Who's that *ladeee . . . ?*" And he'd croon back from the darkness in his salty baritone, "That lovely *ladeee . . .* " I glanced up as he passed.

"Hey, Anwar. What's up with Lopez?"

"Man, the dude finally lost his shit and pushed Waddles."

"Oh, *no*. That stupid kid!"

"Yep, it's bad news, baby."

At Schuylkill you could get away with almost anything except putting your hands on a guard. Guys got caught with smuggled-in cell phones, drugs, booze, porn, all sorts of contraband, and they'd wind up in solitary down in Medium Security, or get denied some visiting privileges. But put your hands on a Bureau of Prisons staff member? You could get years tacked on your time for that, and Lopez knew it.

"He's gone for sure," I said.

"Damn shame," said Anwar. "He was gettin' short. Maybe thirty months."

We never talked about our sentences in years; it was always months. "I'm down to twenty-two." "Ralph just broke sixty." Years were a bitch, but months were easier to take. You could watch them tick away. The guys doing big time had to start off in either High or Medium Security: regular jail cells, exercise periods, lockdowns, shakedowns, and solitary. But if you did that time clean, once your bid fell below 120 months (ten years), they'd move you up to where I was—the Camp. Lopez was in for thirteen years and had less than three left when he lost it.

We called our Minimum wing "Camp Cupcake," a moniker probably bestowed by some wise guy who thought it was easy as pie. And it was. There were three hundred men in two barracks, Camps One and Two, about a mile up a long road from the

Medium wing and sprawled over a grassy pitch the size of a soccer field. There were no razor-wire fences or guard towers with shotgun-toting goons, but the camp was surrounded by miles of thick forests. Sometimes guys would just go for a walk in the woods, or occasionally rendezvous with drug mules or girlfriends who happened to be good with a map. One dude managed to get Chinese takeout delivered and hung from a tree. But everyone always came back. If you didn't, and got caught, your last few months of easy time would get longer and harder, real fast.

Our Camp One barracks had a long four-foot-high concrete wall down the middle separating two rows of cubicles. Inside each was a pair of bunks, two armoires, a writing desk, shelves, and a chair. We rose every day, took the long walk down to the commissary for breakfast, hit our work assignments, took the walk again for lunch, spent the afternoons at the gym or basketball court, walked the walk for dinner, and chilled for the evening. On Tuesdays we had movie night. On weekends the lucky guys had visitors down at Medium. Every night we fell asleep to a chorus of snores that sounded like some jungle symphony. Compared to my experience as a student at Norwich, it was Club Med.

That Sunday when Lopez bolted was a beautiful summer day. I took a walk outside to see if I could spot him. Maybe he was just jogging the perimeter, trying to cool down and hoping for some leniency from Waddles. But Waddles was a fat, ornery prick and I knew Lopez was screwed. He was nowhere to be seen.

The sun gleaming off the dew-soaked grass made me think of another Sunday, the one just after my sentencing in Florida. On that very Sunday at the Farm Neck Golf Club in Martha's Vineyard, President Barack Obama had strolled out onto the links. His golfing partner that day was Robert Wolf, Chairman of UBS Americas. I'm sure it was a fine day of patter and play, guarded by a throng of Secret Service agents, and I wondered if Obama and Wolf had high-fived over my downfall, or maybe sent a "good job" text to Judge Zloch. But I'd never know, because much like Swiss bankers, Secret Service agents don't talk.

That brought me back to another Sunday, the one just after my incarceration, deep in the heart of winter when they finally released me from solitary. *My* partner that day was a prison guard who looked like Roseanne Barr and smelled like bacon. She took me outside to a Bureau of Prisons van and we drove the long mile from Medium up to the Camp.

Schuylkill was still swaddled in piles of snow from the storm of the Friday before, and the cinder-block walls and guard towers looked frozen and brittle. I noticed a pair of black prisoners, also just released from "the hole," trudging through the muck beside the road. I asked Roseanne why she didn't pick them up, but she just smirked and slurped from her Dunkin' Donuts mug. It was my first hard lesson about prison life. White prisoners were eligible to ride; black prisoners were only eligible to walk. It was right then and there that I'd decided to fuck with the system at every available turn.

*So, that's the way it is here, huh? Well, Colonel Hogan has just arrived. You're going to rue the day you met me, and pray for my early release.*

Anyway, Waddles was too fat to catch Lopez, so five more guards came barreling through the block and burst through the door to search the woods. Then they called a lockdown, hauled everyone back from their work duties, had a roll call, and restricted us to barracks. It was after lights-out, about ten o'clock at night, when I heard the fire door open, then squishy footsteps. I sat up in my rack. It was Lopez!

"Dude!" I whispered. "What the fuck?"

"I got hungry." He grinned at me and I saw he was slathered in sweat and pine needles. "And I need a shower."

So while I sat up on my elbows and blinked, Lopez grabbed a shower, changed into fresh clothes, calmly ate some chow mein he'd stashed in his locker, and headed back out for the woods.

"Now I'm *really* gone." He shot me a Boy Scout salute and disappeared.

"See ya, amigo," I called after him. "Good luck!"

*That* was Camp Cupcake.

The place was a fucking joke; a total waste of taxpayer money. The guards would sweep through the barracks, tossing bunks and searching for drugs and cell phones, while at the same time guys were smoking weed in the bathrooms. There were no genuine efforts at rehabilitation; just the occasional course in the Training Room or some silly lecture that everyone laughed at. I'd become a pretty good cook in Geneva, and at one point I'd offered to give a class in French cuisine, figuring some of the guys might use it on the outside. But the staff refused to let me order cookbooks. "No books from outside allowed!" I soon realized that the system wasn't designed to rehab a soul. The Bureau of Prisons' massive budget could only be justified if the cells were chock full. Fewer prisoners would mean less money. "Keep 'em comin', boys!"

I had entered Schuylkill with an attitude; chin up, eyes bright, ears open, and a permanent grin, ready to learn something and also impart what I knew. Being my usual boisterous friendly self, I talked to everybody and got to know their stories. Of the 150 guys in my block, only a handful were a danger to public safety. Most of them were in there on ridiculous drug charges, and the rest were political prisoners like me.

Joe Nacchio had been the President and CEO of Qwest, a huge telephone company. He was close to the Bush people, even visiting the White House on occasion. Shortly after 9/11, the Bush admin- istration had gone to all the phone companies and demanded their customer records and email. AT&T and Verizon had caved right away, but Joe told the Feds to fuck off.

"We're a private company. I can't *do* that!"

"Yes, you can," said the Bushies. "Matter of national security."

"It's unconstitutional," Joe protested. "Without warrants from a judge, on a case-by-case basis, I won't do it."

"Oh, really?"

So the Bushies charged him with insider trading and put him away for seven years. Joe's replacement at Qwest got the message, and the Feds got the records.

Then there was Bill Hillard, a very bright, soft-spoken, well-built guy in his late sixties. Bill had been an Army Delta Force operator with a distinguished career and a list of medals as long as your arm. After the fall of Saigon in 1973, he'd been assigned to guard opium shipments coming out of the Golden Triangle: Laos, Cambodia, and Vietnam. That's right. The US government had kept on funding its secret wars by selling smack to American junkies. And Bill had a second assignment; if he ran across any of the American POWs still languishing in bamboo cages, he was to *kill* them, because most of them had been captured while working "The Program" in Laos and Cambodia. If you don't believe me, read a book called *Kiss the Boys Goodbye*. I've read it twice, and Bill's story checks out. Thankfully, he never found any American POWs.

Long after he retired, Bill made the mistake of accepting an invitation to lecture about his particular skill set at an FBI off-site in Colorado. Believing his story was "old news" at the point, he told it. Six months later, the Feds showed up at his home in Maryland, charged him with revealing state secrets, and put him away for the rest of his golden years. I know; it sounds like something out of a Robert Ludlum conspiracy novel, but it's true. Bill was a career patriot, and Schuylkill was his reward.

Lots of the guys had similar ugly stories. Having nothing better to do with my stint in stir, I did a lot of research and checked them out. It was rare that I discovered a guy had lied about his circumstances. Of course we did have a couple of hard-core types here and there. One Italian-American dude named Joe slept catty-corner to my bunk. He was quiet and friendly, until the night I went around rousting everyone up for the Tuesday night movie.

"I don't give a shit about it!" Joe snapped at me.

"*Whoa*," I said. "Take it easy. Just tellin' you the movie's on! Don't fuckin' bark at me."

Then I tracked down Anwar.

"What's up with Joe? I just told him the movie's about to start and he almost took my head off."

"Well, what's the movie?" Anwar asked.

"*Goodfellas*."

Anwar nearly died laughing. "Don't you know who that is, man? That's Pittsburgh Joe, the guy Henry Hill fingered for cocaine! He got twenty years for that!"

"No shit?" I laughed too. "Guess that explains his lack of enthusiasm."

But for the most part, the average prisoner was a regular guy who'd been in the wrong place at the wrong time. One of my best prison buddies, Cliff Falla, was a simple blue-collar guy from New Hampshire. Down on his luck and out of work, Cliff, who happened to own a pistol, had agreed to do a job for some local toughs. All he had to do was show up at a seedy motel and guard a couple of bricks of cocaine for the night. Well, the Feds showed up too, and Cliff got five years for the gun and another five for the coke. At an average annual cost of $40,000 per prisoner, our taxpayers wasted $400,000 keeping a well-mannered country boy locked up for a decade. Cliff and I hung out together, worked out together, and made each other laugh.

Laughing it up was the best palliative for doing time, and I encouraged it at every opportunity. I'd march through the barracks clapping my hands. "What's going on here? Why all the glum faces? You guys look like you're in fucking prison or something!" That usually stirred things up, and then we'd come up with a new plan to screw with the guards, most of whom should have been behind bars themselves.

Those Bureau of Prisons goons stole food from the kitchens and clothing from the laundry. The prison got thirty brand-new snow-blowers delivered; half of them disappeared and wound up in the guards' home driveways. Same thing happened with a shipment of lawnmowers. Our payback was subtle. They'd snap at us to wash their coffeepots, so we'd sneak the glass pots to the latrine and scrub them in the toilets. "There ya go! Clean as a whistle!" They'd roust us for a roll call, and we'd sing "God Bless America." I'd stride into the lunchroom waving a copy of the *Wall Street Journal*. "Hey, guards, I just read that the BOP is cutting your pension benefits. What an insult!" In my particular case, if a guard fucked with me too much, I'd lean down and squint at his name tag. "Hodges, Francis. Just want to make sure I spell that right for my attorneys. Has to be correct on the lawsuit."

They couldn't do much to you for being a smart-ass. However, you also had to know when to pull back, otherwise you might suffer "diesel therapy." They'd arrange for your transfer to another facility, let's say in a neighboring state like New York. But instead of traveling point-to-point, they'd put you on a rattling, fume-choked prison bus for a week-long haul to a pen in Colorado, and then another week back to Elmira. By the time guys finished those torture trips, their spines were ground up and they'd lost twenty pounds. It was a regular practice, like waterboarding using carbon dioxide. And guess who paid for it? You did.

I never really feared such treatment, because after my first day and my press conference outside, the staff knew who they were dealing with. "Fuck with Birkenfeld too much and he'll have you on the national news." I was generally upbeat and unflappable, although my time at Schuylkill wasn't all laughs. The roughest period was early on in my stint, when Igor Olenicoff read all the newspaper articles about my whistle-blowing status, and realized that in fact I might wind up getting a reward from the IRS. So he sued me and UBS, along with twenty other people, for a "modest" amount: *$500 million*, which was considerably more than the $53 million he'd been forced to pay the government in back taxes and fines (Exhibit 19). He knew I was in a federal penitentiary and wouldn't be able to defend myself. He also knew that my current attorney had just dropped me because I could no longer pay him. But he didn't count on my brother Doug, who happens to be another Birkenfeld pit bull.

The California judge presiding over Olenicoff's suit had given me a flat three weeks to respond. Right away, Doug filed a motion to extend the deadline by ninety days, and got it. Then he tackled the case himself as a highly trained lawyer. He burned the midnight oil, working around the clock, preparing his answer to Olenicoff's spurious claims and countering with cold hard facts; Olenicoff had not only defrauded the US government, but had himself initiated each step he'd taken to screw the IRS. Doug's answer was complex and powerful, forty-five pages long. Adding more pressure to the deadline, Doug had to prepare and print thirty copies of his comprehensive answer to Olenicoff's bogus complaint; one copy for each party involved in the suit. And every copy had to have my signature on it.

Doug shipped them off to Schuylkill in seven FedEx packages. I'd been saving up all my prison postage allowance, so I signed all the copies, licked and stamped and shipped, making the deadline with one day to spare. Doug's answer thunderstruck the California court, resulting in further legal wranglings and a window during which my family could hunt for another legal gunslinger out there. They found him in John Cline, a brilliant attorney with a sterling reputation who quickly joined forces against Olenicoff with . . . none other than UBS! Strange bedfellows, right? But as that old Middle East adage goes, "The enemy of my enemy is my friend." Apparently that adage applied to the other side too. Igor Olenicoff had found a "coach," none other than Kevin Downing! I'd only find out much later that Downing had reviewed every one of Igor's crazy claims and, I am confident, offered his advice on how to skin me alive. Just a faithful civil servant of The People, right?

At any rate, then we waited some more, with me pacing the floors in the block and Doug staring out the window of his Weymouth condo. On the afternoon of the hearing, April 10, 2012, the goons summoned me down to take a call in the visitors' room. It was Doug. *Boom!* The judge had ruled in my favor, declaring what a complete bald-faced liar Olenicoff was, and stating it was patently absurd for a convicted tax fraud like Olenicoff to sue the man who had served him justice!

"Olenicoff and his witnesses repeatedly *lied*," the judge stated in his twenty-eight-page written ruling. "Although it is not this Court's job to make credibility determinations on summary judgment, this coordinated blatant lying does not go unnoticed." He'd thrown the case out of court.

---

I digress for a moment to explain this secret Downing/Olenicoff alliance.

In subsequent litigation, through sworn deposition testimony, the true depths of the Downing/Olenicoff collaboration were exposed. In March 2008 there was a meeting in the office of Edward Robbins, Olenicoff's criminal defense attorney. Kevin Downing flew out to California on the taxpayers' dime to have this meeting. But this was no ordinary meeting.

It was not confrontational. It was rather cordial. Attorney Robbins even left the room for extended periods of time, leaving Downing and Olenicoff alone to engage in private conversations. During this meeting, Downing claimed that I would never get a whistle-blower award. How and why would my potential whistle-blower award even come up in conversation between these two people? The whistle-blower award program is an IRS program, having absolutely nothing to do with the DOJ. There's as close to an admission as you'll get that Downing's actions against me were driven by an almost maniacal desire to deny me a whistle-blower award.

It is critical to understand that Downing had absolutely no involvement whatsoever in Olenicoff's prosecution or his guilty plea the year before. But here they were, face-to-face, enjoying each other's company. Following these meetings, a dual plan of attack emerged.

Downing planned to obtain an indictment of me, and Olenicoff planned to file a frivolous civil lawsuit against me and many other people, trying to shift blame for his own criminal misconduct on to others with blatantly false allegations. But Downing stepped far afield from his official duties as a prosecutor and his fingerprints were all over the pleadings in this groundless civil lawsuit.

Olenicoff had his absurd lawsuit filed in federal court in California in September 2008. The initial complaint had been amended three times, with each amended complaint being filed with the federal court. Subsequent testimony years later revealed that Olenicoff and his advisors shared copies of each of these complaints with Downing for his personal review. He was free to review and comment on them before they were filed. Here you had a federal prosecutor in Washington, DC, working with a private person in the preparation and prosecution of a baseless lawsuit in federal court.

Each one of these four complaints contained blatantly false statements regarding the DOJ which, if believed, would have painted the DOJ as the leader in the UBS investigation and would have denied me an IRS whistle-blower award. "By 2005, the IRS and DOJ approached the UBS AG Defendants about their scheme," read the first complaint. False. Neither the IRS nor the DOJ approached UBS in 2005. I approached both the IRS and DOJ in 2007 about

UBS. Hell, Downing didn't even know how to spell UBS before I walked into the DOJ in 2007 and told them all what was going on.

The first amended complaint stated that "in or around 2004, Birkenfeld was approached by the US Department of Justice which inquired into UBS AG's conduct . . ." No, they didn't. This blatant lie was repeated in both the second and third amended complaints. The DOJ had no clue about any of this until 2007, when *I voluntarily approached them* and handed them the keys to the kingdom. The third amended complaint was filed by Olenicoff's attorneys the very next business day after my sentencing hearing.

Downing reviewed these complaints before they were filed, and each one of these allegations regarding the DOJ was false. Whether Downing played a material role in inserting these falsehoods into these bogus complaints or failed to have them corrected before they were filed with the federal court, we don't know. Furthermore, there is no record of Downing ever alerting the federal court to the false nature of these allegations.

Different witnesses gave conflicting and nonsensical reasons as to why Kevin Downing was reviewing these bogus complaints before they were filed. One of Olenicoff's attorneys, Marisa Poulos, testified that the civil complaints had been sent to Downing to make sure they weren't violating the terms of Olenicoff's plea agreement. However, Downing was not Olenicoff's probation officer, nor was he even one of the prosecutors involved in Olenicoff's case! Nice try, Marisa.

Another one of Olenicoff's longtime in-house lawyers, Julie Ault, gave a very different answer to the same question. She testified that the civil complaints were sent to Downing to be sure he was "happy with it." Poulos and Ault were even reprimanded by the federal court for misconduct in that case.

In my opinion, there was no legitimate reason for Downing to be reviewing the pleadings in this baseless lawsuit; and, in what can only be described as a remarkable coincidence, just one month after this lawsuit was eventually thrown out of court by the judge in California, Downing resigned his position as a prosecutor and slithered out the back door of the DOJ and into a private law firm in DC. His work here was now over. Time to move on.

Furthermore, in 2014 one of Downing's law partners in private practice openly acknowledged, "He [Downing] really hates him [Birkenfeld]." I knew that all along. Nice to have that confirmed by one of Downing's bigmouthed partners. So for those few people who actually believe that Downing and the DOJ were motivated by justice, think again. I now have the evidence that proves otherwise.

I'd always loved my brother, but his help in this case went over the top. Just between you and me, I shed a tear of joy in the prison latrine, and went back to cleaning floors.

That was my primary prison job, by the way—cleaning floors. I've since become a linoleum expert. I cleaned the floors in Medium, I cleaned them in Minimum, and I even cleaned the warden's office. He actually wasn't a bad guy, but he was dumb as a post. Half the time he wasn't there, so I'd empty his garbage can, take the contents back to the janitor's closet, and read all his discarded email and correspondence. The guys in my block always wondered how the hell I knew what was going to happen each week. I'd just smile and say, "Instincts, boys!" They had no idea they had their own secret agent.

I was determined to have fun at the expense of the government, and I did. My first gig was cleaning the floor of the prison's main entrance down at Medium, where I'd taken my perp-walk on my very first day. As new prisoners arrived, often escorted by weeping families, the meathead BOP staff tried to make them feel like slaves being dumped at a Southern plantation. I, on the other hand, made it my business to ease their stress.

"Welcome to Camp Cupcake, brother!" I'd say with a wide happy grin, and then I'd turn to the families. "Hey, folks, don't you worry about him. This place is easy breezy!"

The goons didn't like that much. After a while they told me to stand aside and shut up.

"What are you going to do?" I needled them. "Give me three more years for being too nice to people?"

They could have locked me up in solitary again, but truth be told, I intimidated the hell out of the staff. They all knew who I was and I'd hear their murmurs as I walked on by. "That's the banker dude who had the press conference outside." About a month before my incarceration, *60 Minutes* had done a big story on my case. Steve Kroft interviewed me at the Boston Harbor Hotel, and even though he did his best to edit the piece so I'd look like a scumbag, my message about being the DOJ's fall guy still came through loud and clear. At any rate, after that the media kept clamoring to hear my story. About every three weeks, some crew from *CNBC*, Swiss TV, or journalists from the *Financial Times* or *Wall Street Journal* would show up at Schuylkill for an interview in the visitation room. The prison staff was scared shitless that I'd badmouth the joint, so it was "hands off Birkenfeld."

Plus, I kept the pressure flowing from my attorneys to the various government bodies I'd helped with the whole Swiss banking scam. Steve Kohn from the National Whistleblower Center was an expert at demanding true justice, and expressed his outrage on a regular basis. I don't know exactly how many letters he and Dean wrote, but I think the pile was thicker than the Tax Code (Document 7). I'd suddenly get a call to come down to the prison's "Camp Counselor" office.

"Yes, ma'am?"

"Is everything all right, Mr. Birkenfeld?"

"Everything's peachy. Why do you ask?"

"Well, Senator Kerry's office called yesterday, inquiring about your welfare."

"My welfare's fine, although I think those coffers have been abused by socialists and irrevocably bankrupted by the national debt. How's yours?"

They fucking hated having me there, and I loved that. I wasn't going to let prison change my outlook on life, which had always been about turning mud into money and having fun at every turn. Sure, some guys were jealous of my status, which might have appeared to be "white privilege," and a few of my African American and Latino camp mates grumbled about my role as a government "snitch."

"Park the attitude, brother," I'd say. "If I'm so dirty, what the hell am I doing in here with *you*?"

Then some inmate would say, "You just disrespected me!"

I'd counter with "I would need to *respect* you first before I could *disrespect* you now, which I never did!"

That shut them up, and it was pretty smooth sailing once I set them all straight.

About two years into my bid, Steve Kohn and Dean Zerbe came down for a discussion with me in the visitation room. We'd been having telephone discussions about my application for an IRS whistle-blower award, but up until that point I still thought it was pie-in-the-sky. This time something seemed different.

"We've finished our brief," said Steve.

"Filed it with the IRS," said Dean.

"How brief is it?" I asked.

"All told?" Steve smiled. "About two hundred pages, and half of it's sworn affidavits or signed testimony from high-caliber government people: Levin, Grassley,[3] Khuzami."

I whistled. "That's pretty hefty, especially for something called *brief.*"

"We've also got supporting testimony in there from IRS investigators," said Dean. "It's going to be pretty hard for them to argue against their own agents."

"Okay," I said. "So what are we looking at?"

"Well . . ." Steve grinned and adjusted his smart-guy spectacles. "UBS paid out $780 million. Something north of $200 million of that went to the SEC, so that doesn't figure in the IRS calculations. That leaves about $580 million to work with. We're looking at somewhere between fifteen and thirty percent of that."

I blinked, and as I leaned my head closer across the table, they dipped theirs in too. Now they were grinning like Cheshire cats.

"You're telling me," I whispered, "we might get . . . *$50 million* for an award?"

"We're thinking it'll be closer to $100 million," said Steve.

I blew out a long breath, gripped both their shoulders, and sat back.

---

3   Senator Chuck Grassley is the author of the 2006 whistle-blowing law and is a staunch advocate for whistle-blower rights. He has supported whistle-blowers and passed legislation in furthering the protections and awards to courageous whistle-blowers for decades during his tenure in the US Senate. He is also a supporter of Birkenfeld's case (Document 6).

"You guys can come visit me down here any day! My home is your home!"

At that point I had about six months left in my bid. Time flies when you're having fun, and two years had gone by quickly. Honestly, I think that my prison term was somewhat karmic, if you believe in that sort of thing. For anyone else, it would have been the low point in their lives, but for me it provided an unvarnished look at how things really work in the land of the free. Plus, after years of swinging my sword at government dragons, it was a warrior's vacation. Most folks thought of it as hard time; I thought of it as downtime.

I guess I don't have to tell you that after Steve and Dean's visit my demeanor, which was already chipper, got obnoxiously arrogant as far as the Bureau of Prisons was concerned. I rubbed my good fortune in everyone's faces. Some of my fellow inmates thought I was spinning a fairytale, like I'd gone off my rocker in stir. But the smarter guys who knew me well were convinced I was telling the truth.

"Think you're really going to be rich after this?" Cliff asked.

"Baby, when you get out, we're going to party on a yacht full of Playboy bunnies."

Cliff laughed, but his eyes gleamed like he was already there.

As for the prison staff and guards, they became even more surly whenever I was around.

"You ain't getting paid, Birkenfeld. Keep dreamin'."

"Yeah? Give me your cell number. When you're out there blowing the sidewalks next winter, I'll call you from my convertible Porsche in Saint-Tropez."

Most of the negative chatter died down when a senior guard named Harold starting taking my side. He was a smart, friendly dude with no attitude, a guy who read the *Wall Street Journal*. At times the BOP guys supervised the meal service, and Harold started cruising by my table, grinning and jabbing a finger my way.

"There he is! It's Mr. Thirty-Percent!"

"Told ya, boys." I'd grin at my lunch mates. "Even Harold knows the score."

"Holy shit," they'd murmur. "Birkenfeld's really gonna get *paid*."

My original sentence had been slated for forty months, but had been reduced on account of good behavior to thirty-one months—two and a half years. The Department of Justice didn't fight it. They knew they'd screwed me, and with the rash of media covering my story, the whole world knew it as well. Maybe they thought if they eased up, I'd be less inclined to go after them once I was free. They were wrong. I was just biding my time, making the best of prison life, and keeping faith with that old Mafia adage: "Revenge is a dish best served cold."

No monumental events happened during my time at Schuylkill. Nobody got killed, fights were rare, and the guys generally behaved themselves because once inside Camp Cupcake, they could see the lights of freedom twinkling at the end of that long dark tunnel. Doug came to visit me often, and so did Rick James, my best buddy from the State Street days in Boston, as well as other close friends. My dad and stepmom visited when they could, writing frequently to show their support and bolster my spirits, as did my brother Dave from Seattle and my mom from Florida. I'd call when I could, assuring my family and close friends that all was well with me. I read just about everything in the prison library and thought a lot about my adventures in Switzerland. But I had no regrets, only residual fury at the Department of Justice. I learned a lot about the law and discovered that half the time it was mortally flawed. My fury would not be cured, but it never dimmed my grin.

I woke up one day in the summer of 2012, realizing that it was almost over, getting close. Some of the guys in the block had served out their time and gone home, but my long-suffering buddies were still there. It was a strange feeling; nearing the end, anxious to taste my freedom again, yet laced with melancholy for those I'd be leaving behind. It was much like high school or a military experience; you didn't make lifelong friends with everyone, but some would stick with you forever, at least in your heart and mind.

Anwar had brought me a burger that day. He worked in the kitchen and always slipped something inside his jacket for me or one of our buds. We sat in my cube as I enjoyed the treat and sipped a Coke.

"You're leaving in a month," Anwar said. "Bet you're lookin' forward to leaving."

"Yeah, Anwar, I am. But it's been a good time here. How much longer do you have, bro?"

"Aw, I got another fifty months."

I nodded as I swigged my Coke, but I was thinking *four fucking years*.

"Bet you'll be excited to go too, Anwar."

"No." He shook his head slowly and stared out the window. "I want to stay here."

I leaned back in my chair and looked at him. "What are you saying, man?"

"Brad, you guys are always talking about those mobile phones and computers and the Internet. I don't know what you're talking about. We got nothin' but typewriters here. Like okay, some guys got those illegal cell phones, so I've seen 'em. But when I was on the outside it was before any of that stuff. What am I gonna do out there? I got no skills, no family, no money. I got a warm bed here, a hot shower, and food."

I nodded my understanding, but I was stunned, and the anger and pity welled up in my throat. He'd been totally institutionalized, with nowhere to go, no future. That's what Schuylkill meant to Anwar, and to thousands of guys just like him; the best end of a long rough road paved with hard times and sorrow. I patted his shoulder, but I could barely look at him.

"You'll be all right, Anwar. You should give it a shot."

He just smiled at me. He knew better.

On August 1, 2012, which happened to be Swiss National Day, I turned in my prison uniform and donned a set of Champion sweats and sneakers. The guys gathered around my cube, and I gave away everything I had, except for my box of legal files. It wasn't much; a cheap watch I'd bought at the commissary, all my writing materials, magazines, books. It was just a gesture, but all we could do for one another. Anwar, Bill, and Cliff walked me out into the sunlight and down that long corridor to the front entrance. They couldn't go any farther. We shook hands and hugged, and I turned away for freedom.

Doug and Rick James had driven down to pick me up. In the back of the BMW X5 they'd laid out a mobile picnic for me: steak, pizza, fresh donuts, soft drinks, and coffee. We began the long drive to New Hampshire, where I'd have to report to a halfway house for a two-week stint, and we laughed and bantered and wallowed in the heady breeze of my liberation. It was the best road trip of my life, bar none.

In order for a prisoner to be released, he had to have proof of new residence and a job. For many of the guys inside, that would have been a challenge, but for me it was easy. I'd chosen New Hampshire for a reason; "Live Free or Die" meant no state income taxes. I knew by then that I was going to get paid, so that tactical choice was going to save me millions. The staff at Schuylkill never suspected my motives. They probably just thought I liked maple syrup.

I spent an easy two weeks at the halfway house in Manchester, New Hampshire, a simple brownstone housing twenty other "federal graduates." Less than a week after I arrived there, Doug took a call in his Boston office from Dean Zerbe in Washington. The first words out of Dean's mouth were "We've got white smoke!" Dean told Doug that the IRS was offering me a whistle-blower award of $104,000,000 for exposing UBS's involvement in the largest tax fraud in US history. It sure looked like my award was about to happen, but since I'd learned the hard way to never trust the government, I just carried on.

Then I moved on to my new job. My dad had gone to a Quaker boarding school in Pennsylvania, and one of his old schoolmates, Fritz Bell, owned a small farm and conference center in Raymond, New Hampshire, about thirty miles away. Fritz was a sweet elderly gentleman and he'd said to my dad, "Of course we'll take Brad, with pleasure!" Fritz and his family were delightful. They gave me my own digs in a little old caretaker's house on the property, and I happily groomed the gardens, built rock walls, repaired the barn, and inhaled the crisp autumn air. I've always enjoyed physical labor; it keeps you grounded. I would even have declined the small salary, but the Feds wanted proof of my rehabilitation. Irony of ironies, they'd spent a small fortune in taxpayer money keeping me in prison, then demanded that some taxpayer employ me.

Early in September, Steve Kohn called me from Washington, saying that he was on the way up to see me. He was going to fly up to Boston, hop on a commuter flight to Manchester, rent a car, and drive down to Raymond.

"You're going to be home, right, Brad?" He sounded very excited.

I laughed. "Don't worry. I'm not allowed to leave the state."

That evening we stood face-to-face in my tiny kitchen, me in my muddy work boots, torn jeans, and lumberjack shirt, and Steve wearing his lawyerly suit, though his tie knot was loose and his face flushed. He opened his brief case on my rickety table, and took out a US government check issued by the US Treasury Department (Exhibit 17).

It looked exactly like those refund checks you get sometime after April 15, if you're lucky. It was made out to Bradley Birkenfeld, in the total amount of *$75,816,958.40!* My total reward was for $104 million, but the government had *taken out taxes*. Did I care at that point? Hell no. What's a few dozen million between friends, right?

We didn't say much, because we were both speechless with victory. We shook hands and hugged like a diminutive coach and his quarterback who'd just won the Super Bowl. I turned the check over, endorsed it, and then we walked it over to the conference center and made multiple color copies, for later framing. Steve hurried on back to Washington where, in the morning, he'd be depositing my good fortune in an escrow account. We knew if we tried to deposit it in a Manchester bank, they'd probably call the cops.

On September 11, 2012, Steve and Dean held a press conference at the National Press Club in Washington, DC, where they announced the largest reward in whistle-blower history had just been bestowed upon Bradley Birkenfeld, recently released from federal prison. Still being on probation and forbidden from leaving New Hampshire, I couldn't be there in person. But Doug stood in for me and gave a speech in my stead, saying everything I had on my mind at the time. It was a powerful, damning oratory.

At the Department of Justice, I knew they were kicking the furniture and cursing. Kathryn Keneally, head of the DOJ Tax Division at the time, would later admit that when her BlackBerry flashed with the news, she threw it across the room and yelled, "A hundred and four million?! That's more than my entire annual budget!"

A few days later, I asked Doug and Rick to visit a car dealership in Boston. On the lot was a black Porsche Cayenne Turbo, one of a kind on the whole East Coast. The price tag was north of a hundred grand. Doug and Rick called to ask me if I wanted to negotiate.

"Nah, just pay the sticker price. No sense in haggling over joy."

The beauty was delivered to the farm on a flatbed truck, like an oversized wedding cake. The next day a nice lady leaving the conference center noticed the Porsche and asked Fritz Bell to whom it belonged. He smiled and said, "The gardener."

At the end of November, my home confinement and work-release periods were over. I wrote a $5,000 check to each member of Fritz's family, just by way of saying thanks. After all, they'd been so hospitable and nice, and had never mentioned my good fortune or expected a penny of it. Solid people with a sense of humanity.

Needing a new place to hang my hat, I'd been in touch with a real estate agent in Rye, a beautiful spot astride the Atlantic Ocean. She'd sent me some rental specs and photographs. This one house was a lovely seven-bedroom mansion with a small guest cottage, set out on lush lawns, surrounded by high trees, not far from the beach. But what caught my eye was its towering white flagpole. In my mind, I could already see the giant flag I'd buy for that pole, inky black with a skull and crossbones—the Jolly Roger.

"I'll take it," I said to the agent.

"It's pretty expensive, Brad," she warned. "About seven thousand dollars a month."

I grinned and laughed softly through the phone.

"My dear," I said. "No worries. UBS is footing the bill."

# CHAPTER 15

## RICH MAN, POOR MAN

*"How wonderful it is that nobody wait a single moment before starting to improve the world."*

—ANNE FRANK, HOLOCAUST VICTIM

AS THE LAST LEAVES of autumn left the trees in New Hampshire, I stood on a hard rocky beach, watching a single defiant sailboat brave the curling crests of the coming winter. There in the distance the boat's white canvas triangle whipped and flapped in the wind, its pilot unafraid of the ocean's vast power. I felt a kinship with that man, and had he known me, I know he would have felt the same.

The air was fresh, briny, and pure, though I could still smell Schuylkill in the linings of my lungs. Yet there I stood, head still high, my hands in the pockets of a simple peacoat, an ex-convict with an awful lot of money. Rags to riches, pauper to prince. The millions in my bank account were nearly unfathomable, much more than I ever could have made as a Swiss private banker. It might have humbled me, if I hadn't felt it was a just reward.

Another man might have gone wild, throwing exorbitant parties, bathing in champagne, seducing beautiful women with baubles and promises he was unlikely to keep. But I'd already done all that, and I'd learned long ago that it wasn't about the money at all. I had lived in that world for nearly two decades and discovered that even the most wealthy and powerful people weren't made whole by their riches or influence. I had seen firsthand that the coveted trappings of wealth were often merely bandages for wounded hearts.

Life was about the joy of living, the people with whom you lived it, and if you were suddenly a man of means, it was about helping those you loved who deserved it. In a way, I was like a man who had won a lottery. But instead of just picking lucky numbers, I had fought the fight of my life for this prize, and the scars of that battle would always remain.

Of course that didn't mean that I wasn't going to salve some of my wounds with private pleasures. That sprawling rental in Rye needed some nice new furniture, framed artwork for the walls, and with me being an avid movie buff, an enormous flat screen with surround sound. I also indulged in my two favorite pastimes, NHL hockey and Formula One racing, and started a collection of superstar helmets, uniforms, trophy cups, and classic old posters (Exhibit 20). But that was about it. I already had all the watches I needed, and one slick sports car was enough, at least for the moment.

I was still on probation, and would be for three more years. I had to reside in New Hampshire, but given my luxurious home, that was no trial. The indignities, however, continued. I applied for and received a New Hampshire driver's license, but I couldn't go anywhere outside the state without express permission. The government refused to return my old US passport, which had scores of visas and stamps from many foreign lands. That passport was something of an amulet to me, and it seemed petty and spiteful for them to keep it. I applied for a new one and it finally arrived, but I wouldn't be allowed to use it for years. These things, I knew, were the result of the Department of Justice's residual bitterness over the turn of fate that had left me not only liberated but rich beyond measure. It wasn't as if they feared my mobility. They knew full well that if I'd wanted to return to the ways of my old days, I needed no more than a cell phone.

At the National Whistleblower Center in Washington, DC, my case was the apogee of the Center's accomplishments. As I mentioned before, when Steve Kohn and Dean Zerbe held a press conference to announce the glorious fruits of my historic efforts, I was denied permission to go by the DOJ. I also had a probation officer keeping an eye on me. Eventually the guy stopped visiting my home, maybe because he figured that a multimillionaire with a Porsche, a mansion, fine dining, and plenty of great company wasn't about to flee.

If Kevin Downing thought that keeping me housebound was also going to keep me quiet, he was sadly mistaken. In fact, it had the opposite effect. Rye, New Hampshire, is a lovely place to visit the whole year round. At least once a month newspaper reporters or television pundits appeared at my house to record my story, and I took each opportunity to rail against a so-called justice system that was still ass-up incompetent and completely corrupt. But for the most part, I knew that my words would fall on deaf ears. It was only the actions I'd taken that mattered, and now, across the world, secret banking institutions continued to crumble, and the reverberations of what I'd done would thunder for decades. I knew that I'd been the catalyst for all that, and while I received little credit for my coup, it didn't matter all that much. I had done my part. It was time to spread the joy.

I'm not going to give you a long list of the redemptive things I did, because frankly, I didn't believe I needed redemption. However, I quietly chose some deserving causes and people I loved. My family members and close friends benefited, of course, and a few kind strangers, such as those people on Fritz Bell's farm who'd treated me so well. My favorite hockey team, the Boston Bruins, thought my idea of starting a charity for needy children was a fine idea, and a Boston pediatric hospital benefited as well.

I heard that shortly after my release and reward, Cliff Falla snatched a copy of the *Wall Street Journal* from the prison library. The headline featured my face and story, and Cliff raced around the dining hall waving it like a victory pennant. Since that time, Cliff's been released from Schuylkill and has heard from me again, and I'm hoping that someday Anwar will too. I was never tight-fisted before my award, nor was I careless with money after, yet having so much of it offered me limitless chances to brighten a day, or erase the ones in the past that were hard. What gave me the most pleasure was organizing weekend trips in New Hampshire, taking my friends to luxurious restaurants, handing out the menus and saying with my Birkenfeld grin, "Order anything you want! It's all on UBS, and Kevin Downing's the waiter!"

I had no big plans for the future, but there were a few things I was going to do. If you're of my generation, you might recall an old TV show called *Branded*. The story was about an Old West cavalry officer who's been falsely accused of treachery. His sword broken and his ranks ripped away, he spent the entire series determined to clear his name and serve justice on those who'd betrayed him. It's a classic story often repeated in lore, from Greek mythology to the whistle-blowers of today, and that has been one of my goals. Speak truth to power, serve distasteful facts to those who can't swallow them, show up whenever another Swiss banker raises his ugly head and tries to pretend that he just didn't know. Find other brave men and women who've been scorned and ruined and give them my shoulder to lean on. I've already given more than a hundred interviews and appeared on countless television shows, but the job's not done yet. Apparently it's my vocation chosen by fate, and I embrace it.

One choice fomented in my mind soon after my release and solidified later with clarity—and some sadness. Once my probation ended, I was going to leave the United States, probably never to return. It was the country of my birth, where I had gone from being a patriot willing to die for it to becoming an oppressed citizen, burned and betrayed. To me, America was no longer that shining city on the hill. It was ruled by corrupt politicians, incompetent prosecutors, and greedy financiers, many of whom were my sworn enemies, and would be so to this day and beyond. I knew I'd always be looking over my shoulder, but far from America's shores would be better. I thought about a nice lake in Europe, with a secluded parcel of slope on the shore, a large, strong house, and well-armed bodyguards. I would still visit my friends and family in the States, of course, and they would happily visit my castle as well. But I would never again be subject to the whims of the unjustly powerful. I had lived well before, and I knew how to enjoy it.

But that wouldn't happen for another few years.

Meanwhile, I'm content, wealthy, and wiser. I have enough toys to amuse me, and on occasion indulge in more. There are charities to help, hobbies to pursue, and plenty of good company comes my way. My best friends are still the old ones who knew me before I was rich. I tumbled down that dark rabbit hole, and came out whole and happy.

But since you already know me so well, there's no sense in lying. I'm still a hammer, looking for nails . . .

# ACKNOWLEDGMENTS

*Lucifer's Banker* is the story of my whistle-blowing and the eventual unraveling of Swiss bank secrecy. While many helped me in telling my story, I first would like to acknowledge all those who supported me during my long saga.

My family and close friends stood by me from my early efforts uncovering the scandal, through my long court case, time in prison, and up until today. My father was especially proud for the unethical practices I uncovered at UBS. My brother Doug was instrumental looking after my back through the many legal actions brought against me and worked closely with my whistle-blower attorneys, ensuring the strongest case was made on my behalf. Thank you Doug!

Stephen Kohn and David Colapinto out of Washington, DC and Dean Zerbe from Houston represented my interests under the IRS whistle-blower law. There are no finer attorneys than these guys. They have a keen understanding of whistle-blower legislation, and the workings of Washington DC, and an eagle's eye for the endless machinations of the Department of Justice. I have them to thank for the historic and unprecedented award I received, something only they had the confidence to pursue. John Cline out of San Francisco and Chris Hoge from Washington, DC were instrumental in protecting my interests in actions relating to my former client and earlier legal representation. Charles Poncet was there at the outset in Geneva, Switzerland, providing sage counsel, as I internally blew the whistle at UBS and eventually resigned. Philippe de Guyenro was invaluable coordinating my cooperation with the French magistrates as they investigate UBS's criminal conduct. Gerald Greenberg, my savvy attorney in Miami, strong-armed the DOJ to permit me to travel to Paris while I was still on probation to provide critical assistance to the French criminal investigation into UBS, an investigation the DOJ was not eager for me to support. Thanks to Jerry I was also able to celebrate my fiftieth birthday in the City of Lights with many friends!

A number of non-profit organizations took on my case early on. Jesselyn Raddack, then at the Government Accountability Project (GAP), was instrumental in shining an early light on my case. She exposed the DOJ's attempts to undermine my efforts, as they prosecuted the very person who handed them the keys to the largest tax evasion fraud in history and succeeded in jailing me for what many considered heroic efforts. Her earlier harrowing experiences as a whistle-blower at the DOJ and representations of countless others helped bring early attention to my plight.

In addition to GAP, National Whistleblower Center (NWC), Project on Government Oversight (POGO), Taxpayers Against Fraud (TAF), Transparency International, Global Witness, Democracy Now, No Fear Coalition, Disclosure Watch, Federal Ethics Center, Whistleblowers USA, Federal Accountability for Reform (FEAR), National Forum on Judicial Accountability, Whistleblowers Support Fund, International Association of Whistleblowers, and National Public Radio (NPR) all did their part in shining the spotlight on the DOJ abuse I was subject to and the complicit role of UBS and other private banks in conspiring to help wealthy Americans evade their tax obligations.

Along with the whistle-blower organizations, numerous journalists conducted in-depth investigations and reported on the illicit practices of UBS and other private banks as well as the DOJ's leniency in pursuing and meting out justice. In the US, I want to give credit to the following journalists for their insightful reporting: Sharyl Attiksson, Fabio Benedetti-Valentini, Michael Bronner, Jesse Drucker, Juan Gonzalez, James Grimaldi, David Hilzenrath, William Hoke, Eamon Javers, Janet Novack, Daniel Ryntjes, Laura Saunders, Dave Solomon, Ken Stier, and Vivienne Walt. Outside the US, where the story of private banks conspiring with private citizens to evade tax obligations is still developing, the following journalists have helped expose UBS and other private banks in their complicity in depriving governments worldwide of taxes: Ian Allison, Tom Burgis, Astrid Doerner, Catherine Dubouloz, Siri Gedde-Dahl, Lukas Hassig, Michel Henry, Arthur Honegger, John Letzing, Matthieu Pelloli, Edouard Perrin, François Pilet, Valerie de Senneville, Haig Simonian, Sebastian Sittl, Goran Skaalmo, Noopur Tiwari, Roar Valderhaug, Matthew Valencia, and Maritina Zafeiriadou. I am sure I have missed others' valuable contributions to the uncovering of this global fraud; for my oversight I apologize and extend my sincere thanks.

I took on the then world's largest bank without fully understanding the repercussions whistle-blowers are subjected to for doing the right thing. I have been fortunate over the past few years to meet a few heroic individuals who risked it all to uncover wrongdoing. I would like to thank Harry Markopolos, the man who exposed Bernie Madoff's multi-billion dollar Ponzi scheme, and the many other whistle-blowers for their courageous efforts. We need to recognize these individuals for their important contributions to society and support legislation and programs that protect their work and ensure they are appropriately compensated.

I want to thank all those who helped me in telling my story. To my friends, family, and colleagues, I greatly appreciate your efforts recounting my many experiences around the globe, helping me portray the business and life of a private banker, and ensuring my story did not take unnecessary detours. I would also like to thank Eric Rayman for helping me navigate the opaque world of literary law.

I will always be eternally grateful to my very dear friends Fritz Bell, may he rest in peace, and Will Fregosi who provided me shelter, a job, and company after I was released from prison. They helped me land on my two feet, were very proud of my whistle-blowing, and encouraged me to tell my story to the world.

Lastly, I am forever grateful to Steven Hartov for the many patient hours he dedicated to learning my story, his thorough immersion into the life of a private banker, his thoughtful research of my historic whistle-blowing, and the long drama of my fight against the DOJ. He masterfully captured my voice, and in *Lucifer's Banker* we tell the untold story of how I destroyed Swiss bank secrecy.

# APPENDIX

**Top Ten UBS Scandals**

My historic whistle-blowing uncovered but one of many illegal schemes perpetrated by UBS in recent years. While the offshore tax-evasion scandal I exposed was among the largest, the scope and range of the remaining schemes gives testimony to the rampant disregard for the law with which UBS conducted its affairs across the globe.

1. *May 10, 2004 – Illegal Transfer of US Currency to Embargoed Countries*
   **FINE: $100 million**

2. *February 18, 2009 – Offshore Tax Evasion in the United States*
   **FINE: $780 million**

3. *May 4, 2011 – Securities Fraud in the Muni Bond Derivatives Market*
   **FINE: $160 million**

4. *November 26, 2012 – Rogue UK Trader Lost $2.3 billion*
   **FINE: $47.6 million**

5. *December 19, 2012 – Currency Market LIBOR Rigging*
   **FINE: $1.5 billion**

6. *July 25, 2013 – Mortgage-Backed Securities Fraud*
   **FINE: $885 million**

7. *July 29, 2014 – Offshore Tax Evasion in Germany*
   **FINE: $403 million**

8. *September 30, 2014 – Offshore Tax Evasion and Money Laundering in France*
   **FINE: $1.4 billion**

9. *May 20, 2015 – Currency Market and LIBOR Scandal*
   **FINE: $545 million**

10. *March 10, 2016 – UBS Bankers Bonuses Ruled Illegal*
    **FINE: $130 million**

## Document 1: Swiss Bank Secrecy

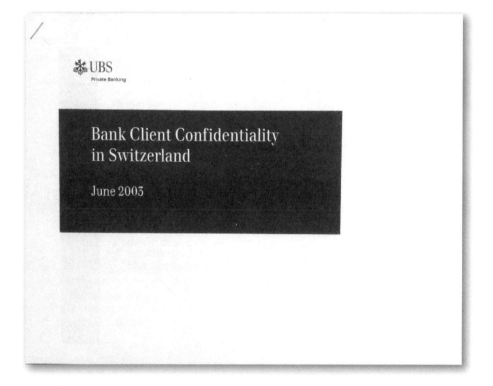

This UBS power point presentation outlined the reasons why UBS clients were incorrectly informed that they were totally shielded by Swiss Bank secrecy.

# Document 2: The Three-Page Memo

## Cross-Border Banking Activities into the United States (version November 2004)

1. **Introduction; Regulated Activities in United States and Status of UBS Entities**

   The U.S. legal regulatory framework draws an important distinction between banking and securities activities:

   **Banking activities,** most important cash and custody services, are governed by various federal and state laws and are regulated by various federal and state banking supervisors, including, in the case of UBS AG's branches, agencies, and bank depository subsidiaries, the Federal Reserve Board (the "Board"), the Office of the Comptroller of the Currency ("OCC"), the Federal Deposit Insurance Corporation ("FDIC") and the Connecticut, Illinois and Utah state banking departments.

   **Securities related activities** (i.e., broker-dealer, investment advisor) are governed by various federal and state laws and are regulated by the Securities and Exchange Commission ("SEC") and state securities supervisors. Broker-dealers also are members of, and governed by, a self-regulatory organization ("SRO") known as the National Association of Securities Dealers ("NASD"). There is a separate regulator and regulatory scheme for providers of commodities services.

   UBS AG has several U.S. branches and agencies and various non-banking subsidiaries all properly licensed, but these licenses **do not** encompass cross-border services provided to U.S. residents by UBS AG offices or affiliates outside of the United States. (Unless otherwise specified, all references herein to "UBS AG" refer to offices located, or employees based, outside of the United States).

2. **Advertising & Events**

   **Advertising:** Some state laws prohibit banks without a banking license from that state from soliciting deposits from that state's residents. States also may prohibit non-licensed lenders from making certain loans to consumers in such states. Any entity outside of the United States that is not registered with the SEC (and, in the case of brokerage activities, with the NASD) may not advertise securities services or products in the United States. Therefore, UBS AG will not advertise and market for its services with material going beyond generic information relating to the image of UBS AG and its brand in the U.S.

   **Events.** UBS AG may not organize, absent an opinion from Legal, events in the U.S.

3. **Establishing Relationships with New Clients Resident in the United States**

   **Securities services/products.** UBS AG may not establish relationships for securities products or services with new clients resident in the United States with the use of U.S. jurisdictional means. Thus, it must ensure that it does not contact securities clients in the United States through telephone, mail, e-mail, advertising, the internet or personal visits.

   **Banking services/products.** To avoid possible violations of state law and/or to avoid establishing and maintaining a place of business in the United States, UBS AG should ensure that:

   - No marketing or advertising activity targeted to U.S. persons takes place in the United States;
   - No solicitation of account opening takes place in the United States;
   - No cold calling or prospecting into the United States takes place;

- No negotiating or concluding of contracts takes place in the United States;

- No carrying or transmitting of cash or other valuables of whatever nature out of the United States takes place; The same applies to actively organizing such transfers or attempting to circumvent this prohibition through other means.

- No routine certification of signatures, transmission of completed account documentation, or related administrative activity on behalf of UBS AG takes place;

- Employees do not carry on substantial activities at fixed location(s) while in the United States thereby establishing an office or maintaining a place of business.

**Outside the United States.** Soliciting and accepting banking business from U.S. residents while they are outside of the United States generally is not problematic.

4.    **Maintaining Relationships with Clients Resident in the United States**

**Securities services/products.** UBS AG may not maintain relationships for securities services or products with clients resident in the United States, unless the relationship is conducted without the use of U.S. means (*e.g.*, telephone, mail, e-mail, advertising, the internet or personal visits into the United States) and consistent with procedures UBS AG has established in this regard.

**Banking services/products.** If UBS AG obtains a U.S. resident client for banking services without violating the restrictions set forth in section 3 above, it may service the account:

- UBS AG may provide statements, account information and transaction confirmations to the client, provided it does so in accordance with the terms agreed by the client and in compliance with all applicable internal procedures.

- UBS AG may provide product and service information subject to the points mentioned in section 6 below.

- UBS AG may certify signatures, transmit account documentation and conduct related administrative activity for existing clients.

Under no circumstances will UBS AG be carrying or transporting cash and other valuables of whatever nature on behalf of clients into or out of the United States. The same applies to actively organizing such transfers or attempting to circumvent the prohibition.

**When traveling cross-border, UBS AG employees always must remember that all clients of UBS AG expect us to take all necessary steps to safeguard confidentiality. Client advisors are referred to separate guidance on the protection of confidential information and other available resources that may assist.**

5.    **Dealing with Financial Intermediaries and other Non-Private Clients Resident in the United States**

**Securities services/products.** UBS AG may not deal with financial intermediaries or other non-private clients resident in the United States in matters relating to securities services and products, except for registered broker-dealers and U.S. licensed banks, provided that it does not directly or indirectly deal with the private and non-private clients of such broker-dealers and banks.

**Banking services/products.** UBS AG may accept referrals from financial intermediaries in the United States, provided that the financial intermediaries (i) do not work for UBS AG, (ii) do not actively market UBS AG services and products, and (iii) make referrals only to accommodate client requests. In dealing with such intermediaries, UBS AG must comply with the restrictions set forth in sections 3 and 4 above.

6.    **Product Offering**

2

**Securities products.** All securities products offered to U.S. persons must be compliant with U.S. laws, which generally means that they must be registered with the SEC. The purchase of securities may be exempt from registration if certain condition are met.

**Lending products.** It may be necessary to obtain a state license to offer lending products, depending on the purpose, amount, interest rate and borrower of the product. There is a reasonable argument that federal consumer protection laws do not apply to products offered by non-U.S. entities, but state consumer protection laws (*e.g.*, anti-usury) may apply.

**Research.** UBS AG research may not be distributed to clients in the United States, except in very limited circumstances.

**E-Banking.** UBS AG has implemented specific restrictions for e-banking for U.S. customers.

3

This UBS memorandum was the quintessential reason for Brad to commence his historic whistle-blowing.

# Document 3: UBS Training Documents

## Case Studies Cross-Border Workshop NAM

- Please go through each case. Put yourself into the concrete situation as it occurs in real life.
- Do not tackle the case with the perspective of what you think that Legal, Compliance, IT or Security Risk wants to hear.
- Compare your behaviours with the ones of your colleagues in the group.
- Identify and note questions you want to raise in the plenary session.

### Case 1

During your trip to the USA/Canada, where you wish to visit various clients, you are stopped at the border by the customs authority or during your stay by the police and confronted with the following questions:

- purpose of your visit
- your profession
- people you are going to visit
- content of your baggage incl. notebook, cell phone, PDA (SMS, MMS, digital photographing) or Blackberry

Question 1: How do you react? How do you prepare for such a potential confrontation? How did you fill out your immigration form?

You get a strange feeling about the way the way the questions are asked. You remember that, with the intention to avoid having to carry those documents with you, you had sent an envelope with some of the sensitive account related data to your hotel (alternatively: a friend in the respective country whom you know very well; a family member; a local business contact).

Question 2: How do you handle sensitive documents you want to use during your visit (such as account statements and similar documents) when planning a trip to the USA/Canada?

### Case 2

During the discussion with a very interesting prospect in the USA/Canada he/she indicates that he/she has a substantial amount of money to transfer from his/her home country to your bank. The prospect queries whether the bank can assist him/her in this respect. He/She mentions in the same token that Bank XYZ had offered him/her very concrete services for his/her assistance.

Question: How do you react? Would it make a difference if the person was a long standing client of the bank?

### Case 3

During a trip to the USA/Canada you intend to meet client X. He recently gave you a telephone call and asked you to bring his latest account statements with you at your next visit. He also mentioned that he would like to hand over to you a number of written trading orders and to discuss them at the proposed meeting. Finally, he refers to the telephone conversation you had with him some weeks ago regarding the advantages of a PM mandate and he asked you to also bring along the necessary documents for the conclusion of a PM contract.

Permanent Subcommittee on Investigations
**EXHIBIT #92**

Due to a conflict of dates you are not able to travel. As you do not want to disappoint your client, you consider making a call to the local UBS branch/subsidiary (where you know one of the officers very well) and ask an officer to meet your client and to satisfy his requests on your behalf.

**Question 1: What do you think of this idea?**

**Question 2: Generally speaking, to what extent and in which activities can your colleague of the local branch/subsidiary be of assistance? Please go through concrete situations as they occur in your daily work.**

### Case 4

After passing the immigration desk during your trip to the USA/Canada, you are intercepted by the authorities. By checking your Palm, they find all your client meetings. Fortunately you stored only very short remarks of the different meetings and no names.

As you spend around one week in the same hotel, the longer you stay there, the more you get the feeling of being observed. Sometimes you even doubt if all of the hotel employees are working for the hotel. A lot of client meetings are held in your suite of the hotel.

One morning your are intercepted by an FBI-agent. He looks for some information about one of your clients and explains to you, that your client is involved in illegal activities.

**Question 1: What would you do in such a situation?**

**Question 2: What are the signs indicating that something is going on?**

### Case 5

As you had a lot of documents to take with you to your trip to the USA/Canada, the carry on luggage was very heavy and you decided to put your notebook in the checked luggage. When arriving at your destination, you realise that your notebook is missing. You are not sure, whether you had a separate excel-file with a client summary still on your notebook.

**Question 1: What would you do in such a situation?**

Later on, when arriving at the hotel, you are contacted by an anonymous caller. He pretends having found your notebook at the airport and offers you a deal: He sends you the notebook if you pay him an amount of USD 100'000. Your notebook is equipped with the latest security features (encryption, token based authentication).

**Question 2: Your reaction**

This UBS training document outlined sample case scenarios for UBS bankers to contemplate answers to as they entered customs in the US and Canada.

# Document 4: Martin Liechti's
# Non-Prosecution Agreement

Case 0:08-cr-60322-JIC   Document 47-5   Entered on FLSD Docket 05/23/2014   Page 2 of 5

**U.S. Department of Justice**

*United States Attorney*
*Southern District of Florida*

*500 East Broward Boulevard, Ste. 700*

*Fort Lauderdale, FL 33394*
*(954) 356-7255*

July 2, 2008

David M. Zornow, Esq.
Skadden, Arps, Slate, Meagher, & Flom LLP
Four Times Square
New York, New York  10036

Re:    Martin Liechti

Dear Mr. Zornow:

On the understandings specified below, the United States Attorney's Office for the Southern District of Florida and the Department of Justice, Tax Division (collectively hereinafter "the United States government"), will not criminally prosecute Martin Liechti for any crimes he committed related to his involvement in a tax fraud scheme whereby UBS managers, UBS bankers, United States clients of UBS and others defrauded the United States and other United States government agencies, including the Internal Revenue Service and the Securities Exchange Commission with respect to United States cross-border banking and investment activities (hereinafter "the UBS tax fraud scheme").

In exchange for these promises, Martin Liechti agrees that should the United States government determine that he willfully violated any of the following conditions, then: (a) Martin Liechti shall thereafter be subject to prosecution for any federal criminal violation of which the United States government has knowledge, including perjury and obstruction of justice, and any such prosecution that is not time-barred by the applicable statute of limitations on the date of the signing of this Agreement may be commenced against Martin Liechti, notwithstanding the expiration of the statute of limitations between the signing of this Agreement and the commencement of such prosecution; and (b) all statements made by Martin Liechti to the United States government or any United States law enforcement agency designated by the United States government, including statements given pursuant to a proffer agreement executed on May 22, May 23, June 2, June 12, and June 18, 2008 and any testimony given by Martin Liechti before a grand jury or other United States tribunal, whether prior to or subsequent to the signing of this Agreement, and any leads from such statements or testimony shall be admissible in evidence in any criminal proceeding brought against Martin Liechti.

This Agreement does not provide any protection against prosecution for any crimes except as set forth above.

1.    Martin Liechti (a) shall truthfully and completely disclose all information with respect to the activities of himself and others concerning all matters about which the United States government inquires of him, which information can be used for any purpose; (b) shall cooperate fully with the United States government, the Internal Revenue Service, and any other law enforcement agency designated by this Office; (c) upon reasonable notice shall attend all meetings at which the United States government requests his presence; (d) shall provide to United States government upon request, any document, record, or other tangible evidence in his custody, possession or control relating to matters about which the United States government or any designated law enforcement agency inquires of him; (e) shall truthfully testify before the grand jury and at any trial and other court proceeding with respect to any matters about which the United States government may request his testimony; (f) shall bring to the attention of the United States government all crimes as defined by United States law which he may have committed, and all administrative, civil or criminal proceedings, investigations, or prosecutions in which he has been or is a subject, target, party, or witness; and (g) shall commit no crimes as defined by United States law whatsoever.  Moreover, any assistance Martin Liechti may provide to federal criminal investigators shall be pursuant to the specific instructions and control of the United States government and designated investigators.

2.    Martin Liechti appoints his attorney, David M. Zornow, as his agent to accept service of legal process, including subpoenas and summonses, in any proceeding instituted by the United States government or to which the United States government is a party with respect to the fraud scheme described above.

3.    Unless and until the United States government decides otherwise, Martin Liechti shall remain in the United States until the United States government obtains from UBS AG or otherwise the compilation of documents assembled by Martin Liechti and his assistant in early 2008 concerning the fraud scheme described above, the existence of which Martin Liechti disclosed to the United States government pursuant to a proffer agreement on June 12, 2008.

4.    Unless and until the United States government decides otherwise, Martin Liechti shall remain in the United States until either (a) UBS AG executes a stipulation satisfactory to the United States government regarding the admissibility of Martin Liechti's affidavit dated July 2, 2008 in any proceeding the United States government institutes against UBS AG to which the United States government or any United States government agency is a party with UBS AG, or (b) until the United States government secures Martin Liechti's testimony in a deposition so ordered by a district court judge pursuant to Rule 15 of the Federal Rules of Criminal Procedure and to which UBS AG is a party.

5.    Martin Liechti shall provide to the United States government the names and identification information of UBS AG United States clients who had or have undeclared accounts with UBS AG. Martin Liechti shall remain in the United States until he has provided this information to the United States government.

6.      Should Martin Liechti commit any crimes as defined by United States law subsequent to the date of signing of this Agreement, or should it be determined that he has intentionally given false, incomplete, or misleading testimony or information, or should he otherwise violate any provision of this Agreement, Martin Liechti shall thereafter be subject to prosecution for any federal criminal violation of which the United States government has knowledge, including perjury and obstruction of justice. Any such prosecution that is not time-barred by the applicable statute of limitations on the date of the signing of this Agreement may be commenced against Martin Liechti, notwithstanding the expiration of the statute of limitations between the signing of this Agreement and the commencement of such prosecution. It is the intent of this Agreement to waive all defenses based on the statute of limitations with respect to any prosecution that is not time-barred on the date that this Agreement is signed.

7.      If the United States government determines that Martin Liechti has committed any crime as defined by United States law after signing this Agreement or has intentionally given false, incomplete, or misleading testimony or information, or has otherwise violated any provision of this Agreement, (a) all statements made by Martin Liechti to the United States government or any United States law enforcement agency designated by the United States government, including statements given pursuant to a proffer agreement executed on May 22, May 23, June 2, June 12, and June 18, 2008 and any testimony given by Martin Liechti before a grand jury or other United States tribunal, whether prior to or subsequent to the signing of this Agreement, and any leads from such statements or testimony shall be admissible in evidence in any United States criminal proceeding brought against Martin Liechti; and (b) Martin Liechti shall assert no claim under the United States Constitution, any statute, Rule 410 of the Federal Rules of Evidence, or any other federal rule that such statements or any leads therefrom should be suppressed. It is the intent of this Agreement to waive all rights in the foregoing respects.

8.      This Agreement does not bind any state or local prosecuting authority. The United States government will, however, bring the cooperation of Martin Liechti to the attention of other prosecuting offices and any other foreign or domestic agency, if requested by Martin Liechti.

3

9.      With respect to this matter, this Agreement supersedes all prior, if any, understandings, promises and/or conditions between the United States government and Martin Liechti. No additional promises, agreements, and conditions have been entered into other than those set forth in this letter and none will be entered into unless in writing and signed by all parties.

Very truly yours,

R. ALEXANDER ACOSTA
UNITED STATES ATTORNEY

By:

KEVIN M. DOWNING
SENIOR TRIAL ATTORNEY
MICHAEL P. BEN'ARY
TRIAL ATTORNEY
UNITED STATES DEPARTMENT OF JUSTICE
TAX DIVISION
JEFFREY A. NEIMAN
ASSISTANT U.S. ATTORNEY

I have read this letter and have discussed it fully with my attorney. I understand and agree to the terms set forth in this letter. This letter fully and accurately sets forth my agreement with the Office of the United States Attorney for the Southern District of Florida and the Department of Justice, Tax Division. There have been no additional promises or representations made to me by any officials or law enforcement authorities of the United States in connection with this matter. I have signed this agreement knowingly, intelligently, freely and voluntarily because I believe it is in my best interest to do so.

MARTIN LIECHTI

I represent Martin Liechti as his legal counsel. I have discussed this letter with my client, and to the best of my knowledge, he understands this letter and agrees to the terms set forth therein.

DAVID M. ZORNOW, ESQ.

4

The secret July 2, 2008 Non-Prosecution Agreement that required UBS Senior Executive Martin Liechti to fully cooperate with the government. Two weeks later, Liechti appeared before the senate subcommittee but refused to answer any questions. Despite the clear violation of this agreement, Liechti quietly left the country the following month and was never prosecuted by the Department of Justice.

# Document 5: Levin Letter

JOSEPH I. LIEBERMAN, CONNECTICUT, CHAIRMAN

CARL LEVIN, MICHIGAN
DANIEL K. AKAKA, HAWAII
THOMAS R. CARPER, DELAWARE
MARK L. PRYOR, ARKANSAS
MARY L. LANDRIEU, LOUISIANA
CLAIRE McCASKILL, MISSOURI
JON TESTER, MONTANA
ROLAND W. BURRIS, ILLINOIS
MICHAEL F. BENNET, COLORADO

SUSAN M. COLLINS, MAINE
TOM COBURN, OKLAHOMA
JOHN McCAIN, ARIZONA
GEORGE V. VOINOVICH, OHIO
JOHN ENSIGN, NEVADA
LINDSEY GRAHAM, SOUTH CAROLINA
ROBERT F. BENNETT, UTAH

MICHAEL L. ALEXANDER, STAFF DIRECTOR
BRANDON L. MILHORN, MINORITY STAFF DIRECTOR AND CHIEF COUNSEL

## United States Senate

COMMITTEE ON
HOMELAND SECURITY AND GOVERNMENTAL AFFAIRS

WASHINGTON, DC 20510–6250

July 28, 2009

**VIA U.S. MAIL & EMAIL (dmeier@toddweld.com)**

David E. Meier, Esq.
Todd & Weld, LLP
28 State Street, 31st Floor
Boston, MA  02109

Dear Mr. Meier:

This is in response to your request that I provide my assessment of the assistance provided by Mr. Bradley Birkenfeld to the Permanent Subcommittee on Investigations in the course of its investigation into tax haven banks and their impact on tax compliance in the United States.

In October of 2007, Mr. Birkenfeld initiated a contact with the Subcommittee and subsequently provided testimonial and documentary information related to his employment as a private banker at UBS in Switzerland.  In a sworn deposition before Subcommittee staff, Mr. Birkenfeld supplied information on the program conducted by UBS Switzerland to attract client accounts in the United States, and the activities and practices employed by UBS private bankers operating out of Switzerland.

Throughout the Subcommittee investigation, which lasted over 14 months, Mr. Birkenfeld voluntarily made himself available for additional staff interviews and provided additional documents to the Subcommittee.

The information provided by Mr. Birkenfeld has been accurate and enabled the Subcommittee to initiate its investigation into the practices of UBS.

Sincerely,

Carl Levin
Chairman
Permanent Subcommittee on Investigations

This letter from the Chairman of the US Senate Permanent Subcommittee on Investigations, Carl Levin, clearly recognizes Brad's courageous efforts that led to multiple investigations, hearings, and reports that toppled UBS.

# Document 6: Grassley Letter

MAX BAUCUS, MONTANA, CHAIRMAN

JOHN D. ROCKEFELLER IV, WEST VIRGINIA
KENT CONRAD, NORTH DAKOTA
JEFF BINGAMAN, NEW MEXICO
JOHN F. KERRY, MASSACHUSETTS
BLANCHE L. LINCOLN, ARKANSAS
RON WYDEN, OREGON
CHARLES E. SCHUMER, NEW YORK
DEBBIE STABENOW, MICHIGAN
MARIA CANTWELL, WASHINGTON
BILL NELSON, FLORIDA
ROBERT MENENDEZ, NEW JERSEY
THOMAS R. CARPER, DELAWARE

CHUCK GRASSLEY, IOWA
ORRIN G. HATCH, UTAH
OLYMPIA J. SNOWE, MAINE
JON KYL, ARIZONA
JIM BUNNING, KENTUCKY
MIKE CRAPO, IDAHO
PAT ROBERTS, KANSAS
JOHN ENSIGN, NEVADA
MICHAEL B. ENZI, WYOMING
JOHN CORNYN, TEXAS

RUSSELL SULLIVAN, STAFF DIRECTOR
KOLAN DAVIS, REPUBLICAN STAFF DIRECTOR AND CHIEF COUNSEL

**United States Senate**

COMMITTEE ON FINANCE

WASHINGTON, DC 20510-6200

June 8, 2010

The Honorable Timothy F. Geithner
Secretary of the Treasury
Department of the Treasury
1500 Pennsylvania Avenue
Washington, DC 20220

The Honorable Douglas L. Shulman
Commissioner
Internal Revenue Service
1111 Constitution Avenue NW
Washington, DC 20224

Dear Secretary Geithner and Commissioner Shulman:

I am writing to express my concern about continued tax evasion by taxpayers using secret Swiss bank accounts, particularly accounts at UBS AG. Swiss lawmakers voted today to block the treaty the United States hammered out with Switzerland last year. While I understand that today's vote in the lower chamber of the Swiss Parliament is not the final word, I am worried that the Internal Revenue Service ("IRS") is doing next to nothing to identify tax evasion by U.S. taxpayers utilizing these accounts while waiting for ratification of the treaty.

It has been over three years since Mr. Bradley Charles Birkenfeld approached the Department of Justice, IRS and the Securities and Exchange Commission about potential tax evasion facilitated by UBS AG on behalf of U.S. clients. The attached letter from Mr. Birkenfeld's attorneys outlines a number of steps that the IRS could have taken with the information he provided in March 2007. It seems this information would allow the IRS to trace individuals in the U.S. that had UBS bank accounts. In addition, this letter also provides information about UBS USA, a wholly-owned subsidiary of UBS AG, and its involvement in UBS AG activities here in the U.S.

Using this information to identify U.S. clients would appear to be more productive than simply pursuing agreements and treaties with the Swiss, especially since those avenues seem limited to specific individuals. It does not appear that you would need a treaty, or other agreement with the Swiss government, to pursue the records of UBS USA.

As a result, I would like a detailed listing of all steps IRS has taken with the information that Mr. Birkenfeld provided. Please note that I am not asking for information about any individual taxpayer so I do not expect section 6103 to preclude you from responding to my request. I would also like to know what IRS is doing to ensure that, if and when it receives a complete list of UBS AG account holders, the IRS will not be precluded by the statute of limitations from auditing those individuals.

Today's vote in Switzerland only underscores the need for the IRS to encourage whistleblowers to come forward. Mr. Birkenfeld blew the whistle on just one bank. What is the IRS doing to encourage more whistleblowers to come forward about offshore bank accounts?

I appreciate your prompt attention to this matter and ask for a written response by June 18, 2010. Please contact me or my staff at (202) 224-4515 with any questions.

Sincerely,

Chuck Grassley
Ranking Member

Enclosure

This letter from the author of the whistle-blowing law, Charles Grassley, clearly outlines the government's lack of action on Brad's unprecedented information about UBS.

# Document 7: Letter from Mr. Birkenfeld's Attorney

**STRICTLY CONFIDENTIAL**

November 17, 2009

*The Honorable Carl Levin*
*U.S. Senate*
*269 Russell Senate Office Building*
*Washington, D.C. 20510*

<u>*Bradley Birkenfeld – IRS Whistleblower- UBS*</u>

Dear Senator Levin:

My firm has been retained to represent Mr. Bradley Birkenfeld on his whistleblower claims.

I would like to take this opportunity to express my gratitude to you and your staff for the July 28, 2009, letter you wrote regarding the nature and extent of the assistance provided by my client, Bradley Birkenfeld (the IRS whistleblower against UBS) to the Permanent Subcommittee on Investigations. This letter was very helpful and was submitted to the Court at Mr. Birkenfeld's sentencing hearing in the United States District Court for the Southern District of Florida on August 21, 2009.

However, I feel compelled to bring a number of very serious matters to your attention. These matters directly concern the integrity of the new IRS Whistleblower Law, and the ability of the United States Government to ensure that the Congressional intent behind this law is fulfilled and the right of whistleblowers to fully and completely communicate with the U.S. Congress. Given the harmful impact of illegal international bank secrecy on the United States, as fully documented by the work of your Subcommittee, we believe these matters should be immediately reviewed.

First, I had the opportunity to review some of the early e-mails between Mr. Birkenfeld's prior attorneys and the Tax Division of the Department of Justice, including the chief prosecutor assigned to the Birkenfeld matter, Mr. Kevin Downing. These early e-mails, attached hereto, demonstrate that the DOJ did not understand that Mr. Birkenfeld was in fact a whistleblower that desired to come to the United States and make significant voluntary disclosures both to the DOJ, the IRS Whistleblower Office and the United States Government. As far back as March of 2007, the prosecutors were refusing to consider Mr. Birkenfeld a "whistleblower," despite his requests for protection under the newly enacted IRS Whistleblower Law (passed by Congress in December of 2006). Mr. Birkenfeld's former counsel attempted to explain to the prosecutors the vital importance of the disclosures Mr. Birkenfeld intended to make, but they were brushed off ("don't minimize the importance of the information that our client is about to give the government . . . We look forward to working on the same side as you and the government in this matter."). E-mail Chain, March 28, 2007.

The misunderstanding concerning Mr. Birkenfeld's status as a whistleblower, and his willingness to voluntarily provide information to the government was not resolved. On June 11, 2007, the prosecutors recognized Mr. Birkenfeld's desire to work with the IRS whistleblower program, but specifically stated that DOJ is "not a part of the IRS whistleblower program." See e-mail chain dated June 11, 2007. Likewise, as a whistleblower, Mr. Birkenfeld had information relevant to the SEC. Yet by refusing to consider him a whistleblower the DOJ interfered with his ability to fully communicate with all relevant federal law enforcement agencies. timony Mr. Birkenfeld provided to your Subcommittee on October 11, 2007. Mr. Birkenfeld Despite the fact that the IRS Whistleblower Law is part of the laws of the United States, the DOJ was not willing or able to alter its approach to Mr. Birkenfeld in light of the new Congressional mandate. Moreover, under the False Claims Act (the law for which the IRS Whistleblower Law is based), the Department of Justice regularly works hand-in-hand with the program offices for which the contracting abuse is material. For whatever reason, the DOJ was not willing to consider Mr. Birkenfeld a whistleblower. These differences also impacted Mr. Birkenfeld's relationship with the U.S. Senate inasmuch as the DOJ raised objections to his cooperation with the Senate.

In this e-mail chain the Subcommittee Investigator asked Mr. Birkenfeld's counsel The disconnect between Mr. Birkenfeld's desire to "blow the whistle" on the UBS tax fraud and SEC violations, and the DOJ's refusal to consider Mr. Birkenfeld a whistleblower, harmed the interests of the United States and federal law enforcement. Mr. Birkenfeld's counsel informed the Subcommittee that Mr. Birkenfeld had fully disclosed Olenicoff during his testimony before the First is the issue of Mr. Olenicoff. At the August 2009 sentencing hearing the DOJ prosecuting attorney stated that if Birkenfeld had disclosed information related to Mr. Olenicoff when he met with the DOJ, the United States would have recommended no jail time in this matter. During the sentencing hearing the DOJ prosecutor, Mr. Downing, stated that Mr. Birkenfeld did not disclose his relationship with Olenicoff. On page 32, lines 12-16 the prosecutor insinuates that Mr. Birkenfeld withheld information on Olenicoff because he wanted to "continu[e] aiding and assisting Mr. Olenicoff committing tax evasion." On page 33, lines 14-21 of the transcript the prosecutor is more specific in his criticism of Mr. Birkenfeld, and states that "Mr. Olenicoff would be in jail had Mr. Birkenfeld come in, in 2007 and disclosed that information." The prosecutor concludes by stating that Mr. Birkenfeld's failure to disclose information on Olenicoff was key to "why the U.S. government seeks jail time for Mr. Birkenfeld." Page 33, lines 19-21.

However, the actual record is very different. Mr. Birkenfeld *did not* withhold information on Olenicoff. Mr. Birkenfeld did *not* "continue" to "aid and assist" Olenicoff in tax evasion. Those statements are completely false.

Mr. Birkenfeld was fully ready, willing and able to provide DOJ with all the information he had on Mr. Olenicoff.

But the proof that Mr. Birkenfeld was ready, willing and able to turn in Mr. Olenicoff (among every other person for whom he had knowledge of the fraud) is confirmed by his whistleblower activities. Whereas the DOJ was not willing to treat him as a whistleblower, the U.S. Senate Subcommittee on Permanent Investigations did. In 2007, before the Olenicoff plea deal was filed in Court (and well before Mr. Birkenfeld was aware that there was a criminal matter pending against Olenicoff), Mr. Birkenfeld provided testimony about Olenicoff to the SEC and Senate. This should be confirmed in your staff files and in the transcript of the testimony Mr. Birkenfeld provided to your Subcommittee on October 11, 2007. Mr. Birkenfeld wasn't hiding or protecting Olenicoff. Far from it. Your Subcommittee staff should be able to fully confirm that Mr. Birkenfeld voluntarily gave them Olenicoff's name and the magnitude of his accounts at UBS.

The fact that Mr. Birkenfeld was not "hiding" Mr. Olenicoff from the government investigators is also confirmed in an e-mail chain between Mr. Birkenfeld's former attorneys and the lead investigator for the Senate Permanent Subcommittee dated March 4, 2008.

In this e-mail chain the Subcommittee investigator asked Mr. Birkenfeld's counsel: "if Brad ever heard of a person named Olenicoff." Clearly, the issue of Olenicoff and his role with UBS had somehow sparked the interest of the Subcommittee.

In response, Mr. Birkenfeld's counsel informed the Subcommittee that Mr. Birkenfeld had fully disclosed Olenicoff during his testimony before the Subcommittee on October 11, 2007:

*"Yes. Olenikov was identified to you during the session we had on October 11, 2007 . . . . Olenikov was Brad's biggest client with over $200,000,000 in accounts . . . . Olenikov just plead guilty to tax fraud and from the press reports I read, it doesn't appear that Olenikov disclosed the UBS Switzerland funds. We went back to the IRS and DOJ-Tax people and told them that Bard had information that would help them with Olenikov, but DOJ-Tax merely threatened Brad with withholding information from them . . . . I hope that someone in Congress takes note of the poor handling that Brad has received from DOJ-Tax."*

The Senate Committee investigator responded: *"You are right. I completely forgot about Olenicoff . . . ."*

3

This letter from Brad's legal team, Steven Kohn and Dean Zerbe, was a thank-you response to Senator Levin and discussed the DOJ Prosecutor, Kevin Downing.

# READING
# GROUP GUIDE

**Q.** After living through the latest banking crisis and learning of the questionable ethics and practices of bankers, were you surprised by the intrigue, action, and corruption depicted in *Lucifer's Banker*? What was the most surprising element of the story, and why? What part of the story made you the most uncomfortable?

**Q.** Swiss banking laws protect the secrecy of account holders. When Brad flies to North America to get wealthy people to open accounts at his bank, he says it's not his job to check up on how these Americans file their taxes. Do you agree? Have you known of an instance of someone not declaring every bit of income on their taxes? Is there a difference between neglecting to declare thousands (cheating a lot) and neglecting to declare a few hundred dollars (cheating a little)?

**Q.** Who is hurt the most by wealthy tax-dodgers?

**Q.** When Brad first starts out at Credit Suisse, he's amazed at how easy it is to do his job of signing on new clients to secret Swiss accounts; plus, the pay is great. Perhaps you thought: Gee, maybe my son/daughter/spouse/self should do that for a few years, build up a nest egg, live in the Alps . . . Who wouldn't love the rich and carefree lifestyle—dining, dancing, driving Ferraris? Would you enjoy this work and lifestyle? Why, or why not?

**Q.** Would you be happier if you had more money? Would you be tempted to put it in a secret tax-avoiding account? Is there such a thing as having too much money? Or would you like to give it a try and report back in a few years?

**Q.** The writer has a wry and relentless sense of humor—the way he describes people; the colorful phrases he uses, such as "useless as a screen door on a submarine." What humorous parts did you most enjoy?

**Q.** When Brad loses his job at State Street Bank in Boston, he hires clowns with balloons to hand out flyers detailing the bank's practices—proving he wasn't one to go down quietly. In what way did this foreshadow his later decision to blow the lid off UBS and its questionable practices? Have you ever revealed a wrong in a public way? Did it work, or did it backfire?

**Q.** The author says when he decided to blow the whistle on UBS, he was considering the hardworking American taxpayer who has to pick up the slack left by the rich folks who avoid paying their share. But he was also peeved at Bovay, his boss, and UBS in general for their duplicity revealed in the "Three-Page Memo." What do you think was the real reason for Brad's decision to reveal UBS secrets?

**Q.** If you'd been in Brad's shoes, what would you have done when your boss tried to cheat you out of your bonus, stole your secretary, and then played dumb when confronted about the Three-Page Memo?

**Q.** Brad was the only UBS banker who was sentenced to prison; his bosses and their bosses pled the Fifth Amendment and were allowed to return to Switzerland. In addition, the judge sentenced Brad to even more months than the prosecutor asked for. Do you think this was fair? Why do you believe the cases played out in this way?

**Q.** Clearly the Department of Justice's Kevin Downing disliked Bradley Birkenfeld, and the feeling was mutual. Do you think Downing's ultimate actions were justified from a legal standpoint, or do you think he allowed personal bias to cloud his judgment?

**Q.** Though it was a white-collar prison, the author was behind bars for thirty-one months, including a visit to solitary confinement.

Would you have been willing to go to prison as he did? Did you think the outcome, taking down UBS and exposing so many tax-avoiding account holders, was worth the price Brad paid?

**Q.** While we all benefit from the actions of courageous whistle-blowers, they are frequently treated as pariahs and marginalized from society. Many ills have been exposed over the years—medical experiments, coal mining practices, nuclear power failures, human trafficking, political corruption, etc. Do you think whistle-blowers should be granted immunity from prosecution after risking so much? Do you think incarcerating one who comes forward, as Brad did, will have a chilling effect on future whistle-blowers going public? Or are there times when such punishment is fitting?

**Q.** Under subpoena, the author was forced to divulge those clients he'd signed up for new accounts at UBS, such as the gentleman at the car show in California. How would you feel if you'd been in that fellow's shoes? What about the movie star and others revealed when Brad named names?

**Q.** When the author sought legal representation on his first trip to Washington, DC, he realized all the big firms were already on retainer by UBS—perhaps some actively working for the Swiss bank. Given what you've learned about UBS, do you think it's harmless or somewhat reprehensible for an American law firm to earn substantial legal fees from companies like UBS?

**Q.** Who were your favorite players in the book? Most despised?

**Q.** If *Lucifer's Banker* became a movie, who would you imagine playing Bradley Birkenfeld? How about his secretary, Valerie? Any other actors for specific roles?

**Q.** If you could sit down to a cup of Swiss coffee with Brad, what would you most like to ask him?

# AUTHOR Q & A

**Q. Bradley, congratulations on writing such a riveting book. What made you decide to tell your story in *Lucifer's Banker*?**

**A.** I wrote this book to share the untold story of how I destroyed Swiss bank secrecy. Swiss private banking conjures up images of wealth, privilege, and lavish lifestyles. With *Lucifer's Banker*, I expose the dark side of private banking and my tortured journey that ultimately destroyed centuries-old Swiss bank secrecy. Without the veil of secrecy, terrorists, corrupt politicians, power brokers, influence peddlers, and the wealthy today face stronger barriers to financing indiscriminate attacks on the innocent, to corrupting elected officials and bureaucrats, and to shirking their tax obligations.

While I remain proud of my successful efforts to end Swiss bank secrecy, UBS and the Department of Justice aggressively attempted to undermine my historic whistle-blowing every step of the way. I also wrote *Lucifer's Banker* to share the story of how UBS and the Department of Justice misled and deceived the public for close to a decade. They perverted the course of justice to protect their conflicted interests and to shield from justice and public shame their powerful and influential benefactors who themselves held secret numbered accounts.

While my efforts were rewarded by the largest whistle-blowing award ever—$104,000,000—the world deserves to know the truth about this scandal. I am satisfied that *Lucifer's Banker* has been able to expose what the US government failed to expose, and that my revelations have been a catalyst for ongoing investigations into corrupt private banking activities across Europe and around the globe.

**Q. Readers often love tell-all books, even though we imagine the writer took great risks to disclose so much. How worried are you about revealing so many intimate details of your case? How about the details of other people's financial lives?**

**A.** I'm not worried about revealing what really happened and why. Rather, it's UBS, the Department of Justice, and the many wealthy Americans with secret Swiss accounts who are worried . . . and for good reason. I now welcome the opportunity to expose the corruption on the other side of the Atlantic and around the globe.

**Q. You speak so fondly of your father, a medical doctor, and your mother, a former-model-turned-parent. Clearly they raised a strong, smart son! What did they think of your career when you were raking in big bucks at UBS? Did they know any of the details, such as how you were helping Americans avoid paying taxes?**

**A.** UBS, Credit Suisse, Barclays, and the many other private banks operating out of Switzerland for generations prided themselves on providing discreet financial services for the wealthy. Many respected, law-abiding families availed themselves of their services. My role at each of these firms was to provide access to stable and attractive investments, as well as discretion, to these clients. It was not our role, nor our responsibility, to address our clients' tax responsibilities. While we may have wondered whether or not our clients were meeting their local tax obligations, just as with making cash payments to cab drivers and other service providers, it was not our responsibility to ensure our clients were making appropriate income tax declarations.

Coming back to your question, my parents were certainly happy for me to have landed positions with such reputable firms after finishing my MBA in Switzerland. The fact that the positions would leverage my interpersonal skills and love of travel in supporting clients' financial needs around the world convinced them I had found the perfect career. I was providing banking services to clients, not tax advice.

The Swiss private-banking model began to unravel when private bankers offered financial services during client visits in domiciles where they were not properly licensed or registered to offer such services, or when bankers actively facilitated clients' tax-evasion schemes. Financial rules and regulations tend to be highly technical and complex, particularly in cross-border situations. Operating in the many markets we did, we relied on internal and external legal and compliance resources to ensure our business practices were not running afoul in any of the markets where we did business. What we did not fully understand was that our firms were aggressively interpreting local regulations, and in some cases crossing the line, with many business practices exposing us to legal risks. What triggered my eventual whistle-blowing at UBS was the uncovering of a policy document (the "Three-Page Memo") where the firm defined *as prohibited* many of the activities we bankers were charged and incentivized to perform. The firm, while enjoying the fruits of our efforts, was ready to disavow our activities in the event of any legal trouble. They were not going to stand behind their "rogue" bankers.

**Q. It was amusing the way you first described how easy it was, when you started at Credit Suisse, to solicit new money from wealthy individuals. Was it really that simple? Or did you underplay the financial acumen that one needs in that job? In other words, was that MBA important to this line of work?**

**A.** Financial services is a highly competitive industry with many players competing for a limited amount of investor dollars. At the end of the day, what differentiated one from the next was the quality of the client service effort. While the MBA was important for understanding the inner workings of the many complex products and services we offered, it was not enough to distinguish you in the field. I suppose I made it sound easy because it actually was for me, as I have a natural talent for developing an engaging rapport with most people I encounter. I genuinely enjoy people, and, on the flip side, my clients appreciated my positive and professional approach and were truly engaged with my company.

**Q. While the turning point for you at UBS was the day you saw the "Three-Page Memo" that practically denied permission to solicit American money, in fact when you were at Credit Suisse you came up with the idea of wining and dining the rich—something it sounded like the bankers there weren't already doing. Was Credit Suisse just slow to pick up on the game that UBS players were already experts at?**

**A.** Credit Suisse, at the time, had not developed as sophisticated an asset-gathering operation as UBS had. Much of the business on the books came from clients with other relationships across the bank (banking, commercial lending, trading, letters of credit, etc.). While at State Street, we bankers had ample opportunities to actively cross-sell other services to our clients. My efforts at Credit Suisse were simply introducing new business opportunities to existing and prospective bank clients. As at UBS, my efforts at Credit Suisse were completely transparent and under the firm's legal and compliance umbrella.

**Q. Upon graduating from Norwich University, a military academy in Vermont, you considered a career in the military, but ended up back in finance, where you'd worked during summer breaks. How did your academic and military training at Norwich impact your life, or even dictate the way you reacted to the battle you embarked on as a whistle-blower?**

**A.** My experiences at Norwich University, America's oldest private military academy, battle-hardened me for the challenges and struggles the future had in store for me. Diligence, perseverance, and self-confidence were all instilled in the cadets at Norwich, and I benefited from that environment. I needed all of these traits—and more—for the ultimate battle against UBS and the Department of Justice.

**Q. Speaking of the military, is what you did patriotic? What about the years before you turned in those bankers—when you**

**were signing up more and more rich people to Swiss numbered accounts? Was that patriotic?**

**A.** This is a tough question. I don't believe patriotism has any bearing on what I may or may not have done. Opening up accounts for US and other foreign clients in Swiss bank accounts was my job, as it had been for hundreds of other private bankers across Switzerland for decades. I performed my job with the understanding that the firm was not asking us to violate laws in their name.

The question of whether clients shirking their tax obligations are being unpatriotic is also a curious one. There are many cash-based service industries in the United States and elsewhere where large proportions of revenues are not declared to tax authorities. Are all of these "non-declarers" unpatriotic? Are the clients of these providers unpatriotic for not "outing" their providers for not fully disclosing their income, or worse, complicit for not reporting cash payments to tax authorities? Or do these people have moral standing for refusing to pay taxes to a government with lax spending controls and discipline? These are complicated, value-loaded questions.

My feelings on the subject have evolved over time. As I explain in the book, it was easy to turn a blind eye to questionable activities when you believed these were sanctioned and vetted by your firm. Unquestionably, it was also easy to turn a blind eye when you were young, invincible, and the money was rolling in. As the years wore on, however, you recognized that what may or may not be legal was not always ethical. Was it right for our clients to shirk their tax obligations, and thus leave the less sophisticated and less wealthy to shoulder a heavier share of the tax burden? You might ask why I didn't act on these ethical instincts earlier. Good question, but the same applies to most of us. Many of us have been exposed to similar ethical quandaries. These are tough situations to face, let alone fix.

In the end, the problem was solved for me when I confirmed through the "Three-Page Memo" that many of my job responsibilities had crossed the line. At that point I realized the game was over. I could have just walked away, but instead I had the courage to take on the most powerful bank in the world as I brought their illegal and unethical activities to light.

**Q. Looking back at your State Street days in Boston, when you were fired for refusing to illegally wiretap conversations with your clients, what do you think of your coworkers who went along with business as usual? Did you find it hard to keep relationships with your buddies who quietly toed the (unethical) company line?**

**A.** My focus during the State Street Bank scandal was on the perpetrators of the wrongdoing more than on the knowing bystanders. Furthermore, none of my buddies at State Street were engaged in the wrongdoing. I realize that some people who were there, like many who work for large financial institutions, did not want to risk their futures by standing up to corporate wrongdoing. They made their choices, and I made mine by going to the authorities.

There is a curious parallel between the State Street case and the way the Swiss private bankers executed duties in violation of the laws of countries where they operated. State Street traders may have accepted the wiretap under the assumption or hope that the firm had properly vetted the legal and compliance ramifications. They did not believe it was up to them to make those determinations. But just as I later did in Switzerland, once I confirmed the wrongdoing, I duly reported the transgression.

**Q. At UBS you were a well-paid star, earning far more than your peers, thanks to the deal you negotiated as a condition of your hire—namely, that you would receive a share of the return on assets from any "Net New Money"—money you brought in from new clients. Did any of your friends know then about your sweet deal? Did you make more money than burglar-tool-teeth Bovay, your boss? If so, do you think that contributed to his dislike of you? Or was his aversion due to the way you got that deal through?**

**A.** There is little question that my compensation contract roiled virtually every UBS executive who was aware of it—not because there was anything untoward about it, but simply because I was more effective than they ever imagined possible. It was an unprecedented employment contract for a Swiss private banker, and it was pulled off by one of "them"—an American—another thorn in their side.

**Q. What became of Valerie, your loyal secretary whom Bovay stole from you and then failed to pay her the proper salary and bonus?**

**A.** Valerie is now happily married with two children, living in Switzerland.

**Q. You aren't afraid to tell the truth, Bradley, even when it paints you in a less-than-ideal light. So forgive me for asking this, but can you tell us what your primary motive was for blowing the lid off UBS's practices and Swiss bank secrecy? Was it to retaliate against Bovay, who clearly had it in for you?**

**A.** It is very important to keep in perspective the events that eventually led to my historic whistle-blowing. While Christian Bovay was clearly a thorn in my side, he was simply a bitter man, resentful and envious of my success, but not loath to take the credit for the success I helped bring to his unit. I had a strong contract in place, and he had limited scope to cause me any harm. I had certainly dealt with more devious characters in the past.

As I mentioned earlier, there was also growing unease with the motivations of many of the bank's clients for opening accounts. As I worked principally with Americans with legitimate business interests, the gnawing ethical dilemma was related to tax obligations. But to be quite clear, I was a banker, not a tax consultant; the client was and still is responsible for their tax obligations. Avoiding taxes arguably competes for the title of the world's oldest profession, raises many ethical dilemmas, and was a battle I was not lobbying to become the poster boy for.

The discovery of the "Three-Page Memo," hidden deep in the bowels of the UBS intranet where no banker would be able to find it, was the trigger for my historic actions. The memo defined the principal activities of our group as prohibited. The firm was prepared to continue to reap the rewards of our efforts, but if ever challenged by authorities, it would be able to point to the memo and argue our efforts were not sanctioned and thus it would not stand behind the efforts of those "rogue bankers." They would hang us out to dry! This was not a philosophical dilemma. The bank understood they were putting us in legal jeopardy; they did not inform us; and they would be easily able to wash their hands of our efforts.

My first action after uncovering the memo was to raise questions directly with UBS legal and compliance. After getting no responses from my repeated written requests, I realized the bank was not prepared to acknowledge the seriousness of the situation; they were happy to continue with the status quo, which placed us bankers at grave legal risk. Based on recommendations of Swiss counsel, I then tendered my resignation and escalated the concern directly with the executive team and board of directors of the bank, invoking UBS's very own whistle-blower policies. At this point the general counsel called for an internal investigation, and after cursory effort, came to the conclusion my concerns were primarily the result of misunderstandings: There was no admission our unit had been charged to perform illicit activities. This was my motivation to then approach US authorities and eventually become a US whistle-blower.

Others have argued my whistle-blowing was motivated by the prospects of receiving a substantial reward. What they conveniently forget is the whistle-blower law that eventually compensated me was not in place when my saga began; even after I applied as a whistle-blower, long after I initially blew the whistle on UBS in Switzerland, the prospects of ever collecting any reward were very remote, given the statutory standards and the difficulties experienced by whistle-blowers in other programs. Not to mention, I received a very hostile response after I first contacted the Department of Justice. But I persevered and continued to provide information, despite knowing that rather than receiving an award for my historic testimony, I ran the real risk of being incarcerated. Which of course I was: I spent thirty-one months in a federal penitentiary for uncovering the largest, longest-running tax fraud in US history; and, to date, no other UBS bankers have been jailed for this fraud.

So, no, my whistle-blowing testimony was not driven by a change in conscience relating to my clients' potential tax avoidance. It was driven by UBS implementing and promoting an illegal business plan, hiring me and my colleagues as unknowing agents, and then making clear their intention to disavow any responsibility for our actions. Simple as that. A collateral benefit of my whistle-blowing is that the US Treasury has been able to recover $12 billion and counting in taxes, fines, interest, and penalties from clients who had evaded their obligations for years. So while tax-avoidance practices of private clients had been gnawing at my conscience, it was my whistle-blower actions against UBS that directly led to the substantial amounts collected from tax-evaders and their enablers.

**Q. It's impossible to read this book without imagining it as a movie—partly because you write the scenes so well and give us a great cast of characters. So when that day comes, who would you like to see up on the silver screen in the role of Bradley Birkenfeld? How about actors portraying other people in the story?**

**A.** I really haven't thought about who should portray these people in a possible film. But I certainly won't allow somebody with a fake, unnatural Boston accent to play me in any possible film. A real Boston accent is like having swagger: you either have it or you don't. As the first Swiss private banker to have exposed this epic saga, the basis for a hard-hitting exposé has been laid.

**Q. What did you learn in all this? If you had to do it over, would you blow the whistle on UBS? Would you do it sooner? Clearly you'd have avoided the DOJ—or maybe not, despite the grimness of solitary confinement?**

**A.** I certainly would do it all over again if I had the chance. My efforts brought more than $12 billion (and counting) into the US Treasury and exposed thousands of tax cheats who thought they were above the law. New tax laws were passed and new tax treaties were ratified as a direct result of my whistle-blowing efforts. I destroyed Swiss bank secrecy, which was thought for years to be impregnable. The one thing that I would do differently would be to bypass the Department of Justice. I've now witnessed their corruption from the inside. Of the many things the prosecutors were seeking, justice was not one of them.

**Q. Have you looked at the recently revealed "Panama Papers" detailing offshore accounts? Any names you found familiar? Will there be more such revelations, in your view, from other places around the world?**

**A.** I am aware of the news accounts about the Panama Papers scandal. One name that was reported as part of that story was none other than that convicted tax felon Igor Olenicoff. My goodness, that Igor certainly gets around!

The Panama Papers were files from a single law firm, Mossack Fonseca, a meaningful player in the offshore trust world. There are sure to be future disclosures involving other law firms, accounting practices, and banks. In a similar but separate vein, Lux Leaks (also uncovered by the ICIJ, the International Consortium for Investigative Journalists) disclosed files detailing the preferential tax treatments that major multinational corporations were able to secure from Luxembourg to reduce their European tax bills. It's not just individuals who have an aversion to paying their taxes!

**Q. And yet, despite cracking down on UBS and the offshore accounts that keep the rich from having to pay taxes, isn't the United States still a country of tax laws that favor the wealthy? Warren Buffett is outspoken about the fact that he, a multibillionaire, pays a lower percentage in income tax than does his lower-paid secretary. How much closer have we come to real tax equity—toward helping out that hardworking American you thought about when you decided to blow the whistle?**

**A.** Rich and powerful people, both inside and outside the United States, clearly play by a different set of rules than do most people. I'm not endorsing it; I'm just recognizing this reality. My whistle-blowing efforts forced many of these people out into the open, into clear view, and many were held accountable. To that extent, I did my share to help level that playing field—while also bringing more offshore money back into the US banking system than any other individual in history.

**Q. Any final words for your readers?**

**A.** It's a known historical fact that Switzerland has never been successfully invaded . . . until I came along.

# ABOUT THE AUTHOR

BRADLEY C. BIRKENFELD is a retired financial industry professional renowned as the most significant financial whistle-blower in history.

Birkenfeld began his banking career in Boston. From there, he moved to Europe and established himself as a successful private banker for Credit Suisse, Barclays Bank, and UBS. In 2005, he objected to UBS management about the illicit practices of its private bankers serving high-net-worth American clients who engaged in tax fraud. Rebuffed by UBS management, Birkenfeld then contacted American authorities, starting the process by which his bombshell revelations helped the US Treasury recover over $12 billion in back taxes, fines and penalties from American tax cheats.

The Birkenfeld case commenced a broader crackdown on tax fraud by European governments. These strikes against Swiss bank secrecy after Birkenfeld's case resulted in a monumental change in the regulatory and enforcement environment, causing changes previously unimaginable before "L'Affaire Birkenfeld." Switzerland yielded to pressure from US and European governments to impose stricter bank regulations. As a result of Brad's historic whistle-blowing, the risks and costs to financial institutions that support clients' tax evasion, fraud, corruption, and terrorist activities have increased dramatically.

Birkenfeld holds a BS in economics from Norwich University and an International MBA from the American Graduate School of Business in Switzerland. He is dedicated to supporting whistle-blower initiatives exposing and eliminating fraud. An avid Boston Bruins fan and major memorabilia collector, assisting the team's efforts to help disadvantaged children ranks high among his philanthropic endeavors.